The Word and the Law

THE
WORD
AND THE
LAW

༺∾∾∾༻

Milner S. Ball

THE UNIVERSITY OF CHICAGO PRESS

Chicago & London

The University of Chicago Press, Chicago 60637
The University of Chicago Press, Ltd., London
© 1993 by The University of Chicago
All rights reserved. Published 1993
Paperback edition 1995
Printed in the United States of America
02 01 00 99 98 97 96 95   5 4 3 2

ISBN (cloth): 0-226-03625-1
ISBN (paper): 0-226-03627-8

Library of Congress Cataloging-in-Publication Data

Ball, Milner S.
      The word and the law / Milner S. Ball.
          p.   cm.
      Includes bibliographical references and index.
      ISBN 0-226-03625-1 (cloth)
      1. Law (Theology)   I. Title.
      BT96.2.B34   1993
      261.5—dc20   92-28701
                                               CIP

For Sarah, Scott, Virginia, and Richard

CONTENTS

INTRODUCTION

THIS IS AN EXPERIMENTAL JOURNEY. It begins with depictions of several people who work with law. These practitioners are not a randomly chosen cross-section of the bar. Two are not lawyers in the currently official sense. All have been selected according to an uncomplicated rule: I cannot think about law apart from such people and their specific practices. Their stories are set down next to literary and biblical texts, primarily William Faulkner's *The Sound and the Fury*, Toni Morrison's *Beloved*, the Gospel of Mark, and the Book of Isaiah. The aim of this juxtaposition is to open possibilities for a nonscientific dynamics of law.

Some fifty years ago, Jerome Frank, who was first a teacher, then a judge, and always a legal realist, inveighed against what he saw as a wrong turn taken late in the nineteenth century and early in the twentieth, when professionals began to present law as though it is a science. He urged students of law to correct the error of exclusive focus on the narrowly conceptual by attending to what lawyers and judges actually do. Although academic jurisprudence has yet to complete a fundamental alteration of the basic direction set a hundred years ago, deviations and course corrections are increasing. With differing degrees of acceptability in the law schools, various discourses have been made available for teaching and writing about law: social science, literary criticism, critical and feminist legal studies, minority narrative scholarship. Even clinical training has become a regular part of the curriculum.

Judge Frank would doubtless take heart from this diversity in the academy and from growing debate about what constitutes legitimate legal scholarship. He might even detect, here near the turn of another century, the makings of an essential revision of priority whereby the actual is preferred over the conceptual. He would surely applaud the triumph of the actual in popular culture, as represented by *The Bonfire of the Vanities*, *L.A. Law*, and media coverage of Supreme Court nominations. The actual practices and politics of law are irresistibly alluring; they have gained the better hearing they could not forever be denied. Insofar, then, as this book draws on nonlegal sources and directs attention to practitioners, it belongs to a general trend and is not exceptional.

Also unexceptional in a profession growing tolerant of different methods for writing about law is the formal, structural medium for the book's substantive experiment. I do not here make a linear argument or advance a set of propositions toward a conclusion designed to compel readers' assent by the force of its logic. I make an argument, but in the sense in which we talk about the argument of a ballet or poem. I try for a performance, for affect and understanding more than agreement. By constructing juxtapositions, I hope to create occasion for the reader's participation and invention. It may not work. But that is the question that concerns me—does it work?—rather than whether it is right or wrong.

A performance that works requires the same discipline of the author as an argument that prevails, but it requires something different of the audience. Instead of demanding a willingness to engage in contention, it asks for trust, or at least a provisional suspension of disbelief. Such a claim on the reader has been pressed by other recent legal scholarship. Its repetition here should not be found novel.

The present experiment may fall outside the range of currently familiar legal scholarship insofar as it is also an experiment in theology. Even in this particular, however, precedent has been set by others whose recent books have established the legal-academic legitimacy of inquiry into the historical, personal, and political relationships between law and religion. Possibilities for misunderstanding still attach to such undertakings—especially one like this, whose primary concern is theology and not religion. And especially when it explores the potential of nonreligious theology, something that, out of context, sounds hopelessly oxymoronic, esoteric, or idiosyncratic.

Instead of arguing that theology is relevant to law, I shall do theology and either perform its relevance or fail to do so. I am clearly eager to engage others in conversation about these matters, but, equally clearly, I do not intend to proselytize or give religious instruction. (However, I would not object if other theologians closeted in law were encouraged to make public confession of their predilections.) If theological talk is troublesome to others, it is no less so to me. I do not hold in mind a slate of self-satisfying dogma that requires only to be transcribed to the page. This book is written more toward than from understanding.

I employ theological categories because I cannot do without them. This is a question of necessity, not self-indulgence. In *The Promise of American Law* (1981) I described the judicial process as a performance that mirrors our nature as a people. *Lying Down Together* (1985) then addressed the presently dominant conceptual metaphor—law as bulwark against chaos—and suggested an alternative—law as medium of community. The first book had a tentative theological beginning. The second was somewhat less tentatively theological. Neither was centered on what lawyers do. As lawyers' practices have claimed increasingly central attention, I have found it increasingly necessary to resort to the explanatory power of theological categories. This convergence has rendered inescapable my responsibility to make a fuller, more explicit theological statement.

It is also the case that two relationships have overcome my great reluctance to attempt a clarification of theology's moment for contemporary legal practice. One is the education I began to receive several years ago from Native Americans. There is much yet to be learned, but already I have been driven back into examination of my own tradition. In a recent meeting between traditional tribal leaders and a small group of non-Indian theologians, lawyers, and others, a Cheyenne medicine man proposed that non-Indians do not understand his religion because they do not understand their own. In the abstract it may seem paradoxical, but in my experience it is the case that appreciation of others' ways and traditions is bound up with appreciation for one's own. In that meeting, as in prior ones, I was deeply, appreciatively moved by Native American beliefs even as I became more aware of differences between those beliefs and my own.

Too often, Christians have taken such differences as a reason or compulsion to do whatever was necessary, including obliteration, to displace others' religious faith (and thereby also betray their own). I am captivated by the biblical stories. This captivation does not entail destructive rejection of others' constituting stories. To the contrary, it seems to me to lead directly to—to require—respect and gratitude for them. The biblical stories are no warrant for triumphalism. In any event, a better understanding of my own beliefs has led to and followed from a better understanding of the beliefs of others and the respect that is their due.

The other relationship is that to the person and work of Robert Cover of the Yale law faculty, who died long before what should have been the end of his life. One of the memorials to him is an annual study group. Another is a public interest law conference that I refer to in the next chapter. Aviam Soifer, a mutual friend, asked me to lead one of the study sessions. The only condition was that I had to address a text of my choosing. I elected a passage from the Gospel of Mark. The work I did on that text in preparation for the study group lies at the root of a later chapter of this book.

Cover was a Jew. I am a Christian. The choice of a tough, even opaque Christian text and my ensuing struggle to understand it was my way of paying tribute to Cover. We had only begun what promised to be a long, complex conversation about our two theological traditions. He was a student of both Jewish law and American constitutional law, and his later writings were as much essays in biblical-talmudic legal theory as they were essays in the meaning of law for American democracy. He took his theology and his law seriously and together. So do I.

Perhaps, too, there was some commonality of faith in the midst of our differences, or just out of sight beyond them, that, given time, might have been brought into view. Or might not have. The trying might have been the thing. In any event, as has also happened in the instance of Native Americans, respect for the other's faith and practice grew in conjunction with a deeper investigation and clarification of my own.

I begin this journey in chapter 1 with vignettes of seven people who work with law. Many other practitioners could have been written about in addition to these few, and as I think of those other friends now, I have once more the strong urge to include them. Also, much more could be said about the few whose stories have been selected. These are sketches. I hope that, although they are momentary and incomplete, they are nonetheless like snapshots that capture something of the person, the continuing work, and the larger life. I place them first because the emphasis is on these people and their labors. The subjects should stand on their own here as they do in life. They have their individual, complete value quite apart from any interpretation I might practice on them.

All seven, but some more than others, will likely disagree with what I make of them. I understand—have begun to understand—their work as indicative of the Word at work in the world. Because I do not employ the term *Word* in a religious sense, chapter 2 is devoted to distinguishing religion from the reality I am attempting to discern. It is in this chapter that I turn to *The Sound and the Fury, Beloved,* and other secular texts. I was surprised to discover how these texts illuminated the implications of the theological critique of religion mounted by Karl Barth. I suspect that Barth would be surprised, happily, to find himself in the agreeable company of Dilsey and Baby Suggs.

Readers of early versions of this chapter cautioned that I would need to identify Barth as a twentieth-century Protestant theologian from Switzerland and not an American author of long novels, a continental literary theorist, or a humorist (although the Barth I mean was full of genuine laughter). The advisability of such clarification is symptomatic of the difficulties that I or any serious student of theology must reckon with. Even during Barth's lifetime, his theology was thought by many to be inaccessible. I am no Barthian apologist and shrink from the wars fought among theologians, the *rabies theologorum* (although I do appreciate the need for intellectual rigor and dissent in theology as in jurisprudence). The simple fact is that I find Barth's work helpful and wonderfully freeing.

Chapter 3 is a brief afterword. It ties up some of the loose ends left by chapter 2 and attempts to clarify the meaning of a theological but nonreligious approach by addressing some of its implications.

Close reading of a hard text from Mark and an equally hard, related one from Isaiah occupies chapter 4. The function of the chapter is to locate and give meaning to my usage of the term *Word,* a usage heavily dependent on the biblical notion of *dabar,* the powerful word, the word that accomplishes what it says. This is the reality I discern in the legal practices I describe at the start.

Chapter 5 is another brief afterword meant to clarify, by drawing them out, subjects introduced in the preceding chapter. It offers two contemporary examples of the phenomenon encountered in the text of Mark. One is taken from George Steiner's exposition of aesthetic meaning, the other from Robert Moses' jail-house experience during the struggle for civil rights in Mississippi.

The last chapter opens with a consideration of the deadening force of law and then returns to the vitality evident in the practices I described at the beginning. The book does not build to a great, enlightening climax at the end. My remarks about the common elements in the seven practices will be more or less plain observations about the obvious. As will be noted, I am influenced in the work of writing throughout by the structural example of Mark, and conclude, as does that text, with unresolved openings rather than finalized closures.

ONE

⮑⮑⮑

Seven Practices in Law

HENRY SCHWARZSCHILD

THE DEFENDANT'S LAWYER in a capital punishment case might bring a moral challenge to the court. As the trial or appeal begins, she might stand, say that she, as a lawyer, is an essential part of the process that proposes to kill her client, that she will not lend herself to it, and that she refuses to take part, and then walk out. Or so Henry Schwarzschild, provoking audiences of lawyers and law students, proposes as something to think about.

Decades of advocacy—of weighing in and staying and not walking out—have purchased for Henry the right to raise such hypothetical possibilities and expect that they will command serious attention. He has the appearance of a durable veteran from the ancient wars still at service: penetrating eyes intolerant of bombast and passivity, facial lines that mobilize easily to express by turns infectious good humor, remembered pain, resignation, impatience. He has dark hair and generous dark eyebrows. ("I wish I had a great shock of white hair," he says, a wish whose fulfillment is impossible to imagine.) He is a heavy smoker. In one interview he had torn the top off a box of cigarettes for the readier access his need demanded. Another time he had just finished at New York University an expensive course on kicking the habit but had proved incorrigible; with cigarette in gesturing hand and deep into conversation as well as tobacco, he unknowingly burned a hole in the visor of the vehicle I drove to pick him up. The smoking and years of talking have contributed to the rich timbre of his voice. He speaks with a gravity and resonance that would be ideal for intoning rites of solemn worship except that there is laughter riding just under his voice, and urgency. He dresses in the kind of dark suit that is ready to go anywhere, anytime: New York, Chicago, Jerusalem, Jackson, jail.

In 1960, he and his wife, Kathleen, had been in the small crossroads town of Richmond, Kentucky, visiting her mother (an old Kentucky-

7

Virginia family: Republican, DAR). Some black women had come to nearby Berea College, Kathleen's alma mater, to talk about holding a lunch counter sit-in in Lexington.[1] Henry had gone to hear them. A couple of days later he found himself driving through Lexington on the way home to Chicago. So he stopped by the sit-in and marched up and down in front of a McCrory's store, the lone white among blacks. He wore a sandwich board. He remembers a "hayseed" trying to make out the sign: In the labor of reading, his lips slowly, silently worked the words denouncing lunch counter segregation. There were no arrests.

Henry became engaged by the movement, but, he says, nothing much ensued until the next year, when he went on the Freedom Ride. A decade of civil rights action on the front lines had begun. He did time in Mississippi jails, became a friend of Martin Luther King, Jr., that way, and ran a civil rights lawyers' group from 1964 to 1969. By the close of the decade, he was worn out. He took refuge in jobs as a staff associate of the Field Foundation in New York and then as a fellow of Kenneth Clark's Metropolitan Applied Research Center. In 1972, energy restored, he took over as director of the ACLU's Project on Amnesty for Vietnam War resisters, a position that terminated with victory when Jimmy Carter granted amnesty after he became president in 1977. Henry had by then already begun work on the ACLU's Capital Punishment Project. He would be its director.

He was still operating out of that position when, not long ago, I paid him a visit at the ACLU's national headquarters on Forty-third Street in New York City. His office is minimal. He said he had recently been moved out of the space he had occupied for nine years, and then had been moved twice more. I expect that any of his quarters, however long he had been in residence, would give the impression of temporality, the momentary location of someone en route. In this room a small, institutional-gray metal desk with two drawers is crammed against a wall. At hand is an old typewriter on a stand. There are metal shelves, mostly empty, and three barely comfortable chairs. Letters and papers lie randomly strewn over most of the floor. Filled archival boxes are stacked around.

One of the boxes is open. It contains simply framed black-and-white photographs. In the first one I see, Henry wears dark glasses and a wide-brimmed straw hat of the type associated with Caribbean sugar-cane plantations and rum; he is in the shade of a tree with Martin Luther King, Jr., and others taking a roadside break from marching. In another, Henry is in the background. The foreground is occupied by a Mississippi highway patrolman and his rifle; the one word on his shoulder patch clearly visible is "VIRTUE." And there is a picture of Dr. King delivering the "I have a dream" speech at the D.C. Mall. Just to his side, standing above Mahalia Jackson, is Henry. The last picture I pick up is one of the stage at a 1961 rally in Norfolk, Virginia. Here the roles are reversed: Henry is giving the speech, and Dr. King is listening. Henry had just been bailed out of jail in Mississippi and was embarked on a speaking tour. He had become, in this episode, William Kunstler's first pro bono client.

In his office now, Henry listens intently and talks easily and thoughtfully in response to questions. What had brought him to that Mississippi jail? There had been the sit-in at Lexington the prior year. What had prompted him to take part then?

His first conscious confrontation with racist treatment of blacks had occurred at a 1944 Passover seder at Fort Bragg, North Carolina. A recreation hall had been filled with 2,000 GIs, including Henry. They were being served by black soldiers. He comments, still exercised: "It is Passover, the celebration of liberation. I am off duty, and the blacks have extra duty." He got out of his seat, walked to the platform laden with VIPs, and, having expressed his outrage to the rabbi on hand, was told to sit down and shut up or be court-martialed. "I left. I was eighteen. I was not involved. It was a momentary impulse. It was the first confrontation."

Why that impulse? Where had that come from?

Henry was born in Germany and grew up in Berlin, the son, as he puts it, of an intellectual, political, theological family, a very old Jewish family that, records show, moved to Frankfurt from Cologne in the fifteenth century. His father had three impulses: pacifist, socialist, and Jewish. He turned toward his Jewish self. Henry was seven when Hitler came to power. The family left Germany for Paris after Kristallnacht in 1939, and then made it to New York two weeks before the war broke out. Henry was thirteen (his Bar Mitzvah had been scheduled for the Sabbath after the Kristallnacht weekend). Five years later he was drafted and on his way back to Germany via Fort Bragg and the offending Passover seder.

As a member of the U.S. Army's counterintelligence corps in 1944–46, he found a difficult moral problem in dealing with defeated Germany and Germans. "Here were people who had had to work. Their resistance to Nazism would have made no difference. They would have died without effect." But there was one lesson he meant to learn: "Whatever the cost, I would not live in a period of major moral, social events and be a bystander. That I would not do. The Germans had been bystanders. I would not be that kind of German." So when the Freedom Rides began, Henry was on board.

Henry has another way of talking about these things. He says he has been "an American Jew acting out of quasi-theological promptings who has deliberately, consciously played the role of witness." In the 1960s, "it was important for blacks as well as society generally to know that the issues contested could not be resolved as a matter of race or skin color, that they were to be resolved in terms of generally applicable moral principles. I was there, a white, committed to act out of commitment to principle. I avoided the disappointment of white liberals who had come to be benefactors and then found that blacks were as thoughtful and as arrogant as everybody else is entitled to be. I was there because I felt moral responsibility. I took on the role of witness. And for the decade of the sixties that is what I did."

He became a regular commuter to the South. "I needed to be there so I would not have to think of myself as a bystander. I would not look at myself as I had at the Germans. This can be overdramatized, but there were three times during the Movement era when death was imminent: on the Freedom Ride, in Montgomery; in Philadelphia, Mississippi, during the Mississippi march; and during the Highway Patrol attack on us in the schoolyard in Canton, on that same march. I expected to be killed momentarily. Real life is not lived at this high a plane, but I was conscious of what was happening at the time and of what I was doing there as a witness to principle."

The spoken word and the specific deed are closely aligned for Henry; his life has been constituted by particular speech-acts. He was never what he describes as an "abstraction monger," but after the war and college, he did enroll in graduate school at Columbia to do political theory. How had he become involved in something for which he was so unsuited? He explains that he and his family were newcomers to this culture. In Europe, if you were a political animal and wanted to do politics, you would first do a graduate degree in political theory. It was not self-evident that in the United States the ticket to public affairs is a law degree.

He is not a lawyer in the narrow, technical sense of one licensed to practice in the legal profession. He did not attend law school. Generally mandatory though it now is, however, law school is not necessarily the only or best preparation for a life at law. Nor is it necessarily American. At various times in the first half of the nineteenth century, Massachusetts practically abolished requirements for admission to the bar, and New Hampshire, Maine, Wisconsin, and Indiana allowed anyone over twenty-one and of good moral character to practice. In 1835 Lysander Spooner called for overturning "the injustice and absurdity of the restraints" on bar admissions. He did allow that "a decent moral character" might be retained as the only requisite for admission, for the sole reason "that otherwise individuals might sometimes put themselves there, from whom the Court would be in danger of insult." On such terms Henry qualifies for licensure. He would not present to a court the risk of insult, although he might well dispute the legitimacy of a tribunal prepared to kill a client. In any event, lawyer or not, he is very much a person of the law.[2]

In 1964 he had put together the civil rights lawyers' group, the Lawyers Constitutional Defense Committee, and so had joined his profession to his vocation. (He had been supporting his involvement in civil rights first as business manager for a North Shore Chicago Jewish congregation and then as publications director for the Anti-Defamation League of B'nai B'rith.) In the LCDC's first year, Henry persuaded three hundred lawyers, including Ed Koch, who went on to become the ex-mayor of New York City, to devote their vacation time to volunteer work in the South. For the rest of the decade, in addition to his own continued campaigning in the field, he deployed law and lawyers on behalf of civil rights.

Since 1972, law and arguments for changes in the law have continued to be integral to his life as well as to his work in the ACLU projects on amnesty and capital punishment. The first of these projects ended in victory. In his lifetime, the second will not. It is already the longest battle he has waged.

He recalls being opposed to the death penalty all his life. In the early fifties in Queens he had received a jury summons that bore two qualifying questions: Was the recipient male or female? (Women were excus-*able* from jury service.) Against the death penalty? (Men and women opposed to capital punishment were excus*ed*.) He discussed with his wife-to-be the moral obligation of his answer. One person could hang a jury and prevent the death penalty. If Henry were seated in a capital case, he could be the one. But the opportunity would arise only if he gave a false reply on the form. "That was not a difficult dilemma. I did not hesitate." He identified himself as a male but not as one opposed to the death penalty. There was no capital case, and he did not serve on a jury.

A brief summary of the ACLU project describes it as a campaign to provide "vigorous advocacy against capital punishment." The "against" is important. Henry makes it clear that he is not an advocate for the people who have committed capital crimes. They are not nice people, and they have done terrible things. Henry is opposed to those terrible things. He is also opposed to the terrible thing of the death sentence. He is an advocate not *for* murderers but *against* the death penalty.

He is critical of people who claim they are opposed to capital punishment but who also claim they are obligated by the nature of their public calling not to act on that judgment. Some judges say that, as individuals, they are morally opposed to capital punishment and would vote against it if they were legislators. As judges, however, they claim their duty is to enforce the law as written. They say that, because legislators have not changed the law, they must continue to affirm the death penalty. In turn, the legislators say they are only voting what their constituents want. "This is a professionalism in which each blames the other. But someone else's failure to do a job should not mean that I do not do mine."

Taking responsibility as a lawyer and attempting to quicken a judge's willingness to take responsibility is the animating sense of Henry's provocative proposition that a lawyer in a capital case might challenge the legitimacy as well as the jurisdiction of a court by disassociating herself from the proceedings and leaving. Whenever I have heard Henry put this hypothetical possibility to lawyers and law students there has been an instant rush to repudiate it. The legal mind recoils at the thought and defends with questions: What about the client? You cannot abandon clients like that. What about your practice? You would be disbarred. What about the system? You cannot renounce the system; if you think it is sometimes wrong, you must stay in and fight for change. Besides, it is always possible to win those cases, or one of them, sooner or later.

Henry reports that he has never discovered among the top attorneys who defend capital cases anyone willing to entertain his proposal for conscientious objection even as a thought experiment. Lawyers keep at their work from a belief in the enterprise and the feeling that victory lies just over the horizon. He observes that "morally radical impulses will not get you anywhere as a lawyer. Still, I would feel better if lawyers had the impulse. Controlled it, but at least had it, the intuition."

He goes on to compose a more general comment. Alexis de Tocqueville, in the course of noting the pervasive influence of law, famously maintained that "scarcely any political question arises in the United States which is not resolved, sooner or later, into a judicial question."[3] That the observation is no less valid of contemporary than of eighteenth-century America is, Henry believes, regrettable. "This society has the sense that every social question becomes a legal issue, and law students are constantly taught to believe in the validity and comprehensiveness of this sense of things. But that is wrong and misleading. No important social matter is a legal issue, including important questions about law. Important questions about law are never legal questions." Henry's argument can be supported by evidence of the way law functioned in, for example, the instances of Watergate, or Iran-Contra, or Jim Bakker: Scandal was put aside without answering or raising the underlying social, political, and legal questions. Law was a medium of avoidance rather than confrontation.

Henry would keep the fundamentals directly in view. He returns to his insistence on principle. "The ACLU is not against the death penalty *because* the Eighth Amendment outlaws cruel and unusual punishment. We would be against the death penalty, whether or not there were an Eighth Amendment, for reasons of principle. We take principle seriously. That is why we represent right-wingers. Defending the Nazis' right to hold a parade in Skokie did not give the ACLU a moment's pause. The commitment to principle is not a façade. We must always pursue neutral principle or abandon to third parties the judgment about what is permissible for us to do. The legal left is against neutral principle. We are not."

I press him about neutral principle: about what a neutral principle is; about who gets to say what is neutral; about neutral principle as a façade, if not for the ACLU, then for others; and especially about neutral principle as sustenance. Are we not sustained by passion? How can neutral principle keep us going? He understands that I am asking about his own enduring ethical energy and its source. "It is in my bones," he says, "ever since Hitler."

And he talks about how Martin Luther King, Jr., was upheld. He recounts the episode in Neshoba County, Mississippi, when a crowd of jeering whites descended on a group of civil rights demonstrators including Dr. King and Henry. Among the pieces brought out for the occasion by threatening law enforcement officers unsympathetic to the demonstration was a Jeep-mounted machine gun. (Two of the officers were eventually convicted for having earlier murdered the Neshoba County Three.) In that charged atmosphere someone set off a package of firecrackers. Henry thought the end had come. Dr. King did not flinch. "Martin's response was not the product of courage in the activist Rambo sense but of the rather extraordinary sense he had of mission, of imitatio Christi, of vicarious suffering for others as redemptive. This was not idolatry. He did not seek out suffering. He accepted his own suffering when it came as redemptive for others. Martin had this extraordinary applied Christian theology. That is not my theology. Vicarious suffering does not redeem, and crucifixion is not intimate to my theology. Martin believed in it."

I wonder aloud about Henry's attempt to end capital punishment. Its immediate prospects are barren of promise. Contemporary political campaigns are won or lost by the test of commitment to the death penalty. Some judges, including the present chief justice of the Supreme Court, are committed to curtailment of death penalty appeals and are ready to get about the business of execution. Success is improbable for the ACLU Capital Punishment Project. Henry rises. He condemns the idolatry of success. "The ACLU knows you cannot afford to fight only the battles that you will win. You cannot fight on the condition of success. You cannot do that as a human being." By way of more personal explanation, he quotes from *The Sayings of the Fathers:* "It is not given to you to finish the task, but neither are you free to desist from it."

Henry would contend with God, for whom he has a great many questions amounting to anger. But he is angry, it appears to me, in the way that only lovers and believers can be. He does seem to have taken biblical texts to heart. I have heard him roundly condemn the violent bloodthirstiness of the Book of Esther. However, his arguments and his objections in this instance and others betray a close familiarity with the texts that is scarcely available to distanced, academic reading. In the course of one conversation, he rejected my suggestion that the Ten Commandments are given meaning by or as biblical story: "In Judaism, commandment is law." There is an edge to his voice. "The Talmud is not biblical stories but law." Perhaps what is in his bones is commandment. "One does not serve God," he says, "in expectation of a reward."

In remarks delivered at a welcome service for Nelson Mandela held in New York by Jews for Racial Justice and Congregation B'nai Jeshurun, Henry said,

> Jews are defined by neither doctrine nor credo. We are defined by *task.* That task is to redeem the world through *justice.* To accomplish that task, the Jewish people needs to stay alive, but survival is not an end in itself but rather a means to enable us to pursue our task. Indeed, to make survival into an end in itself, to seek it for its own sake, is to belie the values of the Jewish tradition, of Jewish law. If the notion of "chosenness" means anything supportable, it is that our portion, our task, is unlike that of other peoples, being in fact the duty to refine, exemplify and apply human and social justice. . . .
>
> The one-time Chief Rabbi of Palestine, Rav Kook, once called the aggressively secularist kibbutzniks of the 1920s and '30s the most intensely Jewish people he knew. Just so, even the unbelievers among us are never so Jewish as when they reject social apathy and confront the desperate needs of their brothers and sisters, here and now, in our own city, our own state, our own country, not because our well-being depends on it, but because Judaism does.

The theologian Paul Lehmann, my mentor for thirty years, observed that believers are the ones who are still there when everyone else has left. Lehmann was talking about Christian believers, but his observation is surely no less applicable to the Jewish faithful.[4] By that standard and extrapolating from the stamina of his remonstrance against injustice, Henry is, in my outsider's judgment, a believer.

He talks about retiring from the ACLU, but not in order to go into retirement. He must give more time to playing again the role of witness—on this occasion in the Middle East. When everyone else has left, he will still be there. "Just as the South was not a black-white problem, the Middle East is not a problem between Arabs and Jews. It is intolerable to let it be seen as an ethnic problem. Crucial for me humanly is not that I change anything but that I do what I can. Arabs must know— and Jews and the world—and I must give evidence that, again, this is not a conflict to be resolved by ethnicity but by principle, universal principles of justice. I must give evidence to the underlying principle. I cannot avoid that." Again, Henry has already been in the field working on behalf of Palestinian groups. He joined with other Jews and Palestinians in Jerusalem in a demonstration for peace. They were tear-gassed by Israeli troops. Henry, ever the connoisseur, sniffed the bouquet and, relying on past experience, declared it to be a '72, a fine year, made in Pennsylvania. For Henry, the law—commandment—is obligation. The obligation is not to achieve the Eschaton but not to not take part. The double negative is his; it reflects what is felt and what is to be expressed in the unrelenting, vigilant action demanded by the divine prohibition of idolatry.

The double negative is also reflective of the tension to be read in Henry's life and words. In a 1965 letter to the newly elected Senator Walter Mondale, he addressed an ideological, political split in the civil rights movement, noting that "the main division . . . is between those who want to win the country over and those who want to win over the country. The latter . . . consider themselves in a profoundly adversarial position vis-à-vis the country, its institutions, and its 'power structure.'" Henry wants to win the country over. Nevertheless he has also felt compelled to place himself—for howsoever long a time being—in opposition. Walking out of court to place in issue the legitimacy of a tribunal that would hand down a sentence of death, like protesting segregation and Israeli treatment of Palestinians, is a profoundly adversarial stance.

Because such opposition, made necessary for him by present extremes, turns neither on expectation of success nor on hope of persuading the opponent, it cannot be a complex form of respect paid an adversary. And yet it may be an appeal to—and therefore an affirmation of or love for—the better self which humanity may be persuaded to become through the appeal. There is tension here not to be resolved.

To another gathering of lawyers and law students, Henry quoted portions of a piece that he finds moving and powerful. It is a 1722 sermon. Moses Paul, an Indian, was convicted of murder and sentenced to death in New Haven, Connecticut. Paul invited a fellow Indian, Samson Occom, to preach at the execution. Henry read the introductory remarks of Occom's execution sermon. They conclude with an admonition to the assembled crowd: "Let us all be suitably affected with the melancholy occasion of the day, knowing that we all are dying creatures, and accountable unto God. Though this poor condemned criminal will in a few minutes know more than all of us, either in unutterable joy, or inconceivable woe; yet we shall certainly know as much as he, in a few days."[5]

JOHN ROSENBERG

The federally funded legal services agency for eastern Kentucky is headquartered in Prestonsburg, Kentucky (Appalachian Research and Defense Fund of Kentucky, Inc., known as Appalred). It occupies an old two-story, dark brick building. The inside is institutionally beige and brown. The color and life come from the people who labor here. The first impression is of soft voices, gentle accents, laughter, and lots of work. In the background is the muffled whine of a computer printer producing the monthly statement of accounts.

In the middle is John Rosenberg, Appalred's founder and director. He is a tough lawyer in tough country who has had to do a lot of what he calls "lawyering uphill." He has done so successfully. He first learned how in eight years as a trial attorney in the Civil Rights Division of the U.S. Justice Department. He litigated controversial cases in the South in the 1960s. When he left the Justice Department for Kentucky in 1970, he was chief of the division's Criminal Section.

He is a heavyweight. You would not know that from his appearance and manner. He takes the steps down from the second floor to meet me in rapid, graceful, soft-shoe style. He is small, has a high-pitched voice and laughter lines at the eyes, and gives the impression of light-footed dancing even when he is sitting at his desk: legs crossed, one foot patting the floor in time to a fast tune, the other simultaneously bouncing in the air to an even faster beat, his fingers playing the chair arms and air, none of the music heard by me. He is repeatedly up and off, darting through the door and back to retrieve documents, to tend to chores, to show me around. He does not care much for sleep, he says; it is a diversion. And, I suspect, just another form of aerobic exercise for him. When he listens intently, which he does frequently, he has a manner of squinting that furrows his brow but widens his eyes and opens his mouth. He is always ready for action.

Among the items he brings to my attention in the course of the visit is an album of photographs, pictures from the first staff reunion held a couple of years ago. Appalred began as a two-state program headquartered in Charleston, West Virginia. The independence of the Kentucky operations was dictated by survival strategy in 1973 when Office of Economic Opportunity director Howard Phillips tried to dismantle legal services in the U.S. Appalred made it through that period and reached a high point in 1981 with forty-eight attorneys, twenty-three paralegals, and thirty-two supporting staff. Subsequent funding losses have cut the number to twenty-five attorneys, nineteen paralegals, and twenty supporting staff. They serve about seven thousand clients a year. The program has ten offices covering thirty-seven eastern Kentucky counties with a poverty population of 280,000. John rides the circuit. ("The time I spend on the road between offices is useful. It is my chance for thinking through problems.") He evokes a strong sense of allegiance. Many of the present professional staff have been with him for a decade. More than a hundred attorneys, past and present Appalred employees, turned up for the reunion. When he has the funds or a vacated spot to fill, John hires in new attorneys at a salary of $17,000. They are as smart and fully qualified as some of those students who are presently offered $72,000 by large firms.

It takes time to get through the album. As we turn the pages, John's forefinger taps every plastic-enclosed photo. He smiles. His eyes light up. He has stories to tell about each person pictured. Most wear one of the apple-red T-shirts commissioned for the occasion. "An amazing group of people," he keeps repeating. He is so obviously proud of them and proud to tell me that "the vast majority are still in public service work—if not here, somewhere else." He is a mentor. He is also a practitioner of community. The Appalred staff and alumni are one of his communities. David, Kentucky, is another.

David is actually on the map. We drive the several miles out of Prestonsburg for a look. On the way we pass one of the tipples where coal is graded, washed, and sorted. A sign identifies this one as "Beverly Ann." Coal and poverty are much in evidence in these parts. If you have seen the film *Harlan County, USA,* you will have the picture. Eastern Kentucky's landscape is rippled and ridged. The elevation here is about 1,000 feet, but with the feel of steep mountain land. People live in the hollows and along the bottoms. To build higher up on the slopes or ridges is a luxury no one can afford.

Prestonsburg has been squeezed into a valley along the Big Sandy River. Much of it is only two blocks wide. At the end of every short crosstown street is a wooded hillside. The only building of any size is a new five-story bank whose architecture is undistinguished except as a reminder of where the area's ownership is centered. It is early December, and the air is chill. The first snow of the season is on the way. Against gray sky, bare trees on the narrow ridges appear lined up in single file, like "tree persons," as I have heard Indians call them.

Below the road to David, along the river and the creeks that feed into it, the residue of a recent flood is much in evidence. Waters can gather quickly in the tight valleys; this time they had risen several feet above the banks. The limbs of trees and bushes combed the flow, and, as the flood retreated, they were left festooned with refuse—strips of colorless plastic, bits of grayed cloth and paper, an old boot—for mile after mile. Dispersal by flood comes free of charge. Strip mining has not brought the luxury of publicly funded waste disposal, but it has increased the flooding.

It has also managed to refurbish the landscape. Entire hills have been taken down by surface mining and then rebuilt. The smooth, rounded forms with freshly planted grass and no trees are the designer hills. The coal they yielded grudgingly is everywhere. Coal trucks rule the roads. Coal dust blows into thick collections on the median strip and in the gutters. Coal smoke rises out of cabin stoves. Coal is disgorged from an active mine within the city limits of Prestonsburg. Before we get to David, we have to wait at a crossing for a coal train.

David is the site of a salt lick discovered by Daniel Boone. More recently it was a coal company camp. The mine closed. The surface was sold to a businessman. The houses fell into disrepair. Residents came to John. He incorporated them as a nonprofit housing corporation, helped secure the necessary financing, and assisted the corporation's purchase of the town and the ensuing resale of residences to the tenants who lived in them. The corporation has built twenty new homes and sold them to low- and moderate-income families. Ridge to ridge, the hollow David occupies includes eight hundred acres, thirty-five homes, and a special school for seventy kids who would otherwise be drop-outs. The school has drawn national recognition. It is housed in a breezy building that once served as the company store. The rumble of coal trucks and coal trains renders classroom conversation difficult. A new school is planned. John helped with the purchase of a tract for the new building. Shortly after the deal was completed, the school was notified that the local coal company intended to develop a mine on and under the site. John helped orchestrate a series of actions, meetings, protests, and public relations campaigns. The company withdrew its mining plans and offered to help with grading of the new school site.

John leads me into the school. It is ramshackle. Some windows are out. Some are patched. The front door opens into a gym just big enough to accommodate its three-quarters of half a basketball court. It features a homemade backboard. The pine floor is warped. Classrooms are tucked around. Students are concentrating on their lessons, working closely with their teachers. In the rear of the building, toward the old feed shed, is the dining room, with its long plywood tables soon to be heaped with biscuits and barbecued chicken. The wonderful, mightily tempting smells of lunch drift into the classrooms. There are bright, eager faces. John breezes into the classes as freely as the aroma and strikes up good-humored conversations with the teachers and students, me in tow. He knows no barriers. He is welcome.

He takes me next door to a shop, David Appalachian Crafts, a non-profit organization for the development and marketing of regional crafts. On display are colorful quilts, bonnets, toys, three blind mice in calico, and Christmas ornaments. The work is impressive, lovingly done. On the wall is a newspaper clipping, a story about Johnny Carson placing a large order for pillow covers with David Crafts; he gave them as Christmas presents to his television staff. (Some items from the shop are displayed in the storefront windows of the Appalred office in Prestonsburg, along with yellowing notices about meetings and available legal services.) John says David is a true success. He is proud of it.

On the way back into Prestonsburg, John stops at a house that serves as headquarters for another of his communities, Kentuckians for the Commonwealth. KFTC is a statewide organization dedicated to land, mineral, environmental, and community-service issues. They have lately scored a major triumph.

"Broad form" deeds have been a curse here, as they have been elsewhere in Appalachia. Beginning a hundred years ago, land speculators, most of them from out of state, purchased the rights to coal, typically for a pittance, from poor, usually illiterate landowners. The customary legal instrument for the purchase was the "broad form" deed, whose stock, general terms severed the property interest in underground minerals from that in the overlying land and conveyed title to the subsurface coal to the speculator. Subsequent purchasers of the surface land years later might have no idea that an unknown company owned the underlying minerals. They would first learn when the company came for the coal.

The ancient deeds often failed to specify the manner in which the coal could be extracted. The Kentucky courts held that companies with "broad form" deed title to the minerals could employ surface mining methods. They could destroy the property of the surface landowners, including their homes, without obligation to compensate for the damages. Landowners began seeking help from John and Appalred. One of the consequences was the formation of a group that was to become KFTC. It succeeded in persuading the legislature to enact a statute, drafted by Appalred, precluding surface mining under "broad form" deeds. That was in 1986. In 1987, the Kentucky Supreme Court ruled the act unconstitutional. KFTC went back into action and succeeded in getting an Appalred-drafted proposal for a constitutional amendment on the ballot. In essence the proposed amendment restated the legislation the court had struck down. It passed with a whopping 82.5 percent of the vote. "There is a lot of citizen activity in Kentucky," John remarks. The KFTC staff is small. The three I meet are young, bright, still flush with success and optimism. I purchase a T-shirt with the broad form campaign logo, out of date except as a fund-raising device. With these young people and their work, John's pride swells again.

Our next stop is Prestonsburg Community College, a low, dark, gray building. Its exterior has about as much welcoming warmth as the stone outcroppings on the surrounding ridges. John's wife, Jean, heads a program here for single parent homemakers. Its official purpose is to provide educational opportunity and financial assistance to people who dropped out of school and now have children. In fact it does that, but also offers human support and hope to women who have been abused by men and poverty. "It does not rescue people," Jean observes; "it gives them a chance to live out their potential." The program takes up a hall of cramped, soundproofed offices originally intended as rehearsal rooms for music students. The soundproofing is still needed: The women who come to Jean and her staff have hard, painful stories to share, and there is much crying to be done. A box of tissues lies close at hand on each desk.

Jean says it takes a lot of courage for her clients to make it to PCC from the hollows. (It took three weeks of driving to the parking lot and sitting there before one young woman found herself able to go inside.) They are usually divorced, with children and without funds. If they go back to school, their food stamps are cut. Once in the program, they work at various educational levels: high school equivalency, remedial college courses, regular college courses, or vocational training. (About the latter, Jean notes: "We have a lot of cosmetologists in the area.")

As we approach the college, John observes that his wife's clients drive clunkers, and when we pull into the parking lot, sure enough, there is one, rusted and red, hood up, a woman of about thirty bent over the engine. We try to help, but there is a major problem. Her options are neither good nor affordable. She has regularly survived much worse situations and will not be defeated by this one. She takes charge, calling a mechanic and then a friend who will take her home.

Jean is a Quaker. John is a Jew. They met in the Department of Justice, where she was a paralegal. There is neither a Quaker meeting nor a synagogue in the Prestonsburg area. With their children, Mike (a Duke University student) and Ann (a high schooler), they have kept the feasts of both traditions at home. As they talk about their practice, they give the impression of being doubly sustained, doubly delighted. John's commitment to justice and the service of others, he says, is a clear but hard-to-articulate function of his Jewish heritage. He also finds himself heavily influenced by Jean's Quaker tradition.

John's family sailed to the United States in 1940 aboard one of the last boats to leave Holland before the war broke out. John's father, a cantor and schoolteacher in Germany, found work in Spartanburg, South Carolina, sweeping the floors of a shirt factory. John became a southerner. He graduated from Duke in 1953 and served as a navigator in the Air Force. When he was discharged ("I left my sneakers in the Pentagon and never went back"), he went to work in Philadelphia for a chemical manufacturer and then returned to the University of North Carolina's law school (class of '62).

John Doar brought him into the Justice Department. Rosenberg refers to his former boss frequently and admiringly. Doar, he says, is the person who taught him how to try cases, which I take to mean trying them with intense and thorough preparation. Rosenberg continued into the Nixon-Mitchell Justice Department. His colleagues induced him to stay by reminding him that if he left, he would be replaced by an entirely different kind of person with an entirely different kind of civil rights agenda. He remained as long as he could, until 1970. It was not only the change at Justice that caused him to leave. He had necessarily been an itinerant, traveling from place to place as cases required. He and Jean wanted to settle into a community where they could invest themselves over the long term and help make life better for others. They left D.C. with their infant son on a cross-country camping trip, stopped with a friend in the fledgling Appalachian Research and Defense Fund in West Virginia, and decided to give it a try. "We thought we'd stay a couple of years at the most." John opened the Kentucky branch office in 1970. "It was tough," he remembers, "but then the kids were in school, and the place does grow on you."

I get some idea of the difficulties they have faced when John talks about how hard it has been for him to live where there are few like-minded attorneys. Legal services lawyers become objects of the hostility aroused by the program. In this part of Kentucky John has been determined that his clients would have "first-rate legal service and a square fight. I want to make sure that when people go to court, they have as good representation as somebody with money." That does not always go down well with the local bar. Early on he asked the bar to establish a system that would provide a fair way of referring clients to local attorneys. A committee was appointed for the purpose. Instead of devising a referral system, the committee passed a resolution that legal services did not belong in the area and ought to be defunded. "I am on decent terms with the other lawyers now," he says, "but there is little social interchange with them. Members of large law firms have a different value system."

Where some would have thought the prospects bleak and unpromising, the Rosenbergs have devised ways to become fully, happily settled. When I have to leave Prestonsburg early in order to stay ahead of the snow, John is disappointed: "There is so *much* more to see." Speaking for them both, Jean says they have found a lot of satisfaction in Prestonsburg. "It is satisfying," she adds, "when there is not a difference between your principles and your work."

John took it as a major show of respect for the program and his direction of it when he drew local support for appointment to a federal judgeship in 1988. He was one of eleven people out of forty interviewed for the position, although his name was not submitted to the president. I expect signs of change and encouragement can also be seen in the election of Janet Stumbo to the Kentucky Court of Appeals. The thirty-five-year-old Ms. Stumbo was chair of Appalred's board last year. After taking the Kentucky-required oath of office when she was sworn in as a justice, she was administered another, at her own request, in which she swore to give equal justice to rich and poor.

The private bar has stopped taking black lung cases that are not sure winners, which means that Appalred provides attorneys of last resort. The work can be discouraging. Black lung cases are brought before the Department of Labor under the Federal Coal Mine, Health and Safety Act of 1969. As the statute is presently administered, claims are difficult to bring and are seldom successful. When Congress recently held oversight hearings on the statute, John testified about the grim details:

> [A] miner's chances of prevailing in a claim are four out of one hundred, and he/she is faced with a claims process that takes years to complete. It is a national disgrace. The present system provides a steady source of income to doctors, radiologists, and medical technicians; to lawyers who are employed by insurance company claims examiners and other personnel; and to Department of Labor personnel and administrative law judges; but it does precious little for the coal miner whom Congress intended to help with this law; and it has abandoned his widow.

Black lung cases are what he means by "lawyering uphill." There are other, equally difficult cases arising from coal production: miners fired because they refused to work in hazardous conditions (in one instance a mine roof was about to give way; in another, handling an electrical cable in water had produced repeated shocks), landslides caused by strip mining, labor disputes, and the like. Appalred became involved in the devel-

opment of regulations under the strip mining acts and represented the
Black Lung Association in the development of regulations under the
Black Lung Act.

John shakes his head in disbelief as he talks about a case with a long
and ongoing life: *Samuel J. Meek v. UMWA Health & Retirement Funds.*
Mr. Meek was born in 1904 and began underground mining in 1919. He
had last worked as a miner in 1956. In 1973, he applied to the United
Mine Workers of America for a pension. To qualify for a pension, a
miner must establish that he has worked the mines for twenty years, five
of which must have been with a company that had signed onto a national
UMWA contract. The Funds denied Meek's pension. One of its grounds
for doing so was that, although he had over thirty years of underground
work, only four and a quarter were with signatory companies. Appalred
filed suit on his behalf in federal district court. The court held that the
Funds erred in finding that Meek had not worked a signatory mine in
1956 and sent the case back for a determination of the time to be allowed
for that year. The Funds then found that Meek was still short of the required five years. He had been injured in a mine accident in the early
part of 1956, the year in question. That injury, coupled with black lung
disease, had prevented his return to the mines. The Funds allowed no
pension credit for the period after he was forced to stop mining work.
Appalred went back to District Court, where he lost again. Meek died in
1986 while the case was pending. His widow has perfected an appeal to
the Sixth Circuit. "He had worked the mines for thirty years and more,"
John reflects, "and we're still fighting to get three-quarters of a year for
his pension credit."

Appalred has spread into counties without coal mines, with the consequence that black lung, mine safety, and other cases directly related to
coal are now only a small percentage of its work. The major areas of
practice have become public benefit/disability (40 percent), family (35
percent), consumer, housing, environmental, and civil rights law. The
cases involve denial or termination of social security benefits, sexually
and racially discriminatory hiring practices, defaults on mobile home
payments, child custody and termination of paternal rights, and bank-
ruptcies. In one case the money received for a prepaid funeral had been
misappropriated. In another, all the available nursing homes and hos-
pitals had refused to admit a ninety-four-year-old man wrongly thought
to have AIDS.

In subjects like strip mining, mine safety discrimination, black lung,
and consumer law, Appalred undertakes law reform efforts, but John is
quick to underline "the importance of daily individual representation. I
have always thought that, when you represent an individual client in an
individual case—the social security or Medicaid benefits you obtain for

someone, or sometimes even the divorce that needed to take place because someone's mental condition depended on it—that particular case is as important as any major law reform." He finds it easy to justify the positions of Appalred's clients: "They are asking for justice, and what they ask for is usually right."

He talks about the need to improve the system. "This is a class society, and we have a large underclass of the poor. But this is a wonderful country, the best place going. I came here on the boat. We've just got to make the system better."

On the way out of town I stop for gas and a copy of the local newspaper, the *Floyd County Times,* which I cannot read until the following day. It carries a farewell editorial by a member of the paper's staff who is moving to Texas. In it she pays tribute to John for his determination "to help set the local school system on the right track." He has faithfully attended school board meetings and related functions, she reports, and "generally served as a guardian of What is Right."

MARGARET TAYLOR

The Civil Court of the City of New York is housed in an undistinguished, tall, dark office building in lower Manhattan. As soon as I enter the ground floor shortly before 9:00 A.M., I am drawn into a noisy mob surging toward elevators. Most of these people appear to be lawyers. In the crush, they hold their briefcases and documents above their heads. I have come to see Judge Margaret Taylor. I do not wish to take the elevator yet. I want to look around first and talk to some of the clerks. But the individual will counts for nothing in this crowd, and I cannot separate myself from it. We are being drawn into elevators. I remember once when, as my family watched late evening swifts feed on insects and sweep low over the street to ride thermals given off by pavement still warm from the day, a signal was given or a common biological switch was thrown, the independent action stopped, the swifts rose above the trees in a flock, circled a nearby chimney, and disappeared into it as though they had been vacuumed from the sky in the last light. This pack of lawyers is being sucked from the lobby into elevator shafts. I cannot *not* be pulled into one of the cars. Up I go.

I push my way out—am released—on the eleventh floor, where Judge Taylor is scheduled to hear landlord-tenant cases. Courtroom 1164B, the provisional location, is not easy to find in all the corridors and corners. In the search, I take occasion to step into other courtrooms where trials and hearings are under way. All are uninviting. Some are in ill repair and cramped, with barely enough room for the minimum furniture necessary to a judge and a couple of attorneys. There is a small round window in one door that opens in. I peer through. I see that if I try to enter the close quarters, the door will strike the back of an attorney standing to make an argument before a judge. When I do find 1164B, it is empty. No one I ask in the halls knows when court will begin or where Judge Taylor will, in fact, be sitting.

I wait long enough for the lobby to clear and ride back down to confirm the court schedule. I hope to give my visit a different, independent beginning. First I check the schedule and see that Judge Taylor will indeed be holding court in 1164B. I have time to go to the Housing Court office. I want to see how the system works. In one of her reported decisions, Judge Taylor notes: "Complying with Housing Court procedures is ordinarily a challenge to any *pro se* litigant," and "approximately 77% of all tenants in Manhattan's Housing Court appear *pro se*."[6] The particular lawyerless tenant before her in that case had "been fighting a confusing battle from the outset. In this sense, his experience has not been unique."[7]

What if I were a tenant who had come to this place in response to a notice that the landlord was seeking to evict me? The Housing Court office is jammed and chaotic. There are long lines and confusing forms to fill out. One woman, addressing everyone and no one in particular, is pouring out her woes; she is destitute, she is about to be put out on the street, she and her children have nowhere to go. Except for clerks, I am the only white person I see. I join a line before a counter where a hanging sign declares "information." Behind it is a tough-looking male in his late twenties: multicolored dyed hair, short on top with a long tail trailing down the back; one earring; forbidding, noncommunicative. He seems to think he is standing guard. If he has information in his keeping, he will not release it, and no one can find the combination of words that will make him give it out. Help and advice come only from other members of the crowd.

In the case in which Judge Taylor noted the challenge and confusion of the process, the landlord's attorney had asked the court to strike the tenant's request for a jury trial. He argued that the request had not been made at the specified time. In explaining her denial of the motion, Judge Taylor wrote: "The court is ashamed to admit that in the course of reconstructing the history of this case, it became aware, for the first time, that a *pro se* tenant is *not* informed in any manner whatsoever that she/he has the right to demand a jury trial. . . . Discussions with the clerks in the Housing Court office indicate that the clerks do not ask the *pro se* tenants . . . whether they want to demand a jury trial. An inspection of the office failed to reveal any posted signs, directives or memoranda containing information on how to go about requesting a jury trial."[8]

How can tenants invoke the right to a jury trial they cannot know exists? "*Pro se* tenants leave the Housing Court office without ever having been advised of their rights while our judicial system at some future point in time may deem this to be a waiver of this important right. . . . Our official reports are filled with beautifully worded decisions which exalt the constitutionally-protected right to a jury trial, but without providing clear and accurate information to *pro se* tenants, this protected right is no more than an illusion."[9] Eviction is a terrible prospect, and the introduction to Housing Court is daunting, Kafkaesque, as Judge Taylor knows from her own field inspection.

Courtroom 1164B, to which she has been assigned this day, has, in addition to the raised judge's desk and a table and chairs for attorneys, fifty green metal chairs for spectators and a table bearing stacks of books and papers along with a computer terminal. The linoleum-covered floor, fluorescent lights, and blond wood wainscoting give it a harsh air. Above the wainscoting, the white walls are scarred. Broken chairs are piled in a corner.

The room fills up. People will continue to file in and out throughout the day. One expensively dressed attorney huddles in his trenchcoat, drawing it around him not against the cold—it is warm inside—but against being here. It is not his kind of place. No one stands when Judge Taylor walks in energetically but unceremoniously to begin the session. There are fifty cases on the docket, and all will be disposed of, one way or another, before day's end. The judge prepared for today well into the night last night and will prepare for tomorrow until late tonight. (In the course of the day, she tells one attorney: "I must have sleeping time and shower time, but if you will get all the papers to me, I will make a decision that day. I may have to sleep and shower on your motion, but I will have a decision in twenty-four hours so long as you have the papers.")

Before she takes her seat, the judge swaps banter with the attorneys, the court officer, and the court reporter. The officer and reporter smile when they see her and remain in good humor all day. Judge Taylor is dressed, as she typically is, in a black pantsuit and a powerfully pink blouse. Even with her graying hair gathered loosely on top of her head, she is no more than five feet three or four inches tall. Her voice is authoritative. From the Manhattan accent and manner, you would not know that she is from Klamath Falls, Oregon. Over the outside of each eye, wrinkles form an upward-slanting, open *S*, the top of each tilting inward toward the other at a forty-five-degree angle. They allow her to appear penetratingly attentive or quizzical or on the verge of total absorption in laughter. She can be uproariously, raucously funny. She both commands and enraptures audiences.

One of her more frequent expressions in court is: "What's *this?*" said, brightly smiling, with deliberate innocence, rising slightly in her chair. "What's *this?* No one told Mr. Slenis he has a right to a jury trial? No one told him how to invoke it? And you want me to find that he waived the right?"

Or, "What's *this?* You really want me to proceed against this tenant without appointing a guardian for him when he is *non compos mentis?*"

Or, "What's *this?* The process server's affidavit says he delivered notice to the tenant, whom he identifies as a fat lady, and the affidavit of the attorney's investigator says he met with the tenant, who is a thin lady?"

In this instance, there is an explanation. The lady was the same. She was pregnant when the process server had come and had delivered before the visit of the investigator. The more unusual aspect of this case is that the process server and investigator had actually gone to the premises as they swore they had.

The usual circumstance is spelled out by Judge Taylor in one of her reported opinions in a more typical housing court proceeding.[10] The tenant failed to make one or more rent payments. The landlord initiated legal proceedings. Notice of the proceedings was supposed to be served on the tenant by a process server. The tenant did not appear at the appointed time. The landlord applied for default judgment for possession of the premises. The court was asked to evict the tenant. In these instances, the court's jurisdiction over the absent tenant depends on the tenant having been served with the necessary papers (the notice of petition and petition). When process servers cannot find the tenant or gain admittance to the premises—they must show that they made "reasonable application"—New York law allows for conspicuous place service, also known as "nail and mail service" or, derisively, as "sewer service."

Process serving is not nice work and can be dangerous. How often attempts at personal service are actually made in tough neighborhoods is uncertain. One report found that at least one-third of all default judgments are based on affidavits of service that are perjurious.[11] In this case the process server alleged

that he attempted to serve the tenant personally by ringing the bell and knocking on the door of tenant's home. . . .

Although the process server was unable to effect personal contact with the tenant in this case, significantly, one Nesto Diaz, the investigator employed by petitioner-landlord's attorney to ascertain whether tenant was a member of the armed services, had no such difficulty. Mr. Diaz swears that at an unspecified time on the very same day of the alleged conspicuous place service . . . he called at [the] apartment . . . and conversed with the tenant. Mr. Diaz swears that the tenant personally stated to him on that date that he was not in the military service.[12]

This fact pattern is pervasive in applications for default judgments of possession in landlord-tenant summary proceedings. . . . In 196 of the 201 [default proceedings before the court during the week of January 11, 1982,] the process servers were unable to effect service either by personal delivery to the tenants or by substituted service and, instead, claimed conspicuous place service. In 162 (or 83%) of these same matters, investigators employed by the attorneys representing the landlords were successful in making direct personal contacts with the tenants for the purpose of ascertaining that such tenants were not in military service so that affidavits of compliance with the Soldiers and Sailors Civil Relief Act . . . could be filed. These contacts between the investigators and the tenants occurred in some cases before the petitions were even prepared, in some cases between the date of the petitions and the date service was attempted, in some cases (as in the instant matter) on the very day the process servers could not locate the tenants, and in some cases after there was conspicuous place service. . . .

That the process servers in all these matters were unable to gain admittance and make any contact whatsoever with the tenants, when the investigators employed by the landlords' attorneys had no such difficulties, taxes the credulity of the court. . . .

The court submits that the inescapable conclusion to be drawn is that there is either widespread violation of [the Soldiers and Sailors Civil Relief Act] or that the process servers are not making any good faith reasonable applications to obtain admittance for the purpose of effecting service by personal delivery or substituted service.[13]

Similar realities with a similar response are evident in another of Judge Taylor's past decisions, this one involving the application of Consolidated Edison to search a private apartment in order to terminate electrical service and seize the meter for nonpayment of a bill.[14] The application was accompanied by an all-purpose affidavit form. Before issuing the necessary order in such cases, the judge is required by law to find that "the facts are as stated in the affidavit." The affidavit was unhappily drawn for this purpose and had been too hastily filled out.

The written opinion does not include the phrase "What's *this?*" but it can be heard nonetheless:

[What's *this?*] Plaintiff alleges that the meter is both in the apartment and in the public area (e.g. apartment/basement/public area) and that it made a meter reading on May 10, 1988. Par. 6. If this affidavit is based on personal knowledge . . . presumably an actual meter reading would have revealed the actual location of the meter. . . .

In Par. 9 . . . plaintiff contradicts Par. 6 by claiming that the amount due is based on "actual and/or estimated meter readings"?[15]

In one of her many talks with law students and lawyers about her life as a judge, she told about being assigned to hear cases in Brooklyn Civil Court. The courthouse had a bathroom for women—an accommodation unavailable in a Bronx building she had once been assigned to—but it was not furnished with toilet paper. Judges could request a roll of toilet paper to carry with them. This meant first checking out the roll and then clutching it while standing in the women's bathroom line with those who had to do without, a circumstance that called for solidarity and meant that Judge Taylor usually emerged empty-handed with no roll of toilet paper to check back in. Appeals to the judicial and administrative staffs produced no changes. Toilet paper for all was not in the budget. The city rented the building from a private landlord. Judge Taylor summoned him for a conference: "What's *this*? No toilet paper for women?" He produced the lease: "Look at Paragraph 22. Look at that, sweetie. It says the city has to supply toilet paper." Back to the city's staff she went. Still no result. "They said since they hadn't furnished toilet paper for five years, they wouldn't do so now. I called the Human Rights Commission. I said this is discrimination against women. I also announced I would no longer hold court in cases where there were female court officers, attorneys, or parties, because I would not subject them to such discrimination." That did it. At last, toilet paper arrived, a huge box of it, delivered to Judge Taylor's chambers, which then doubled as the women's toilet paper dispensary.

Long after her Brooklyn assignment ended and she had left, she saw some of that courthouse's personnel. They reported the toilet paper stopped with her departure. "Sometimes you can't make a dent," she says, "but they know I've been there. They remember."

She laughs about these things—as she does about many others—with the kind of genuine heartiness reserved to those who know more than enough of the pain, discouragement, and long, repeated hard work that are required to win incremental improvements in the legal system.

When she first started sitting in the residential landlord-tenant part of Civil Court, she was, she says, stunned by the routine. Weekly, every judge would be presented with a stack of hundreds of applications for default judgments for possession. The papers in each case were wrapped together, folded, and then stapled in a way that left available only a line at the bottom of the judgment form where the judge was expected to sign. Discrepancies in the record—one affidavit describing the tenant as red-haired, another as gray-haired—or facts indicating a tenant in need of medical or other help were stapled out of view. It was not easy for a judge who chose actually to read the documents. "It would take me two days just to pull out all the staples."

So she persisted in raising the issue in meetings with her fellow judges and the administrative judge. "Why staple the papers? Why not assume that the judges will read them?" She made arguments from the efficiency of judicial administration as well as from justice: Default judgments on unexamined records do not issue in finality. Instead they evoke orders to show cause why they should not be vacated; tenants come in after the default judgment has been issued and prove that they have paid their rent. She also made arguments from landlord recompense: In many cases tenants prove eligible for public services that will cover owed rent, and judicially supervised settlements insure a greater regularity of future payments. She says it took years but that she finally achieved this victory: Now the stacks come stapled only if the particular judge requests it. And, she adds, now about half the judges actually read the papers and hold hearings on default judgments.

When there has been service, with no answer from the tenant, and the landlord applies for default judgment, Judge Taylor has made it her habit to send a postcard from the court to the tenant (at her own expense; there is no administrative budget item for postcards). The postcards may provide useful information even when they do not produce the tenant. For example, in the case in which Consolidated Edison applied to enter an apartment and seize the meter, Judge Taylor noted: "In previous applications by Con Edison, notices of the application sent by the court itself were returned indicating that the defaulting defendant had moved and that a new tenant . . . was residing in the premises. If the court had not sent out its own notices, the court inadvertently would have terminated utility services of a person against whom there was not even an allegation, leastwise acceptable proof, of a refusal to pay an electric bill and a concealment of a meter."[16]

If the postcard does not produce the tenant's presence in court, Judge Taylor then holds an inquest as provided by law where default judgments on claims do not involve liquidated sums. In one that takes place while I am there, she goes over the affidavits of service carefully. She wants to question the process server and the investigator. Neither is on hand. She will go no further until the lawyer brings them in. She is not only concerned that the correct process be observed; she wants also to get on to what she describes as "the real questions." She wants to know if the tenant has small children, or is ill or is old. Another inquest reveals that the room in issue is part of a single-room-occupancy hotel and that the tenant concerned may be suffering from mental illness. She will not give judgment until she can determine whether the tenant is unable to protect himself and will require the appointment of a guardian.

In 1984, a sixty-six-year-old mentally disturbed woman, Eleanor Bumpurs, was shot to death while she was being evicted for failing to pay a month's rent of $96.85. When the police officer involved was acquitted, newspaper editorials observed that Ms. Bumpurs's death could have been prevented by proper police procedures. Judge Taylor wrote the *New York Times* to note that her death could also have been prevented by appropriate civil court procedures.[17] She observed that the Bumpurs case was one of those in which the judge had merely signed the default judgment. Ms. Bumpurs had never been personally served. A hearing would have revealed that fact, as well as the facts about her condition and her eligibility for an emergency rent grant.

Landlord attorneys that I observe are not happy about inquests. They are evidently unaccustomed to such examinations in housing court. But Judge Taylor insists that the process function in fact as the statute books and cases provide. Some attorneys are vehement in the arguments they make to her. They want their default judgments now, without delay. Judge Taylor is equally forceful in explaining why she will not grant them until the process that is due has run its course. Occasionally in these interchanges, she has to remind attorneys that she is the judge. Some landlord attorneys seem grudgingly accepting, even respecting. They are affirming a bond: the mutual regard of well-matched opponents; the common love of well-made, lawyerly arguments; the belief in process. Others just want to get on with the day's work. Others are angry. One, maybe half the judge's age, mutters to his companion in the hall as he leaves: "A wild and crazy girl. That's her calling card."

Not all the landlords are faceless corporations. Some who come to court are, literally, little old ladies in tennis shoes. Another is a housepainter who has come to court directly from a job and is still wearing his spattered overalls. He has been in Judge Taylor's court before. He does not get the default judgment he seeks, but he does get sympathetic attention. Judge Taylor explains to him what she is doing and why and promises early resolution of the case. She concludes: "I am the one doing the evicting. I need to know who is there. I may need to bring in an agency. You will get your money. There are things I can do. I really do want to know who I am evicting." She thanks him for coming and waiting.

Landlords, too, have rights. In one of her published opinions, she noted that the circumstances in the case "call for an early trial of all the

legal and equitable issues raised. The landlord's right to a speedy determination of the issues should not be delayed by the tenant's right to
pursue his rights in this Court."[18] And landlords, too, appear in court
without attorneys. When they do, Judge Taylor helps them with the process just as she helps tenants. "It is," she tells me, "one of the joys of
knowing myself. I have strong feelings about due process and equal
protection."

Of the cases where an inquest is held, some 12 percent end in a judgment of possession and warrant of eviction. Not all of those issue in an
eviction. After the judgment and warrant are signed, there is a five-day
stay before the eviction is effected. Judge Taylor sends out a second
postcard: "Come NOW." Some do, and the eviction is avoided. "Merely
sending postcards," she reports, "results in a lot of people showing up."

Today's cases prove to be largely hearings rather than inquests, for
in the majority of instances tenants have appeared. This means action
takes place outside the courtroom in the long, narrow, chair-lined corridor. It is full. All the tenants I see have come in response not to service
of papers but to the postcards Judge Taylor has mailed (the first card,
not the "Come NOW" second one). Many are women with children. Some
speak only Spanish. One or two are accompanied by a legal services lawyer. The remainder are unrepresented. They are a help to each other:
where to go for financial assistance, where to seek medical care for the
children, where to look for work. Most of the immediate help comes
from Judge Taylor's clerk, Bob Erlich, who has recently graduated from
law school but is not yet a member of the bar. He is the judge's agent and
alter ego as well as clerk. He bounds back and forth conferring with her
and working the halls. He relates well to both the attorneys and the
clients. He gets tenants together with their landlords and the landlords'
attorneys. He starts them talking to each other.

In one colloquy, a tenant, a woman with a child in hand, tells her
landlord's attorney: "I didn't sleep." She looks very tired. "I worried all
last night about this eviction." In another, it turns out that the landlord
has made an accounting mistake. In others there has been a misunderstanding that is easily rectified. In yet others, the tenants have simply
run out of money, and Erlich moves the conversation toward settlement.

I surmise that default judgments are about all that many of the landlord attorneys do. Throughout the day, they run from one courtroom to
another where housing cases are being called. They sweat with the
burden of large, battered briefcases bulging with stapled forms. They
are in a hurry. They neither offer nor attract sympathy. Judge Taylor's
courtroom and the corridor outside it represent to them the loss of time
and money. Tenants may not perceive the opportunity: High-volume

practitioners who represent landlords prefer settlements quickly achieved to those favorable to their clients.

One high-volume landlord attorney is young and understanding. He listens to the tenants. He evinces humane concern. He is the exception. I learn later that the landlord is the City of New York. The building in issue is one of those places, in terrible condition, that the city has had to take over. One tenant owes $1,940 in back rent. Terms are worked out for payment of $1,000. She says $940 was paid by a company check and that she has not yet been able to get a copy of the cashed check. She says there have been repeated problems with the computer on which the building accounts are kept. She says the halls in the building are coming apart, the peephole in her door is broken, the inside security chain on her door is off, and there are roaches and rats. The attorney takes notes. He promises to find out about the computer. He says the repairs will be made and the exterminator called.

Every conversation I observe ends in a settlement, and every tenant appears relieved. After they reach agreement, the parties enter the courtroom. Erlich explains the terms to Judge Taylor privately, and then she calls the tenant forward. She reviews the stipulations with the tenant. (She later tells me that the stipulations rarely fail.)

At these times, in conversation with tenants, compassion renders her uncharacteristically still and quiet. "Can you pay this rent?" she asks. As she listens to tenants tell about the conditions of their lives and how they believe they can find rent money, she is unguarded and vulnerable. Fatigue shows in her face. She shares exhaustion with the person she attends. The moment passes. She urges the tenants to come back if they see there is going to be a problem in meeting the payment terms they have agreed to. "Just come back in. To my court. You can always come back in. Just walk in. Any day. From 10:00 to 1:00 and 2:15 to 4:00. There may be something I can do. Maybe not. But come in *before* you can't pay. When you see it is not going to work out, come back. Don't wait. If you wait too long, it is much more difficult. I have very little bargaining power then. Once I sign an order, I have only tears." And then, quickly, she smiles, and the Manhattan banter begins again.

An attorney who has returned to Judge Taylor's court to complete a case begun last week discovers that papers he filed in the meantime have not reached Judge Taylor. She tells him: "You must bring the papers to me personally. You have to be sure to deliver them to me personally. The clerks don't like me and won't send them. You have to hand deliver them to me, otherwise it is not done. Do what I say."

There is more than eleven floors of difference between this courtroom and the Housing Court clerk's office below. Trouble with the landlord is only one of the assaults of poverty endured by the people who come before Judge Taylor. Tenants who survive the bureaucratic chaos of the clerk's office and make their way here enter a human space that opens onto other possibilities. The judge treats them with serious respect, attempts to help order their housing difficulties, and then tries to summon appropriate assistance for the multitude of other, related problems they suffer. In doing so, she acts in consonance with her experience at Mobilization for Youth.

Mobilization for Youth was her way out of the world of corporate law. She had graduated from Oregon's Reed College in 1951 and come to New York, where she could work as a legal secretary by day and attend New York University Law School by night. She completed her law degree, high in her class, in 1956 and went to work for a large, respected firm, Cahill, Gordon, Reindel & Ohl. At the time jobs were not easily found by women, especially by women who had graduated from night school, and especially by women with her political views. (Reed College's students had been thought to pose enough of a threat to the republic to warrant a visit from the House Un-American Activities Committee.) But, she says, Cahill was the son of foreign-born parents; he was not only sympathetic to the marginalized but also knew how hard they would work when given the chance. So she was hired. And she worked hard. And she did well. And she was a highly regarded litigator and corporate counselor.

She has told law students thinking about public interest work to take it up directly upon leaving law school. She confesses to a divided mind about this advice when she reflects on her own career. Her Wall Street, big firm experience, she says, has repeatedly functioned as a cure: When people see that at the top of her résumé, they do not pause at her gender, her night school degree, or her politics.

The corporate and securities work became "increasingly unacceptable. There was a difference between my clients and my beliefs." So in 1965 she left corporate practice for Mobilization for Youth, an experiment on Manhattan's Lower East Side promoted by Robert Kennedy, who, in Judge Taylor's description, "wanted to learn how people became poor." MFY offered a comprehensive response to poor young people who found themselves in trouble. Available under one roof were, in addition to lawyers, doctors, dentists, psychologists, educators, social workers, and job specialists—many of them drawn from the neighborhood. "We offered full service. We had the help right there. And it was successful. If we could just get kids out of scrapes and keep them out of jail, get them a job, keep them in school—if we could just keep them going until they were twenty-one or twenty-two they would be OK. Eighty-five percent of them straightened out after they were twenty-two. I don't know how it is now with crack, but then they straightened out. I keep running into 'alumni' of the program. Many of them work in service agencies, helping the next generation." It was, she says, "an exciting time, and I worked very hard."

Then "the clients began to organize. They were going to change the conditions of their lives." The expectable happened. "First the organizers were taken out of the program, and then the educators were taken away, and then the labor people." Judge Taylor left in 1968 to maintain her own practice and continue, in essence, her MFY work of representing indigent defendants in criminal cases without fee. She worked out of the offices of Ira Gammerman, now her husband. She took some cases for his firm's clients. (Her husband, with whom she lives on a quiet, tree-lined Greenwich Village street across from Public School 41, is a Supreme Court judge. In New York, "Supreme Court" designates a trial court and not, as in most jurisdictions, the highest appellate court.)

The MFY experience was formative. The wholeness of response offered by that program in that setting is a guiding image for what Judge Taylor provides through her present office.

The courtroom is a natural setting for her. A novel whose title she does not now remember decided her, at age fifteen, to become a judge. When the unexpected opportunity finally came, she seized it. She had joined the New York University law faculty in 1972 to teach in the criminal law clinic. In 1976 "someone called." A Democratic reform group was looking for judicial candidates. She went before an examining panel which recommended her to the club, and she became the reform candidate. In what the *New York Times* described as "an upset on the East Side," she defeated the organization candidate by a margin of two to one.[19] The term was for ten years. (She was reelected in 1986.)

She had offered for Civil, not Criminal, Court: "I have problems about sending people to jail in cases where the criminal courts are just dealing with the end result of poverty." This is an objection not to incarceration as such but to jail as an answer to poverty. Civil Court jurisdiction extends to landlord-tenant, consumer, and other disputes involving sums less than $10,000. In talks, she encourages people to become judges, especially in Civil Court or courts similar to it: "We need good judges in Civil Court. There are few lawyers for the tenants. We see people just trying to get by."

Before assuming office, Judge Taylor attended judges' school. "They told us: 'If you screw up, you'll be sent to Family Court.'" Ostensibly because she had been the reform candidate and was a woman, her first assignment was to Family Court.

She was appalled by what she found there, by "the terrible things you are asked to do." She was asked to take children from their parents and send them to foster homes or to "'evaluative centers' that always had some name like Pleasantville or Cloud 9 but were really jails." Then she would be asked for "permanent termination" of the legal relationship between a child and her natural parents and to grant adoption of the child by the foster parents.

In one case, the child had been sent from Manhattan to foster parents in Westchester. Termination and adoption were sought. The agency reported to Judge Taylor that the mother did not have "a good relation" with her child. "What's *this?* The mother is allowed only one visit a month? In a little room at the agency? In the presence of the foster mother? And you say she doesn't have a good relationship?"

She still does not understand why foster homes are not provided in the child's neighborhood. Or why, instead of a foster home, the city does not provide a housekeeper from the neighborhood. "What these mothers need is help. They can't get all their kids' teeth brushed in the morning. Send in a housekeeper, and let the children stay with their families."

Family Court remains, she says, "beyond my comprehension." She lasted there a year. She had been heating up the Siberia to which she had been exiled. *In re P.* was decisive, the case that convinced the administrative judge to bring her in from the cold.[20] Mayor Koch condemned Judge Taylor for the opinion. He called it "ridiculous."[21] But he also described it as dismissing a charge of prostitution on the ground that the sex involved was recreational. He was mistaken and, as a lawyer, should have known better.

P. was a fourteen-year-old female. She was charged, among other things, with making the complaining witness an offer to engage in sex acts with him for a fee of ten dollars. He accepted the offer. Under New York law a juvenile could be found delinquent only if she did an act that would constitute a crime if done by an adult. For adults, prostitution was a crime. But P.'s attorney argued that the prostitution statute was unconstitutional and that, if it was unconstitutional as applied to adults, it was unconstitutional as applied to juveniles. Judge Taylor agreed and dismissed the sexual conduct charge.

New York's prostitution laws were originally directed against women only. They were not rendered gender neutral until the 1965 enactment of a statute that proscribed patronizing a prostitute. Even so, Judge Taylor observed, the "historical sex bias has endured."[22] For example, prostitution carried a penalty of up to ninety days; patronizing a prostitute carried a penalty of up to fifteen days or a fine of $250. Also, the prostitution statutes had been selectively enforced against females. Of 3,219 people arrested in the first six months of 1977, 2,944 had been females.

Only sixty male patrons of these 2,944 females had been charged with a violation. (The male patron in this case was not charged with a crime.) The methods of enforcement included the use of male undercover police officers posing as patrons to entrap streetwalkers, but did not employ plainclothes female officers to entrap male patrons. For these reasons, Judge Taylor found the statute in violation of equal protection.

She also found it in violation of the constitutionally protected right of privacy. She examined the state's claims that the statute was aimed at harmful activity and found them insubstantial: Less than 5 percent of venereal disease is attributable to prostitution; there is no proof that prostitution causes ancillary crime or encourages the spread of organized crime; and if prostitution threatens marriage and the family, the burden lies with patrons, most of whom are married, not with the prostitute, who is punished more severely. Public solicitation by prostitutes is offensive, and the state may legitimately prohibit it. But such public activity is distinguishable from private sex and must be dealt with separately. "Private, consensual sexual conduct between adults, whether or not performed for a fee, is protected by the right of privacy. If the state has a legitimate interest in curbing public disorder, it can and must accomplish this objective without depriving the individual of his or her right to engage in private, consensual, sexual relations. The constitutionally protected right of privacy makes it incumbent upon the state to implement its policy by more reasonable, less intrusive means."[23] The decision was reversed on appeal.[24]

Judge Taylor is no advocate of prostitution ("C'mon, sisters, we've got to get our act together"). But she is committed to the exposure of sex bias and to keeping kids out of the penal system long enough to allow them to "straighten out." She is also committed to creating a voice for the poor out of law. Like her other published opinions, *In re P.* is careful and lawyerly.

There has been talk about running her for a seat on the Supreme Court, the next highest trial court, on which she sometimes sits by special appointment. She declines. "I have never been in such a good place to help so many people." Later she adds: "I sleep so well at night."

At Mobilization for Youth, and Family Court, and then Housing Court, she has been stunned and appalled by what she has seen. She finds the system is deployed fundamentally against the vulnerable. So why is her presence on the court, her acceptance of the forms and discourse of law, and her emphasis on process—why are these not simply subsumed by the establishment and made a badge of legitimation? Will not any system that can exhibit a Margaret Taylor claim to be inclusive and sound?

"You can't sit back and let people's lives be so miserable. Is it time for the streets? It's either the streets or this. If the revolution is not there, you have to give up marching around. You have to give that up as a judge." When she was growing up in Oregon and had first thought to become a judge and make things better, she must already have been able to see beyond present realities. She describes Klamath Falls at the time this way: "Twenty miles to the north, Indians were kept on an 'unofficial' reservation. Twenty miles to the south was the site where Japanese-Americans had been held in a concentration camp. In town, there were three KKK groups and no black people."

Asked how, in that environment, she had developed as she had, she says that Klamath Falls was the kind of place to which young ministers, radical and fresh out of Yale, would be sent for tempering. She was attracted to them, to the discussions they led, and to their sometimes daring ideas. "The values of Christ were always key," she remembers, "the kind of values you got from going to Sunday School, and we all went to Sunday School." She also remembers that a populist spirit ruled Klamath Falls, as it did much of Oregon and the Midwest. "I grew up with the values of Christ and midwestern populism."

When last I visited her, she was scheduled to attend a Washington, D.C., meeting of an association of women judges. A meeting with Supreme Court Justice William Brennan was on the schedule. "I hope I get a chance to speak to him. I want to thank him." She paused and, reflecting on the earlier conversation, said: "Christ was the human for poor people. You're to be like him. The system is not for poor people, but the Warren Court was a shining moment. It's all over now, but at one wonderful time the system was responsive to the poor." I take this as a statement less of nostalgia and weariness than of possibility and challenge. "I think things *are* better to some degree."

DAVID HARDING

The road from Eugene to the Warm Springs Reservation in interior Oregon climbs the Cascade Mountains through towering, dark conifers. Logging trucks rumble by intermittently, taking timber off the mountain. Three logs—occasionally a single one—are large enough to make a huge load. In early April patches of snow remain, enough at the higher elevations for limited skiing. Snow and rain from the evaporated waters of the Pacific drench the Cascades' western slopes and heights; little is carried further inland. First glimpses of lands to the east below bring to mind the arid Southwest. Over the divide and into the lowlands, I cross a distinct natural border near the town of Sisters where pine gives way to scrubby growth, and the air is suddenly sweet with juniper and

sage. Further on, the road passes a deep green surprise: a field of cultivated mint. And, later, rows of hazelnut.

The boundaries of the Warm Springs Reservation enclose some
600,000 acres stretching from high on the eastern slopes of the Cascades
well down into the plains, from snow-capped Mount Jefferson through
old forest to dry tableland. It is a feast for the senses.

The reservation was established by an 1855 treaty as the exchange
for ten million acres granted by the Indians to the United States. Its first
residents were the Warm Springs tribe (made up of bands of Walla
Wallas) and Wascoes, both of them peoples whose original home was
land along the Columbia, where they fished for salmon. Paiutes were
first sent to the reservation in 1879 from Vancouver Barracks, where
they had been held as prisoners of war. Today the three form the Confederated Tribes of Warm Springs. Some 3,500 people live on Warm
Springs, including several hundred who are either nontribal Indians or
non-Indians.

I am told that, according to local stereotypes, the Wascoes are aggressive, and therefore most like whites; the Warm Springs are river Indians and the most cultivated; and the Paiutes, the only true fullbloods
on the reservation, are displaced and, ironically, discriminated against. I
am also told that the three are beginning to mix, a goal of United States
policy in forcing the tribes into the same place, but that the process of
mixing is bringing into being a new Indian with new Indian conscious-
ness, an outcome United States policy did not anticipate and did not
desire.

Extreme poverty ruled Warm Springs until the 1940s. The culture
was rich with stories and dances, but survival was in doubt. Whites
wanted the Indians' land. With World War II came a demand for timber,
and the Confederated Tribes could begin turning a profit from sale of
their principal marketable resource. By 1955, the annual revenue had
risen to $240,000. The tribes now own a sawmill and plywood plant, a
resort and convention center, a home-building corporation, and a
garage-repair shop. A short "official" history of the reservation concludes:

> The Confederated Tribes have received praise from government
> officials and others for their numerous self-help programs. Much
> of this praise resulted from what Vernon Jackson, then tribal gen-
> eral manager, described in 1966 as "a transition to the white man's
> way of looking at things." And he added, "It was kind of hard."

In 1990 the unemployment rate on Warm Springs was around 40
percent. For a recent tribal employment program, forty-six of one hundred applicants failed to pass a drug/alcohol test. Annual dividends paid

to tribal members out of profits from the tribes' businesses are down to $500, from a high of $1,500 in the 1970s.

On this trip, I have come to see Judge David Harding. He is a Turtle Mountain Chippewa whose mother left her old home in North Dakota for Oregon in the 1940s. He lives outside the Warm Springs reservation in a spacious, two-story log home that he built halfway up the steep slope of a canyon carved by the Deschutes River. The sheer, well-defined canyon rim above is a colonnade of reddish basalt. The soft greens, browns, and ginger along the river below are punctuated by a willow glowing orange for early spring. This is a fly-way for eagles. I see only ravens; David puts out dinner scraps for them.

Shortly after I arrive, David's wife, Megan, drives up. She is a Cour d'Alene. Her van is loaded with their four children, all boys—like their parents they are black-haired, black-eyed, gold-skinned. The two youngest, not yet two years old, are twins. The next morning I hear the four of them wake, all laughing and happy.

David is thirty-eight and is a tribal judge. Just now he is judge of the Burns Paiute Tribe in Burns, Oregon. A former president of the Northwest Tribal Court Judges Association, he has been a judge for or consultant to several Northwest tribes, notably the Confederated Tribes of Warm Springs.

As a kid, he says, he had done chores for a gun maker, cleaning a bluing bin and the like. The gun maker gave him some career advice that David remembers taking seriously: "With your size, you need to use your brain." (He is an efficiently built five feet, six-and-a-half inches. I think of him as vigorous and athletic. His height had not registered with me.) He says his high school prepared its students for athletics and farming and that he was disqualified from both by his size and inability. He took advantage of government programs for Indians and enrolled in the University of Oregon in Eugene in 1974. He became a frenetically busy Indian activist.

This transformation involved, in part, the reawakening of early memories. David recalls returning to his mother's tribal home for pow-wows, where she would speak only in her original tongue and in French. He particularly remembers the train rides to and from North Dakota. That was when he heard the stories, swapped among Turtle Mountain Chippewas traveling together. "My mother would tell stories to her friends, and we children would overhear. I would sometimes catch her looking at us out of the corner of her eye. She intended us to hear. That was how she taught us, telling those stories."

He learned more about being an Indian during college. "Indian issues came alive in the mid-seventies," he says, "and I was on a roll." He got to know "the Indian business" and became heavily engaged in it. "I had changed. From knowing nothing about Indians, I became completely Indian and proud to be one."

In Eugene, he was instrumental in the establishment of the Eugene Indian Center as well as the Indian Program on Alcohol and Drug Awareness, and he was made a special agent for Indian inmates in the county jail. He made frequent trips to Washington, D.C. He was brought into contact with the Smithsonian, which named him a coordinator for Northwest Native American Arts and Crafts. He remembers filling a plane with Indians and taking them to the D.C. Mall to perform dances during the 1976 Bicentennial celebrations—"they gave us our own jet." His graduation in 1978 was a memorable triumph. He wore an eagle feather. His mother embroidered a rising sun and tepee on the back of his robe. The university president paid tribute to him. It was a high and heady time. It was about to end.

He started law school the next fall. He did not readily settle into the study of law, and the school was unaccustomed to Indian law students. His first grades were poor. A misunderstanding arose. He was accused of wrongly working with another Indian law student to complete an assignment. And then tragedy struck Megan's family.

He had met Megan in 1977. She was so beautiful—she still is—it made his chest hurt. He saw her next after law school started and was infatuated all over again. They were soon married. In the midst of that first year of law school, her sister was killed in a car accident. Her brother was given a two-week furlough from the service so that he could attend the funeral, a central ritual in the tribal tradition. After the funeral, before his return, her brother, too, was killed in a car accident. It would be years before Megan would recover. Her world came apart, and so did David's.

Just when he needed to concentrate on legal studies, he could not. He was depressed, angry, and short of money. "I was so emotionally disturbed," he remembers, "I could not study." The pain of it all seeps back into his voice. "I sat for hours trying to read and couldn't. I had done all those things in college and had been on that high of graduation and now my ego was battered. Megan was in terrible shape. I was in terrible shape. I sought advice from school officials. They said to drop out and come back the next fall. But I couldn't quit. I was too arrogant about getting that far. I still thought I could power through. I didn't. I flunked out. I applied to the academic standing committee for readmission but got nowhere. It is hard to explain how much I was hurt. I was lost, basically. It really hurt."

He went to work for one of his brothers in the construction business cutting concrete. "I didn't want to work in a family business, but what else could I do? I had changed. From knowing nothing about Indians, I had become an Indian completely. I had to figure out how to use my education, how to use my background." An opportunity shortly presented itself. Late in the fall of 1979 he attended a meeting called to organize a job training program under the federal Comprehensive Employment and Training Act. The Warm Springs Confederated Tribes was to be one of the sponsors. By the turn of the year, David had moved to the reservation to serve as the assistant director of the Warm Springs office. In the spring he became director.

Because he worked in the tribal administrative office, he happened to see a notice calling for applicants for an opening as tribal judge. He talked to some of the staff about it, and they encouraged him to apply, remarking that they would be lucky to have someone with a college education, to say nothing of a year of law school. He was appointed. He went home to tell Megan—"You're not going to believe this. You will have to dress me as a judge." He began serving on July 1, 1980, a year after the debacle at the University of Oregon Law School. There were two other judges: the chief judge and a juvenile judge. Both were women.

When he went to work the first day, he had no idea what to do. At 8:30 A.M. the chief justice handed him a copy of the ninety-five-page law and order code, said his first case was scheduled for 9:00 A.M., and added: "Good luck, kiddo." At the appointed hour he walked into court and began with arraignments. On the afternoon calendar were divorce, probate, and child custody cases. "I had been in law school. I wasn't taught there how to conduct court." The clerk led him through it.

He sat on the Warm Springs tribal court from 1980 to 1986. During that time, he explained in a 1986 talk, he had gradually begun "to consult with other tribes that were establishing tribal courts, and now I sit as a judge in sixteen tribal courts throughout the Pacific Northwest: I'm Chief Judge for the Burns Paiute Tribe in Burns, Oregon, and Chief Justice for the Lummi Tribal Court of Appeals as well as an associate judge in fourteen other courts. I am, you might say, a very busy judge."[25]

Tribal courts are a non-Indian imposition. Not all reservations have them. Contemporary tribal courts and Western-style governmental structure were primarily the product of the Indian Reorganization Act of 1934. Before that there were some Courts of Indian Offenses begun in the last century by the Secretary of the Interior. David notes that "they were operated by the Bureau of Indian Affairs for the support and benefit of the Indian agent, and in many cases they deliberately refused to take any cultural differences into account."[26] More recently, the Indian Civil Rights Act of 1968 introduced further changes to tribal courts. The type and structure of tribal courts differ among the reservations that have them.

"The realities of the reservation," David reports, "are that the democratic forms of government imposed on the tribes caused the people to abandon their old values that made Indian societies very law-abiding. When a tribal court administers justice, the old rule of restitution and reconciliation that families used is eliminated. Government institutions become distanced from the people, and that leads to a good deal of confusion and animosity."

Other commentators agree and note that tribal courts, made in the image of the federal judiciary, dislodge the "informality of Indian life that had been the repository of cultural traditions and customs, and transpose tribal society's understanding of itself as a complex of responsibilities and duties . . . into a society based on rights against government [thereby eliminating] any sense of responsibility that the people might have felt for one another."[27]

Warm Springs has had a tribal court since 1946, about the time its desperate economy took a turn for the better. As is true on most other reservations, the court on this one is an arm of the Tribal Council, ostensibly the ruling body. There is not a rigid separation of powers. Initially the Warm Springs court heard disputes the reservation's BIA agent did not want to handle. It tried to resolve conflicts, David says, in the old way, by seeking consensus and trying to work things out communally. The Indian Civil Rights Act of 1968 provided that individual Indians could claim, against their tribal governments, the protection of certain rights, a modified selection from the Bill of Rights. In response, the Warm Springs court implemented formal procedures in 1971–72.

When he was appointed to the tribal court in 1980, David says, it was still not really engaged in law on the U.S. model. There was no substantive guidance for civil cases, and the criminal law, which followed a model written by a non-Indian lawyer and supplied by the BIA, was a few pages of crude enumeration of crimes. "I was the first judge with law school experience, and I demanded that things be done right, with common sense and fundamental fairness." He worked with the tribal attorneys to have the law and order code rewritten. By 1986 the code ran to four hundred pages. Rules of court that he advocated were adopted.

The changes helped to revise reservation attitudes about the court and brought it increased business. In 1980 each of the three judges had two hundred to three hundred cases a year. By 1986, each judge had a thousand cases, of which six hundred were criminal.

As David points out, there is federal Indian law and then there is the very different law of the reservation and its courts, which remain very much *tribal* courts. A Warm Springs tribal judge's continuation in office depends on reappointment by the Tribal Council. (The council also appoints panels of lay appellate judges as needed. Of the trial courts' three thousand cases in 1986, only three cases went all the way through the appellate process, and only one of those was partially reversed.) The judges are not bound by precedent ("We don't want to be like the white man"), and lawyers, if any are present, may be little in evidence in the proceedings ("We might tell them to shut up sometimes when they get in the way"). Parties may be unrepresented or have a lay advocate instead of a lawyer.

The tribal character of the court is nowhere more evident than in the nature of David's—Judge Harding's—decisions. He points out that "when a defendant has no legal counsel, you learn very quickly what law is supposed to do for a community. It is to solve problems and to seek justice, and tribal judges are much closer to dispensing justice because of their willingness to move beyond established procedures and probe for the understanding of the nature of the offense and the motivations and consideration that were operative, and to seek a just settlement and the good of the tribe. Judges in the non-Indian courts have the luxury of sitting back and allowing the courtroom skills of the attorneys to determine the course of the case." His probate cases frequently concerned who was rightfully in line to inherit and tend a family's allotment or possessions handed down from ancient times. "A final accounting might keep a family together or tear it apart. I had to get to know the people. I'd go out to their homes and talk to them. I'd look at the property or valuables. I sought advice. I'd ask as much as I could find out."

(I surmise that his findings were extensive. He begins to talk about the case of a woman who, in anticipation of death, marked her valuables with the names of the intended beneficiaries. David's account is arrested by the memory that one of her legs had been amputated. She wanted to be buried whole. She took the amputated leg to the funeral home, where it was kept in formaldehyde for ten years until she died and it could be placed in the casket with the rest of her body. The leg went to its rightful place, but arguments arose about whose name had been attached to which valuables.)

Tribal judging, he says, "is moral in nature. It requires a knowledge of the people." He seems to me to have worked at the necessary knowledge in two ways: through involvement in the community and with Olney Patt.

The life of the community engaged much of who David was and what he did. Because he was not a member of the Warm Springs tribes, he was not an insider. But because he is a Turtle Mountain Chippewa, neither was he altogether an outsider.

He had been very poor as a child. "There were white people who sincerely cared about me and my family," he says. "They showed that sincerity in the way they helped us. It is ironic, I suppose, but I learned from white people. I learned that sincerity is expressed in actions. I really cared for the people of Warm Springs. I loved them. I tried to let my sincerity show in my actions. I attended funerals, and I danced. I had to learn the dances, but I did and I performed them. Sometimes my dancing encouraged others to dance. It helped Warm Springs to revive some of its traditional culture. And it helped me to judge. When John Doe would come before me on some criminal charge, I could say: 'John, I know you can do better. I've seen you in the longhouse. I know you can do better, and I know you know that, too. I've seen you at funerals. I know you are not lying. I know you betrayed yourself.'" At lunchtime he played basketball with the young people. "It was good for them to see me, the judge, out there with them." And he was an ambulance driver for the Warm Springs emergency medical service.

He distinguishes his approach from that of the white tribal attorney, who, he says, "divided law from his life and community. For him law was a business. He was only here during business hours."

David got to know the land as well as the people. In his home I notice a map of the reservation. Small sections of it have been marked in one of three colors to record where he has gathered huckleberries, wild celery, and roots. (Several years ago I saw in his office another map of the reservation. It was a checkerboard of four colors denoting different forms of ownership: tribal, individual tribal member, nontribal Indian, and non-Indian. Under the Allotment Act, which was forced upon the tribes at the end of the last century, reservation land was divided and subjected to individual ownership. Today, a tribe, the federal government, or the state government may have separate or concurrent jurisdiction, depending on who owns a given piece of land. It is a mess. In many instances, there is no constitutional or legal basis for anything but tribal jurisdiction. In these instances, the intrusion of federal and state governments is a usurpation legitimated only by force.)

David's immersion in Warm Springs was complemented by his relationship to Olney Patt, an old-time statesman. Olney was a member of the tribal council for thirty years, a reservation administrator, and a rancher. His jobs kept him very busy. His time was also consumed by the fact that he had the gifts of leadership in the old tribal ways in which he had been raised and which he still practices. He both played an influential part in the government installed by whites and had the respect and influence of a traditional tribal statesman.

This bridging, mediating role was singular. David explained: "Democracy doesn't necessarily always work on the reservations. It depends on circumstances and varies from one place to another. When whites came, Indian names were too hard to pronounce. So they gave Indians new names, white names. Some Indians simply accepted their new names and their new position and sold out to the whites. The whites dealt with the accommodating Indians and overlooked the real people, the traditional leaders, who were too proud to do white men's tricks. They recognized the 'good' Indians, what we call the 'hang-around-the-forts.' The descendants of the 'hang-around-the-forts' are the ones in power now in the recognized government. They have to hire a lot of white management because they think Indians are incapable. Today's successful tribes are the descendants of the real guys, like the Passamaquoddy and Six Nations. On Warm Springs, the old leadership structure did not survive past the 1950s, the second generation after the IRA [Indian Reorganization Act]. Until then, they still could have exercised power in the traditional ways. But the need for jobs and food was too great. The Indians here were in pitiful circumstances. So the IRA government won out. Olney is different. He has the gifts of leadership in the old ways, but he harbors no resentment for whites. He tried to mediate, to help the reservation make good both ways. He preserves the old ways and is 'progressive.'"

David takes me to see his old friend and mentor. We drive a pickup deep into the reservation, well beyond houses and businesses. The sky grows larger. We encounter no other vehicles. Occasionally, we pass large farm machinery—combines and the like—rusting in the sage and wholly out of place. David refers to them as "artifacts of another failed government experiment on Indians." He talks lovingly of Olney and remembers how, late at night, Olney would sing old Indian songs. "He would give us their meaning by telling us the event for which they were sung and where he learned them. He knows the old language so well and the old people. Not many people understand anymore."

Olney suffered terrible tragedies and then an increasingly terrible struggle with alcohol. He determined to put both behind him and returned to the spot where he was raised and the old house. To get there we drive miles beyond the ranch he had made into a success and turn off the dirt road onto a smaller one, the driveway. Vehicles have sunk into it during long-ago rains. The deep tracks are now brick hard. If the pickup drops off the thin ridges David gingerly follows, it will be suspended on its frame; the wheels will not touch the bottom of these ruts. Olney's straightforward, one-story frame house faces southeast. Several deerskins hang outside drying on racks. The inside is comfortable and neat, everything in order. There are a few traditional ceremonial instruments close at hand. Olney is not exceptionally tall, but he is large and solid. He is old.

David greets him in a loud voice, practically shouting, so that he can hear. Some while later, David's voice has gradually dropped to normal, and Olney hears everything. I surmise that Olney has a great capacity for distancing himself when the need arises. David is an old friend whom Olney is glad to see, and for that reason he accepts me as well and is willing to hear. He has great dignity and *gravitas* and also much sweetness. His most frequent response is a soft, musical *ooouuu,* uttered in a slow dying fall.

He talks with a soft voice and well-spaced silences as he recalls the difficulties of tribal politics. "Some people thought I was moving too fast, but I wasn't. We always got to one place before we stepped forward to another." He says some of the new ways are better. He says this is so particularly of the tribal court during David's tenure, when the court rules and revised law and order code were put in place, and the court became less beholden to the influence of reservation power brokers. (He allows that David was a good judge.) This is what he saw as progress, but he was and is very firm in the conviction that progress did not lie in any direction that would diminish the tribe's land holdings. No matter how great the need or temptation, the land base could not be allowed to shrink. The tribe could not allow that to happen. Many years ago when he was a boy, Olney remembers, his grandfather had sat by the fire late one evening, in this house. "I can see him sitting there, drawing his knife down a long stick, making shavings, and saying that the tribe must hold on to its land. The old guy got it right."

David and I take our leave as daylight thickens. I shake hands with Olney. Later, as we are driving out, David explains that the traditional response to Olney's extended hand would have been to touch my palm to his instead of grasping his hand. It would have been an apt ritual expression of mutual respect. I see anew how the non-Indian custom of the handshake is the ritual expression of a power struggle. David also explains to me that Olney's detail about his grandfather's whittling was a way of saying how hard it had been to hold on to the land. Wood fires were the only source of heat in the extreme cold and great poverty. Even the elderly had to contribute to the work of survival, in this case helping with the fuel.

When he sat on the Warm Springs court, David made it his habit to consult regularly with Olney, the authority of whose gifts is palpable. "I'd talk to him two hours about a two-minute problem." He was trying to absorb Olney's perspective. "I wanted to see these people through his eyes. I wanted to act through Olney's knowledge of his people. He knew the families and how they got here and their reputations. He knew who was lying and who was not, who was truly in line to inherit valuables and whether they practiced the old ways. I wanted to do what was right, what was right by the culture of the people involved. I think I succeeded. Someday we will have to stand trial before God. You will have a split second to pass before him. Your split second may be something you didn't even know. You may not know when you have been judged. I always tried to do the right thing."

Success like David's is difficult and fragile. He had immersed himself in the reservation's life, as much as was possible to a nonmember of the tribes. Through Olney he had absorbed as much as he could of the local universe. Thus fortified, he tried to act appropriately within what was possible for a tribal court in that time and place. I get an idea of the complexity of the possible from his docket sheets.

He keeps all his docket sheets from the Warm Springs court. In going through them I realize how disproportionate are the number of entries for contempt. One, for example, has 947 entries. Of these, 347 are "contempt." The next highest is "disorderly conduct" (134), then "minor in possession of alcohol" (109). David explains that many of the contempt citations were for people who simply had not appeared in court when they were summoned. They would be found and brought in, and the contempt charge would be dropped. But there were also people who would come to court, not like what happened there, tell the judges where they could go, and then walk out.

One of the original theories of American federal courts is that they are powerless. Lacking force or will, they have only judgment. That is theory. Tribal courts are powerless in fact. They really do have only judgment. They have to exercise care about who is held in contempt. They may not have the power or respect or tradition to do anything about it. If a fledgling tribal court that is trying to build its authority issues many empty judgments of contempt, it may only exhibit and increase its powerlessness. But the same result would obtain if nothing were done about displays of disregard for the court. David says, "I usually found a way to dismiss the case and save the contempt." And save the future of the court.

But subtle judgments have their limits. David's success created jealousies. He was not a Warm Springs tribal member. He had never penetrated the power structure. And, as he said, "I couldn't show everybody my sincerity—not everybody was at the funerals or the longhouse or on the basketball court." He and Megan had difficulties which they resolved, but rumors started. Those who were jealous of him used the rumors. "I couldn't convince some people that the rumors were untrue. I began to lose my footing in the community. I began to lose the power to persuade." The critical event came when the niece of the Tribal Council chairman was accused of a crime. "The chairman sent a message around to me: 'Don't treat her like everyone else.' I treated her like everyone else, and I never recovered." He was not reappointed.

His judicial work with other tribes continued, but he began to limit it. His demise as a judge at Warm Springs "felt like flunking out of law school all over again. I wanted to get in the woods and get healthy." He took a job with the Bureau of Indian Affairs working as a forester.

Now he is a branch manager of the Children's Service Division in Oregon's Department of Human Resources. He is supervisor to ten social workers. His energy and enthusiasm have been restored. He is deeply involved in the care of children. "I can do good here just as I could as a tribal judge on Warm Springs. Maybe kids' cases are where the most good can be done. You can help to shape a child's future. You can look out for them. You can affect a lot of children's lives in a positive way."

He remembers that, at the start of law school, the incoming students were told, "Learn to love the law." He adds: "That's misleading. I never learned to love the law. Law is a tool. You don't love it; you use it. I certainly got to know the law, and I can run a court and keep up with any lawyer. And once I had to teach a federal judge. He had granted a habeas corpus petition and ordered me to release a person I had sent to jail. He did not know Indian law. I told him he was full of it, that under federal law his court had no jurisdiction over the subject matter. Exclusive jurisdiction lay with the tribal court. He had no basis for issuing the order. He had to drop it.

"I can do law. I just didn't allow law to get in the way. I could always show that my decisions were based in law. I could always say where they came from in the books. For white man's law, you read books. But in a tribal court, you have to stop and get to know the people. You try to do good by what the community believes is just."

David still serves as a tribal judge for the Burns Paiute Tribe. "Basically," he reflects, "I have lived a lifetime in the last fifteen years." David was once the singer for a rock-and-roll band. Just as I leave, he pulls out a guitar and sends me away to the strains of "Lone Star Buckaroo": "Sunsets are picking up stardust . . ."

TIM COULTER

Several chiefs and other leaders of the Six Nations Confederacy (the Iroquois or Houdensaunee) have come from upstate New York to confer with Tim Coulter, head of the Indian Law Resource Center. The center occupies an 1865 townhouse on Capitol Hill in Washington, not far from the John Phillip Sousa house and the D.C. Marine barracks. It is nicely appointed, comfortable, and welcoming. Boots, jeans, and open-collar shirts are the dress of the day. Tim, a Potawatomi raised in South Dakota and Oklahoma, is tall, with striking good looks, in his mid-forties. He is distinguishably trim among these large men, all of whom move with lightness of foot.

The subject for the meeting is Six Nations land claims. The talk ranges over cases, politics, and strategy. Occasionally there is small talk about people and events of the present and, with equally easy familiarity, of the eighteenth and nineteenth centuries. ("He was on the booze," it is said about a distinguished chief who signed a disputed document one hundred and fifty years ago. "The people overrode the chiefs. The chiefs didn't want this, but the people and the whites did, and the whites brought in the booze. It was the fault of the people.")

Since Tim founded it in 1978, the center has devoted much of its work to the Six Nations. The land claims turn on old documents and require massive historical as well as legal research. As he explained in one of the center's annual reports:

> In 1784 the United States, in the Treaty of Ft. Stanwix, recognized and promised to protect all the Six Nations' territory which then comprised almost the entirety of western and upstate New York. Yet the State of New York in combination with unscrupulous land companies and speculators contrived a series of fraudulent "treaties," leases and other arrangements to deprive the Iroquois of their lands. . . . By the end of the century, the Six Nations were living on tiny reservations, defrauded of some 18 million acres of their land, land which was supposedly protected by the Treaty of Ft. Stanwix. Almost all of the lands were lost through transactions which were plainly in violation of United States law, the Articles of Confederation and later the United States Constitution. (1979 Report, pp. 4–5)

The Supreme Court agreed with such arguments—advanced by Tim and other attorneys representing the tribes—and in *Oneida County v. Oneida Indian Nation,* 470 U.S. 226 (1985), upheld the validity of the treaty-based Indian claim. The prospect is that the Six Nations have legal title to much of the disputed land. But Tim is cautious: "Turning this court victory into practical final results of land recovery and compensation is, of course, very arduous, time-consuming work that will not be completed for several years" (1988 Report, p. 6).

Some of that work is what leaders of the Six Nations have come to Washington to do. Those who speak do so softly, with assurance. They are realistic and politic. And wily. They also have a bemused sense of irony. They smile as they discuss how recent assertion of their claims brought belated remedial attention from the State of New York. One of the provisions in a contested transaction called for the state's annual payment of, among other things, 150 bushels of salt. There had been an extended lapse, and then a delivery of nine tons.

These representatives of the confederacy would like to achieve public understanding. They readily agree when Tim suggests that they not merely take advantage of loopholes and that their bargaining list be "clear, sensible, upright—things the average citizen will agree with and understand." Negotiations on claims are under way, but it may be necessary to file more lawsuits.

Tim outlines the status of various legal steps and options. He is interrupted by a telephone call from Australia. He jots down notes with a thick fountain pen, hangs up, pushes the note pad to one side of his well-ordered desktop, and returns to his review. His words are accompanied by quick, easy laughs, shoulder hunches, and small shakes of the head that ripple his long, flowing hair (brown, touched with gray). He talks now, as always when I have heard him, with huge, quiet patience. I cannot escape the impression that his patience rests on and compresses a taut, steely spring.

He is confident and optimistic about the Six Nations' legal position. He likely knows more than any other attorney in the United States about the law involved—the ancient treaties, transactions, and statutes. His knowledge comes from the claims of others as well as the Six Nations.

On the wall of his office is an 1845 plat of Seminole lands in Florida. The center represents the Traditional Seminole Nation. One of its reports explains that these clients

> have refused to live on federally established reservations or to join federally chartered tribal organizations. These deeply traditional people have shunned virtually all involvement with federal and state "benefit" programs. . . . [They] have lived primarily in remote camps and villages in South Florida since the end of the Seminole Wars in the 1850's. Practically all are full-blood and most speak little or no English. Their goal for generations has been to realize the promises made to them in the treaty ending the [wars]: that their lands will be respected and that they will be "left alone." . . . Today most of them live as "squatters" on the land that they fought successfully to keep . . . land which was illegally patented to others by the federal and state governments. (1983 Report, p. 7)

Among the center's other clients are Western Shoshones, Hopis, Yuroks, Chippewa-Crees, and Alaska Natives, as well as the Oglala and Rosebud Sioux Tribes, which together comprise more than half of all Sioux. "The United States confiscated nearly all the Sioux land in the Dakotas, Nebraska, Wyoming and Montana during a particularly ugly period in the second half of the Nineteenth Century. The Sioux began at once to seek a return of their lands, and at last retained an attorney in 1923" (1988 Report, p. 4). The lawyers never told the tribes that the claims for compensation they were pursuing could have the effect of extinguishing Indian title to the land. "In the 1970's the Sioux began to realize that the money claims could mean they would never be able to recover the land itself" (ibid.). The Oglala and Rosebud Tribes fired their lawyers and tried to halt their money claims. Even so, the lawyers continued to prosecute the claims and entered a settlement and judgment without the two tribes' knowledge and in opposition to their directions. The center was brought in to help, but the courts ruled against them. The judgment stands. The tribes have rejected the compensation awards. The fired lawyers were awarded four million dollars in fees.

The case is typical of the increasing, and increasingly bitter, losses inflicted on tribes by American courts. Tim finds a way to snatch something positive from this one. He terms it a "Pyrrhic loss": "We made a strong record of the tribes' opposition to the money award. We are in an unassailable political position. No one can say the Sioux voluntarily surrendered their legal claims to the land. They did all they could to oppose and reject the settlement. They did all they could. So we can say: Give the land back."

The focus on land is necessary but treacherous. It is necessary in the first instance because "[a] unique and vital relationship to the earth remains essential for the continued existence of most Indian peoples and Alaska Natives" (1985 Report, p. 3). Then, too, land claims register in courts and in politics in ways that other tribal claims do not. They offer a starting point, a point of leverage. They provide "crucial bargaining power to defend and to develop Indian rights, including those of jurisdiction and self-government, [immunity from] external taxation, and hunting and fishing" (1988 Report, p. 5).

But such claims may have deleterious side effects. For example, they may trigger non-Indian guilt about the way the land was taken. The guilt leads to defensiveness ("You want to take my home?") and then to blaming the victims ("You didn't know how to use the land; we've made it produce").

Or the claims may feed sentimentality. Aggression against tribes, to the extent that it is thought about at all, is reckoned to have ended long ago. Massacre of Indians, according to this assumption, was the unavoidable work of cowboys and cavalry. Such land as may have been seized was an inevitable cost of Western civilization's irresistible advance. In any event, the land has been developed and cannot now be returned without unwarranted harm to innocent landowners. Land claims based on ancient treaties are then taken as a confirming anachronism. They locate tribes in the fading memory of a lost frontier. A well-known sculpture, *End of the Trail*, portrays a lone Indian warrior halted by a canyon's rim. Both man and horse are bent into cold defeat before the wind and snow. The figure is that of a vanishing relic. The Indian and his world are irretrievable.

This is a false image that Tim is committed to cure. He hopes to change minds. He uses every opportunity to do so: lawsuits, lectures, publications, annual reports, bar association committees, visits to law schools, conversations. His message has the character of supplication that must be repeated over and over because the established powers, to whom it is addressed, are amnesiac and unmovable. It runs something like this:

Indian nations are not an anachronism. They "are increasing in population and working as intensely as ever to maintain their distinct ways of life" (1985 Report, p. 2). They are to be valued "not only for what they preserve of the past, but perhaps more for what they can say about how we may live for the future" (1983 Report, p. 1). Their grievances are not the hangover of yesterday's aggression. "The government and the legal system *today* continue to deprive Indian people of fundamental rights and to divest them of their land, resources and other rights. The wrongs which are being carried out today are, in some cases, even more serious than the historic injustices" (1981 Report, p. 2). Therefore, "Indians are not trying to reverse all the historic wrongs, but are trying to correct present day injustices and to stop the suffering that is the result of inadequate land, water and resources" (1985 Report, p. 3). Indians do not ask for privileges or exceptions or handouts for themselves. They are calling attention to a severe moral crisis in American law. The absence of any legal or constitutional limit on the federal government's power over Indian peoples "is the root of the most serious injustices to Indians. It constitutes the greatest single legal obstacle toward substantial progress in alleviating the conditions of poverty, social and political disintegration and economic and political powerlessness which exist in most Indian communities."[28]

It is not only with non-Indians that Tim must contend. Indians are as free to be internally divided as any nation, political party, or religion. Among Indian and sympathetic non-Indian attorneys, a taboo has prevented involvement in inter- and intra-tribal disputes. Tim is not constrained by the taboo. He takes sides.

He says he is influenced in his choices by such things as which government is legitimate, who may have inappropriate or grossly disproportionate outside help, who may be backed by gambling racketeers. The lines of division do not run cleanly between traditionalists and assimilationists, the elderly and the young, conservative and liberals, but Tim does tend to take up the cause of people clearly identifiable as traditionals. His longstanding relationship with the Mohawks is an example.

The Mohawk Nation is a member of the Six Nations Confederacy. The others are the Onondaga, Seneca, Tuscarora, Oneida, and Cayuga. Tim has worked for both the confederacy and for some of its member nations and subgroups. This alone has been the subject of conflict. In one land claim case, Tim represented both the Oneida of the Thames Band and the confederacy. The Oneida Nation of Wisconsin, represented by opposing lawyers, sought to have him disqualified on the ground of conflict of interest. The trial court dismissed him, but a federal court of appeals reversed the decision and permitted him to represent both groups.[29]

One of his clients was the Mohawk community known as Ganienkeh, a group of traditionals who reclaimed an area of their homeland in the Adirondacks. The State of New York asserted ownership. The ensuing dispute alternated between negotiation and intense conflict. At one point Tim was helicoptered in as armed war between the Indians and state police was about to erupt. His intercession was successful. A settlement was achieved in 1977 with the relocation of the community to seven thousand acres of state land near Altona, New York. The land, placed in the hands of a charitable trust created for the purpose, was given over to the exclusive use of the Mohawks. Non-Indians living nearby were disgruntled by the arrival of the community and brought lawsuits against it. Ganienkeh prevailed. Later, it won again when it contested governmental proposals for aerial spraying to kill gypsy moths. The pesticide would have wiped out Ganienkeh's honeybees along with the moths.

Tim has also been involved in negotiation and conflict on the St. Regis Mohawk Reservation, or Akwesasne. Akwesasne, which straddles the border between New York and Canada, was recently in the news because of armed clashes over gambling. Tim's participation in earlier troubles on the reservation began with a volatile face-off in 1972. The reservation had two governments. One was a traditional Longhouse government recognized by the confederacy. The other was an electoral system of government created by New York law. The Longhouse government opposed state and federal jurisdiction on the reservation. The state-created electoral government sought to gain dominance on the New York side of the reservation by first declaring traditional Longhouse members to be no longer members of the tribe and then seeking state court orders to have them removed as intruders. The courts ultimately refused to grant such orders. Some years later, the electoral government began to receive large amounts of state and federal funds and secretly participated in negotiations with state and federal officials to settle Mohawk land claims. It again sought to consolidate its power on the reservation, this time through a police force.

Tim worked with the Longhouse leaders. A dispute arose between one of the traditional chiefs and some workers responsible to the state-imposed government. A showdown was precipitated when state police and county officers arrested the chief. The confrontation continued for months. Further arrests and gathering threats by the state police finally promised to erupt in armed violence in 1979. Tim helped rechannel the hostilities into negotiations and legal actions.

Something of a resolution was achieved in 1981 when traditionals gained control of the imposed government, repealed its law and order code, and disbanded the police force. The state and federal governments finally had to recognize the legitimacy of the traditionals they tried so hard to suppress. Now fresh controversy has broken out on the subject of whether to permit gambling. By attracting outsiders to the reservation, bingo could grow as a major source of badly needed revenue. Tim is not delighted at the prospect. "After all that," he says, reflecting on the reservation's past struggles, "I hate to think what we ended up with are bingo parlors."

He notes that Mohawks are being forced to contend with legal and illegal attempts to take advantage of the tax and regulatory immunities of the reservation (smoke shops, filling stations, and cigarette smuggling, in addition to bingo). The "large influx of cash into poor communities has been a very serious threat to the social and civil controls which the Indian governments normally exercise" (1988 Report, p. 13).

In the instances of Ganienkeh and Akwesasne, Tim's use of law was a necessity. But it had costs. Not the least complex difficulty at the intersection of Native American and American cultures—and it is acutely felt by an Indian lawyer—is the discrepancy between Indian aspirations, claims, and grievances and the available American legal language for expressing them.

In part this is an issue of politics and language.

For example, Vine Deloria, who is a member of the center's board of directors, points out that non-Indians have tried to force Indians to use English and abandon their own tongues. Indians must confront a majority culture that not only does not speak their language but also forces them "to use a language that conveys very little of what [they] want to say."[30]

In part it is an issue of the way American law functions.

Law distorts authenticity of feeling in the claims brought to it. According to Chris Stone, "In every legal system, every time and place you get involved with law, you get involved with a legal vocabulary and a technical vocabulary. No matter what the specialty, such an approach bends human feelings and experiences to its own needs and logic."[31] He adds: "I'm pained to see that the presuppositions of the American legal system . . . force people to take the true feelings that are cultural feelings and re-express them in atomized, individual rights terms which aren't really what they seem to be about."[32]

In part it has to do with a singular, persistent incapacity of American law for Native Americans and their culture.

Tim has noted that "many Indian governments, particularly traditional governments, have always maintained the position that they are separate nations. . . . These Indian nations, knowing that essential Indian rights are not protected under United States law, have refused to acknowledge the right of the United States to exercise legal dominion over them" (1980 Report, p. 2). Even so, the United States asserts jurisdiction over tribes; in many instances, these assertions are based only on superior power and have no legitimate, constitutional basis. "Often, the federal government has forced its jurisdiction on Indian people; just as often the federal and state governments have gradually, almost unnoticeably, taken over certain government powers; in some cases, Indian governments have willingly given up some of their jurisdiction in treaties or other agreements."[33]

So Indian nations must contend with American law. When they do, they find that they "are gravely disadvantaged and discriminated against"; moreover, "increased access to the courts and increased use of legal mechanisms by Indians has not materially changed this fact." Their

> apparent legal "victories" in . . . recent years have left Indian peoples . . . subject to the "plenary power" of Congress with no real constitutional limitation, subject to the uncompensated taking of their lands and property by the federal government, subject to the unilateral abrogation and violation of their treaties with the United States, subject to the absolute termination of their historic rights of self-government and nationhood, and subject to the self-serving and lawless actions of the federal government as the self-proclaimed trustee of Indian lands, water rights, and other property, all without legal protection or legal remedy under present federal law. (1980 Report, p. 2)

When I first heard Tim talk about these things I thought he was exaggerating. The extensive research I undertook in response convinced me that he was understating the case, especially in regard to aggressions against tribes carried out by the Supreme Court in recent years. The newspaper *Akwesasne Notes* commented on the difficulty of finding ways to protect the rights of Indian peoples within the American legal system: "The U.S. laws and the way those laws are interpreted by the courts, are the major barrier to the recognition and implementation of even the most basic rights for Native peoples."[34]

The problem is exacerbated, Tim points out, by attorneys who have represented the tribes. Tribes' contracts with attorneys must be approved by the Bureau of Indian Affairs. Until recent years, representation of the tribes was the province of a small coterie of lawyers who, he says, "routinely approached Indian sovereignty with shuffling feet, downcast eyes and hat in hand, and some still talk of Indians as 'wards of the federal government.'"[35] He adds: "It is a disgrace that attorneys purporting to represent Indian nations or 'tribes' have not challenged the legal doctrines which have for so long made Indians subject to exploitation."[36]

Certainly, better lawyering helps, as Tim's advocacy demonstrates. But the problem is not simply that of unprofessional or unsympathetic or unknowing attorneys. The law is unresponsive. Tim compares the present legal status of Indian tribes to that of African-Americans decades before *Brown v. Board of Education* in 1954. Change "will require a sustained and long term effort which will not be unlike the historic legal effort to end racial segregation with regard to the Black population" (1981 Report, p. 35). Given the present makeup of the Court, its attitude toward tribes, and its relative youth, an equivalent to *Brown* for Indians appears out of the question until the middle of the twenty-first century—if then. A new departure will be necessary. The equal protection jurisprudence developed by African-Americans to produce *Brown* is not readily adaptable to the tribal cause. It protects individuals and their right of participation in the dominant culture. A tribe determined to preserve its independent, sovereign identity as a nation can draw little succor from current equal protection doctrine and may even find the rhetoric of equality deployed against the tribal cause.

One avenue of relief is appeal to international law as a kind of higher law. Tim and some of his clients are developing the possibilities of such appeals. The center has been granted formal consultative status with the United Nations. As a Non-Governmental Organization, it is allowed to participate in UN Human Rights Commission proceedings on behalf of its clients. So, for example, in the course of representing the Mohawks, Tim filed a formal human rights complaint with the commission charging violation of that nation's international human right to self-determination. It was a way to draw attention to the Mohawk's status and to make common cause with indigenous peoples from around the world. International human rights law could prove more receptive to Indian claims than domestic constitutional law. However, Tim knows that "the development of human rights law has been strongly influenced by Western legal concepts which favor individual rights over group rights."[37] It is the same problem he confronts in American equal protection jurisprudence, but, he says, at the international level, there is change under way "and group or collective rights are being given increasing recognition."

Law and the improvement of law are not ends in themselves for Tim. The end he has in mind is tribal life. Law is simply a means—one among others—to gain time and place for the tribes. His work and that of the center, he says,

> is not simply to win and protect Indian rights. Our purpose is to respond to human suffering and to serious injustice. By this I mean the continued mistreatment of Indian communities and the suffering of tens of thousands of individuals from poverty, ill-health, deprivation and violence. . . . Reducing this human suffering depends upon protecting and strengthening Indian civilization, Indian social systems and the "natural helping systems" of Indian society. And so it is essential to preserve native cultures, societies, languages and religions, and to preserve native nations and tribal governments. [The center's] role is to give the legal assistance that so many tribes and Indian leaders need in fighting for their existence and trying to remedy the suffering of their people. (1988 Report, p. 1)

A self-defining, self-limiting career at the bar seems never to have entered his mind. To him law has always been intended for something else. As a child, he was encouraged by his family to entertain thoughts of running for Congress and even the presidency. These thoughts translated in college—two years at the University of Oklahoma, two years and graduation at Williams—into the assumption that he would undertake some form of public service. Columbia Law School came next and was, he says, "easy." I tell him that I have never before heard that comment about law school. He says the curriculum left him plenty of time to help start a human rights journal, to work on civil rights and welfare rights cases, and to offer draft counseling for people opposed to the war in Vietnam.

The draft counseling had led him to the possibility of helping people who objected to the war but were already in the service. He ended up at a coffeehouse near Fort Dix. It was a refuge for service dissidents. He performed as a folksinger, a role essential to every authentic coffeehouse of the time. Folk music had been one of his media. He and his brother had formed two professional music groups in Oklahoma. One did pop music; the other, bluegrass. Tim played guitar and banjo. He has a gift for stringed instruments. He has also been a classical bassist, and is now an active cellist. I can as readily imagine him picking and singing as concertizing with the cello.

Whatever people thought of his folksinging, the coffeehouse was perceived as a threat. Military bases are unfriendly neighbors to dissident watering holes; a hand grenade was tossed into this one. No one was seriously injured. Tim seized this violent finish of the coffeehouse as an opportunity. He patched up the damage in a nearby storefront, and, upon graduating, opened a law office there. He defended GIs who were involved in antiwar protests or who raised issues like stockade conditions. "My legal services," he remembers, "were a catalyst for GI organizing. I may have been some help, but they did the organizing themselves. My practice of law was a mechanism for letting other things happen."

Tim's extracurricular activities during law school taught him two important lessons for which he had remarkable aptitude: how to raise money for public interest issues and how to use law to achieve objectives at the public, political level. The first lesson he learned in gathering funds for the military law project as well as for the human rights journal he helped to found. The second lesson he learned in the coffeehouse across from Fort Dix. He was well schooled for it when the time came to start the Indian Law Resource Center.

He graduated from Columbia in 1969. The military law project wound down in 1971, and he moved to Baltimore to direct Maryland's Inmate Grievance Committee. He made his way to Washington and Indian law in 1972 when he became staff attorney to the Native American Legal Defense and Education Fund. After a couple of other stints (the U.S. Commission on Civil Rights, then the short-lived American Indian Treaty Defense Program/Institute for the Development of Indian Law), he began the center with a Columbia Law School friend, Steve Tullberg. It was another shoestring law office, this one with two full-time attorneys, one half-time attorney, and two staff people. By the end of the first year there were four full-time attorneys and four staff people. The first annual report showed an income of $209,577 made up of grants and contributions from private foundations, churches, and individuals.

Now, as then, the center "provide[s] legal expertise to Indian governments in a way that reaches and challenges the fundamental legal problems affecting Indian peoples" (1979 Report, p. 1). *Akwesasne Notes* has pointed out that the center is one of the few organizations attempting to address the problem of protecting tribal rights within the American legal system, and it is the only one "which responds to the serious legal needs of Native peoples and governments . . . without bowing to the abusive limitations of United States law."[38]

I have heard Tim argue passionately that tribes must work with and under American law. "The Constitution is the best possibility we have. Where else in the world will you find something so good?" At other times I have heard him argue with equal passion that American law is a principal, seemingly irremediable means of aggression against tribes.

The two arguments do not necessarily conflict, and, in Tim's case, are not duplicitous. I read them as expressions of the singular tension in which he must live as a Native American who accepts a complex vocation to give voice to tribes with the available resources of American law.

He has never allowed the strain of that tension to become ethically paralyzing. He retains the belief with which he grew up: "You are morally responsible to make judgments and act upon them. My father taught us that we were to do what the biblical stories suggested. We were just supposed to do it, actually expected to do the right thing."

Perhaps making decisions, acting, and living with the consequent tension helps explain why, after talking about it for several years, he recently moved to Montana with his wife. The time had come for a change. The Indian Law Resource Center now has a second office in his gold-rush-era home in Helena, Montana. He is as much at home there as I found him to be in the urban East. "The mountains," he has written a letter to say, "suit me well. I am able to leave work and be on a blue ribbon trout stream in a matter of thirty-five to forty-five minutes."

STEVE WIZNER/CARLA INGERSOLL

Yale Law School's clinical program in New Haven is known officially as the Jerome N. Frank Legal Services Organization, an imposing title for an unimposing series of offices spread around the third and fourth floors of a hidden back corner of the law school. The building is pure Ivy League Gothic. The leaded panes of the office windows are set in arched stone openings. Most offices have fireplaces. At least some are still operational. Stove wood is stacked in a shower stall in the fourth floor men's room.

There are no signs to indicate the existence or location of the clinic. I am uncertain how unguided clients ever find the place. It is the occasional domain of large squirrels that seem to come and go freely. When I happen into an office, two of them are nosing around the desk. I try to shoo them away. They give me a brief, contemptuous look and return to their business. They leave the impression of doing me a favor by allowing me to withdraw unharmed. Steve Wizner, the director of the clinical program, calls them "attack squirrels."

Steve, a large, graceful, enthusiastic man, has been at Yale since 1970, when the clinic was first made an official part of the curriculum. He has the boyish manner and appearance of a person much younger than his fifty-two years. His eyes have the look of someone who has just taken off a pair of glasses. I had arranged to meet him at 6:30 P.M. on a recent early-spring evening at the conclusion of a class he was teaching on trial practice. He emerges from the classroom, precisely on time, trailing students and peppered with questions. He has a quick mind and a gentle voice. He speaks rapidly. I snatch only part of the answer to one question: "Some witnesses make good storytellers. Let them talk."

He has been trying cases for almost thirty years and knows his business. A year after graduating from Dartmouth, he had been uncertain what to do with his life. His father arranged for him to meet an attorney. After the meeting, the attorney sent him a biography of Clarence Darrow. "That was it," Steve recalls, "I read that book and enrolled in the University of Chicago law school." After graduating in 1963 he joined the Criminal Division of the Justice Department. Fresh from law school, he was sent to Louisiana to try an unpopular case before a local jury and, surprisingly, won a conviction. He still savors memories of the victory and the fine New Orleans coffee. After three years at Justice, he moved to the Center for Social Welfare Policy and Law at Columbia University in New York and was then an attorney in Mobilization for Youth Legal Services before he was invited to Yale.

Just now, for class, he wears a gray herringbone coat, gray flannel pants, a white shirt with buttoned-down collar, and a red tie with white stripes. Snappy. I have usually before seen him in much less formal settings and much more informally dressed. He has to break off the post-class exchange to go to supper with me and talk about his work. He does not end conversations with students comfortably. He is an exacting teacher because he is a loving one who becomes fully absorbed by his students and their questions. The attention he gives individual students out of class authenticates his repeated in-class stress on the centrality and importance of the individual client as a person.

We stop by his office to drop off his class material. This is not a simple transaction. In the hall outside his office, a colleague waits with a problem that must be resolved: One of the students has a client who is about to be evicted by a landlord. A year or so ago the landlord had been the client of another student in the clinic. What to do about a potential conflict of interest? "What does the student think?" is Steve's first question. Investigation reveals that the landlord had been represented on a matter wholly foreign to the present case. Still further inquiry establishes that no real conflict exists. The student, who wants to continue representing the tenant, may do so. We enter the office. It is modest and obviously much used. There are more places for people to sit than there are shelves for books. The swivel chair is Steve's. The next day I will see him roll and pivot in it as he moves with the flow of activity. During the rare stretches when there are no students, he is subject, while seated, to attacks of happy feet.

He lives not far from the school, but his home is another world. It is serene. The house was built in 1919. Years ago he and his wife, Rachel, converted the attic into rooms for their two sons, both of whom are away in college, Ben at Harvard and Jake at Swarthmore. This third floor, reached by narrow, curving stairs, now serves as guest quarters. It would have been wonderful for growing up in: snug under the eaves, safe, just the right amount of connection to parents below and distance from them. Rachel, once a dean at Yale, is a scholar of Jewish history. She talks movingly about her current work, which is centered on translating essays written by Jewish young people in Poland in the 1930s before the coming of the Nazis. She herself was born in Vilna, Poland. Her family fled east to Japan and then to the United States.

The house is not wholly removed from work. There are telephone calls in and out. One call is from a former client whom Steve now counts as a friend. Some days he calls seven or eight times. He is retarded, can be violent, and gets into trouble. The next morning another call from him is waiting at the office. He is in jail again. Steve will try to help.

This kind of continuing care is consistent with the type of lawyering taught in the clinic. A client may have a group of students working on the case. Some may be involved in securing medical or social services. Their obligation to the client may continue long after the "legal" file has been closed. The client is to be attended to as a person; lawyers, as lawyers, need not be impersonal or inhumane. Students in the clinic are encouraged to explore the roles attorneys may usefully, professionally perform.

I seize the chance to watch Steve work in a clinic seminar. He is adept at guiding conversation about the day's heavy assignment. He also draws upon the students' reading of Holmes, Llewellyn, Frank, Unger, and Dworkin—reading assigned for other classes. He elicits connections between the work done in other courses and in this one. He turns discussion to the cases that the students have taken on: What has happened in the last week, what is coming up, difficulties with clients, etc. He and the students are careful to protect the confidentiality of their relationships to clients and do not identify clients by name while I am present. Steve finds different ways to reemphasize the centrality of each student's client. His enthusiasms show.

The history of clinical legal education can be read in Yale's Legal Services Organization. At the end of the nineteenth century, Christopher Columbus Langdell invented the casebook method for teaching law and installed it at Harvard. The theory informing the method held law to be conceptual and scientific; all that students needed to know could be learned from books, especially books of edited appellate court opinions collected under discrete subject matter headings. The casebook method and its ideology soon dominated contemporary legal education.

In 1933, Jerome Frank, who then taught at Yale, urged law schools to include clinical training in their regular curriculum. "Something important and of immense worth was given up," he wrote, "when the legal apprentice system was abandoned as the basis of teaching in the leading American law schools."[39] Frank thought exclusive reliance on books of neatly arranged appellate opinions oversimplified the study of law and rendered it hopelessly artificial. He contended that, without giving up the casebook method entirely, "the law schools should once more get in intimate contact with what clients need and with what courts and lawyers actually do."[40] In 1947, after he had become a federal judge on the Second Circuit Court of Appeals, Frank lamented the absence of response to his recommendation in the intervening thirteen years. He termed Langdell, the father of the case method, a "neurotic escapist"[41] and once again called on law schools to "repudiate Langdell's morbid repudiation of actual legal practice."[42]

Frank did not know about the pioneering work of John Bradway. Bradway had not been called to his attention, Frank reported in a footnote, until shortly before publication of the 1947 article.[43] Bradway had introduced clinical teaching at the University of Southern California in 1930. He wanted law students to see "the case in action rather than as a dead thing lying in the Case Books."[44] When he later moved to Duke University's law school, Bradway started a clinic there as well. So two experiments in clinical education existed when Frank wrote. There would be a long delay before more would follow.

Not until the late 1960s and early 1970s was there a general movement of legal aid clinics into law school buildings. They are now accepted, but not necessarily welcomed. A school's clinical and academic faculties may be formally as well as informally divided. The division may extend into the student body: Students who are activists or are inclined toward public interest law may tend to the clinical side, while those interested in business or academic careers may stick with the nonclinical courses. An uneasy alliance is not what Frank had in mind. He had envisioned a necessary and mutually enriching marriage between practitioners and theoreticians, for "practices unavoidably blossom into theories, and most theories induce practices, good or bad."[45]

Lingering suspicions about legal aid clinics may be aroused by their politics. They teach technique, but not technique at random. If they work, they are an education in social responsibility. When people who cannot afford to hire a lawyer come to clinics, they represent to students a chance to develop practical skills and to connect abstractions from classes to real people with real needs. In the process, clients also expose their lawyers-in-training to the failures of justice in a hungry world. They constitute an opportunity to employ law to make life concretely better for particular people with particular needs. Insofar as the opportunity is seized, clinics are some realization of law schools' responsibility to their immediate communities and some education in the bar's responsibility to society.

Beginning in the 1940s, Yale students organized a voluntary program for assisting legal aid and public defender clients in New Haven. The program continued as a student-run, extracurricular undertaking until 1970, when the school hired its first clinical teachers, Dennis Curtis and Steve. Dennis is now at the University of Southern California, where John Bradway introduced modern clinical teaching. Steve stayed on at Yale. In 1989 (but not until then), as a show of respect for the person as well as for the clinical program and its place in the curriculum, Steve was made the William O. Douglas Clinical Professor of Law. (The *Yale Weekly Calendar* reported that he had been named to the O'Douglas chair.) He is still not a fully enfranchised member of the faculty.

Yale's clinic has grown to include five full-time, one half-time, and several part-time faculty. More students apply than can be accommodated. More than a hundred are included every semester. More than half of each graduating class have taken part in the program. Judge Frank would be particularly delighted by the fact that this clinic emphasizes participation in the first year of law school. (It is singular in this respect; most programs are limited to second- or third-year students.)

There is talk of renovating the interior of the Yale law school. The clinic might be relocated or given a separate client entrance directly to the street. It might also be given an electronic upgrading. A recent American Bar Association accreditation report described the clinic as "short of the kind of technology that is considered mandatory in most places to provide quality legal services." Undoubtedly, good use could be made of more and better computers, photocopying machines, and various sorts of administrative help, as well as office management and design. However, technological, architectural, and administrative gains might add little to the pedagogical capacity of the present clinic. The professionalism taught here is not that of an efficient bureau. It has to do with responsibility in complex human relationships rendered more complex by the limits and potential of law.

The clinic is run like a law firm, but of an unusual sort. The untidy halls and offices have the air of rooms occupied by a large family; fully engrossed in important common work, they would have paused to straighten up a little and drive off the squirrels had they known company was coming. When Steve and I arrive in the morning, knots of students are in conference with each other and with teachers. A student and a client sit on a bench out of the way. The student is taking notes on a legal-size pad of yellow foolscap as the client answers her questions. The paper recycling bins are overflowing.

Under the supervision of a faculty member, participants in the clinic engage in a full range of legal services. The principal activity is divided into seven projects, and students enroll in a seminar related to the work they do: advocacy for disabled people, advocacy for homeless people, a workshop on providing shelter for the homeless, representation of indigent tenants in eviction proceedings, legal services for people in prison, representation of urban poor people in civil matters, and representation of persons seeking asylum. In 1970, students were more or less shown how to handle cases by their supervising mentors.[46] Now, in addition to the same kind of supervision, they have weekly classes, simulations, and collaboration with experts from various disciplines other than law.

Some of the student triumphs in the clinic may appear to be small victories from some perspectives. They are often of great importance to the individuals involved: an eviction prevented, an educational program developed for a disabled student, a domestic relations dispute successfully negotiated. Others may have an immediately broad impact; one grew out of the clinical work in homelessness. Part of it was a case recently argued before the Connecticut Supreme Court by a student, Graham Boyd. Steve speaks glowingly of him and says his argument before the court was "fabulous." Graham is from Spartanburg, South Carolina. He is reed thin, has long, black hair, and wears little wire-rimmed glasses. As he leaves after a brief stop by the office, Steve sends him out the door with a wry encouragement: "Graham, strive for excellence." (To others he has offered: "No lawyer should think on his feet." "A person always serves her purpose." "Law is not about law.")

I chase Graham down later. He has worked very hard on the project—to the destruction, he reports, of his relationship with a girlfriend. "I felt really good about the work, but I can't live like that all the time. I've got to back off some before I'm overwhelmed." The case is *Savage v. Aronson.*[47] Connecticut provides emergency housing to eligible impoverished families. A 1988 regulation imposed a one-hundred-day limit on such housing. Some of the clinic's clients were among seven hundred families statewide who were about to be evicted in April 1989, pursuant to the one-hundred-day cut-off. The clinic brought a class action suit challenging the limit and seeking an injunction obliging the state to continue providing emergency housing. The superior court granted the injunction. It was this action that had been on appeal before the supreme court.

A number of students besides Graham had been involved. Although clinical faculty were counsel, the students prepared the case and presented it in the superior court hearing. Among other things, they had their clients tell the stories of what life was like for them. As the emergency housing limit was reached, the state agency tried stopgap measures. Some clients were told to "double up" with friends or relatives, many of whom were in public housing where "doubling up" is illegal and places the host family at risk of losing their home as well. Others were offered subsidized housing, but packed up and moved only to find the units already rented, uninhabitable, or boarded up. One, a struggling mother with a sick child, was put out on two hours' notice and lost her placement in a nearly completed fifteen-week job training course. The stories reportedly moved the judge to tears. In his memorandum of decision, he took note of the "detailed evidence and hundreds of pages of outstanding briefs" that had been presented.

The project is not limited to this case. Graham talks about how he and other members of the group are attempting to stimulate legislative as well as judicial action. They inaugurated lobbying efforts a few weeks ago with a large press conference at which they presented a report, "The Broken Promise of Welfare Motels."

The report gives the one-hundred-day limit on emergency housing a context. Temporary shelter had been provided to a predictable 400 to 450 families a year until January 1989, when a Connecticut budget deficit led the state to discontinue a rental assistance program that provided subsidies to indigent families so that they could remain in their homes. With the end of rental assistance, people could not afford to stay in their homes, and the number of families needing emergency housing began to rise quickly. The report demonstrated that, by cutting rental assistance to save money, the state had in fact multiplied its spending. The increase in emergency housing was several times more expensive than rental assistance. The report goes on to note that the change was morally as well as fiscally irresponsible. Emergency housing is provided in "welfare motels" whose owners are paid up to $110 a night for a dingy, cramped room. Since there are no cooking facilities in motels, an additional cost for restaurant food vouchers has to be added. Families who are forced from their homes into welfare motels suffer the costs of dislocation. The motels are often far from the childrens' schools and from public transportation. Parents, usually single mothers, are forced to cope with getting children to school and themselves to work without easy access to either or to social services and health care. Children suffer emotional, psychological, and educational deprivation. The report is a well-documented, persuasively presented call for legislative action.

(The Connecticut Supreme Court reversed the trial court's decision in the *Savage* case.[48] Steve has written to say that the clinic's clients "all received rent subsidies and obtained apartments, and none of them, to our knowledge, suffered as a result of the Supreme Court reversal.")

The homelessness project spawned another, the shelter project, whose purpose is development of nonadversarial forms of representation instead of litigation. Its emphasis is on planning and representation of nonprofit companies serving the housing needs of the poor. It helped to organize Housing Operations Management Enterprises (HOME) Inc. and now has a couple of dozen clients and "other matters." It has secured over five million dollars in grants and tax benefits for its clients. One of the "other matters" is the recently published *Homes for the Homeless* (1990), a handbook for groups elsewhere who want to respond to the needs of homeless people and are puzzled about how to begin. One of the internal, pedagogical benefits of the shelter project is that it has drawn into clinical work faculty and students with business skills and business orientation.

The attention to homelessness began in 1985 when students in the clinic started making weekly visits to the local shelters, soup kitchens, and welfare motels of New Haven in an effort to make legal services available to displaced individuals and families. Carla Ingersoll began law school at Yale with the 1984–85 academic year. Her presence animated the clinical seminar on homelessness. She credits the work that people like Graham have done in bringing impact litigation and organizing nonprofit housing organizations. It is important, she says, but she also says that there are other people in the clinic who believe it equally important to spend time with clients instead of projects—"those of us who like to get down and dirty; *need* to get down and dirty, Steve would say." This is not just a figure of speech for Carla.

In the fall of 1988, the two fifty-bed New Haven shelters were full. The homeless people who had no other place to go moved into the train station. Some were Carla's clients, whom she had gotten to know from work in the soup kitchen that moves from one church or synagogue to another. Amtrak was not pleased to have the new occupants. There were tense moments. Carla made it her habit to wrap in a blanket and sleep on the train station floor—"like the rest of the folks"—to help protect her clients from being hassled by the police. She induced other Yale law school students to join her.

One of her clients had a clever idea. He would buy inexpensive tickets for himself and his wife for a late night train out of New Haven. They would arrive at the station after the train had departed. When they were asked to leave, he would show the tickets and say they were waiting for the next train out the following morning. Carla reported the idea to Brother Denys. Brother Denys had been a Trappist monk and then a Benedictine. After he met Mother Teresa and worked with her, he founded a new order, the Order of Emmaus, dedicated to serving the homeless.[49] Carla is an active member of the Protestant United Church on the Green in New Haven, but she is also a member of the Order of Emmaus as one willing to accept its discipline of prayer and of service to the homeless. The order has become a constitutive influence in her life.

Brother Denys's response to news of the train ticket idea was to buy fifty tickets for distribution to people who needed to sleep in the train station. That night when the tickets were shown to the Amtrak police, in Carla's words, "they went crazy. They called in the New Haven police to help them throw out the crowd."

As Steve describes it, Carla saved the situation by engaging the police in conversation. Instead of approaching in a spirit of confrontation, she talked to them as the individuals they were. She got other Yale law students talking to the police in the same way. She explained the plight of her clients and said she knew no one really wanted to banish them to the bitter cold. She pointed out that the nighttime occupants were keeping the station clean and causing no harm to people or property. They just needed a way to get through the night. "She helped the police," as Steve puts it, "to be better, to act as people instead of institutional representatives. She appealed to their private selves." The homeless people stayed. She then approached station officials in the same manner. They eventually agreed to allow sleeping at the station. Subsequently, New Haven legal services brought suit against the city and successfully argued that the Connecticut constitution includes a right to shelter provided by the city. The number of shelter beds has been doubled.

There is a homeless church. One recent Christmas Eve, members of the community of homeless people held a midnight service in the train station. "There was a circle of guys with candles singing 'Silent Night.' It was a five-handkerchief night," Carla says, referring to the flow of tears. The church was started as a result of the homeless people's response to the service. "They said they felt a spiritual void in their lives."

Much of Carla's participation in the clinical program is devoted to nonconfrontational approaches. Some of what she does looks like social work. She identifies it as an attempt to help clients make use of the institutional help available. She gives the example of a client whom she had represented in criminal proceedings. Sentencing would go better for him if he had a job. Carla told him to find one, and he did. It required that he wear black pants and a white shirt. He appeared for work in the appropriate attire. He had stolen it. "It never occurred to him that there were other ways to get clothes. I assume the system will take care of me and didn't realize relying on the system was something he did not know how to do. I have to fight people's cornered despair. They have no faith in the system. They do not find themselves supported by institutions. I hope to do something about that as a lawyer." Her view is "not to ask: Is this law, is this social work? The question is what it means to be an advocate. I am tired of people who want to instill an arbitrary sense of limits. In the clinic, we figure out what ought to happen and then find out how to do it."

Carla is slowly, painfully working her way back to health from the devastation of a severe bout of CFIDS, Chronic Fatigue and Immune Dysfunction Syndrome, that was slow to be diagnosed. She has had to drop out of school temporarily with only nine hours of classes remaining to be completed. For a time she had been too weak to feed herself and was kept alive by friends she had met at church. She is able now to participate in the clinic seminar Steve teaches. In the course of the session I attend, she turns distinctly gray with fatigue.

Suffering is not new to Carla. She is now in her forties. She did not have an untroubled time as a child growing up in the eastern United States and the Midwest. She began college at Bryn Mawr but dropped out. By 1969 she was impoverished, divorced, and the mother of two children. That year she met Jack and in 1971 was back in college at the University of Massachusetts at Amherst, where she would graduate. In conversation, I had referred to Jack as her husband. She later corrected me. In seventeen years of life together, they had not become officially married. By 1976 she had founded two businesses, one for contracting and the other for managing rental property. She had wanted to attend law school since leaving college. "I thought most lawyers went around fighting for justice. I thought I'd really go after white-collar criminals. It was disturbing to me that privileged people should be stealing." When she finally had the money and security to do so, she started at Yale Law School in 1984 and commuted from Amherst to New Haven. Jack grew seriously ill. Carla suffered a pinched nerve ("I'm sure it was stress, like Jack being sick, that did it") and was put in traction. Classmates recorded lectures for her: "I did law school on tapes." Nursing Jack finally required that she suspend her legal education.

Jack died in 1986 on a Saturday night. The following morning, for the first time in a long while, Carla attended worship services. The church has occupied a central place in her life since. "I wanted to do law long before I became seriously involved in the church. In hindsight, it looks much different. I have come to see that law was a form of calling that I did not understand at the time."

Jack's illness and her own needs have exhausted the money she had made from her businesses. When finally she does graduate she will be deeply in debt. Last summer she worked for a New Haven law firm that wanted to have her back as an associate. She needs both to earn money and to represent poor people. Her years make her impatient. She speaks of joining a firm where she might do family law and estate planning ("I am good with old people"). Both would allow her to "represent people in ways that are personal." The New Haven firm where she was employed encouraged the pro bono work that she regards as essential: "There is something suffering inside me. Others who are suffering seem to see that. They are drawn to me, and I am drawn to them. There is a bond of empathy, an enlargement of self, a passion born of suffering."

Carla has lots of curly blond hair that adds movement and extension to her expressiveness and good humor. Her eyes appear sometimes blue, sometimes gray, always lit from within even when her physical stamina has faded. She speaks softly, but her delivery is fast, like Steve's. When the two get together, they work like a team of improvisational actors specializing in ribaldry.

During unaccustomed serious interludes at dinner in one of New Haven's treasured neighborhood Italian restaurants, the two of them talk about the disjunction between what many lawyers do and what they care most about in life. The possibility of poverty law work in large law firms may constitute the great new frontier for public interest lawyers. Carla is intrigued by working from the inside and encouraging other members of a firm to represent poor people. "They think pro bono service is scut work meant for others. They have a fear of poor people because they don't know them. It would free them from their fear to do some in-service poverty law with guidance from those of us who are comfortable with it."

Steve has doubts. He worries about the quality of service poor clients might receive from lawyers unfamiliar with the fields of practice involved. "They would have to be afraid of malpractice." Carla has an answer for him: "*Teach* the fancy lawyers how to do anti-eviction work and the like. They *already* know how to do things like bankruptcy and criminal defense. After all, if first-year law students can do it, so can fancy lawyers."

Steve talks about his own work in service to poor people as advancing what he cares most about. He refers to Robert Cover's "integrated life. His life had integrity. He was willing to sacrifice, but he was happy. It was not that he was altruistic. It was just that his work life and his moral life were together." He adds that, in his own case, "law is something I do to act on my obligations."

Carla responds that law for her is "acting on and from my passions. I feel pulled." Steve, isolating a difference as well as a similarity, remarks: "You feel pulled, and I feel pushed."

From New Haven I drive with Steve and a load of students to a cold camp in New Hampshire for the annual Cover Conference on Public Interest Law, where students from around the country get together with each other and a group of practitioners each spring. It is a way of honoring the memory of Robert Cover by establishing and maintaining exchange among lawyers committed to types of public service.

This year the conference weekend coincides with the Jewish festival of Purim, which commemorates Esther's role in the deliverance of the Jews from a massacre planned by Haman. According to the biblical story, King Ahasuerus banishes his first queen and, when he grows to miss her, is advised to find another. Young virgins are assembled for him. One is Esther, the adopted daughter of Mordecai. On Mordecai's advice, she does not reveal that she is a Jew. She becomes the king's choice. Haman, the king's favored courtier, is the enemy of Mordecai. He plots a massacre of all Jews. Esther outmaneuvers him and saves the Jews. Haman and his sons are impaled on stakes and all other enemies of the Jews are slaughtered.

A scholarly comment concludes that "Gentile and Jew alike are represented in the story as actuated by the basest motives of pride, greed and cruelty."[50] Steve has brought copies of the biblical Book of Esther, and on Saturday night invites anyone interested to join in a discussion of it.[51] Its violence is a surprise to some in the group who are familiar with Purim but not with the full text. The text provokes a lively conversation. It is on this occasion that Henry Schwarzschild repudiates the blood-thirstiness of the story. One student—knowledgeable, like many others in attendance—advances my understanding of the Book of Esther by pointing out its many similarities to standard Persian court tales of the period that he has studied and that ordinarily truck in violence.

Before the discussion started, we had done a serial reading, with each person in turn taking a paragraph. As it turned out, there were an equal number of participants and paragraphs, and the paragraph that fell to me was the one part of the text that has stuck in my mind for many years. It occurs just after Esther learns of Haman's plot to kill the Jews. She has sent a message to Mordecai asking what to do:

> Mordecai had this message delivered to Esther: "Do not imagine that you, of all Jews, will escape with your life by being in the king's palace. On the contrary, if you keep silent in this crisis, relief and deliverance will come to the Jews from another quarter, while you and your father's house will perish. And who knows, perhaps you have attained to royal position for just such a crisis." Then Esther sent back this answer to Mordecai: "Go assemble all the Jews who live in Shushan, and fast in my behalf: do not eat or drink for three

days, night or day. I and my maidens will observe the same fast. Then I shall go to the king, though it is contrary to the law; and if I am to perish, I shall perish!" So Mordecai went about [the city] and did just as Esther had commanded him. (4:13–17)

This portion of the story raises troublesome questions about gaining prestige and power within an alien system, about the time for keeping silent and the time for speaking out, about the actions to take although they are contrary to law, about response to crisis. The story deals in extremes. But extremes instruct. To bend the ordinary, breaking it open, allows discernment of the internal structure and dynamics of the daily.

Critical to me in the text is Mordecai's message to Esther. I understand that it can be variously interpreted: Is he attempting to manipulate his adopted daughter? Threaten her? Use her and her body in a male power struggle? Inspire her? For the present, I read his message as a statement of fact. Esther may indeed have achieved her status exactly to wield power upon just such an occasion as this. (How can she know? Note Mordecai's "perhaps." Neither he nor she can be sure. And the proposed act is "contrary to the law." There is risk and uncertainty; a decision must be made.)

Esther's dilemma draws the reader's attention. But there is a second, larger focus for attention. Her wrong choice will be fatal for her and her family—but not for the Jews. If she fails to act, their deliverance will come "from another quarter." She may become a medium of the dynamics of freedom; her opting out will not frustrate them.

I think modern American lawyers may be located in something close to the same position.

TWO

〜〜〜

Dilsey, Baby Suggs, and the Nonreligious Word

THIS BOOK'S EXPERIMENT will end, as it has now begun, with the people just presented. In between I hope to develop a way to understand their lives in law. My intention is not to supplant the independent value of their work or their own self-descriptions, but to discover whether theology may help to illuminate their practices. One of the criteria of success for such an endeavor must surely be whether it keeps in focus what lawyers and judges actually do.

For the meantime, however, I must shift attention away from these people and toward others, primarily Dilsey, Baby Suggs, and Karl Barth. Like the population of the last chapter, they are not illustrations of a set of principles but are strong, multidimensional people who command attention on their own, for who they are. Dilsey is found in William Faulkner's *The Sound and the Fury;* Baby Suggs in Toni Morrison's *Beloved.*

Karl Barth is less easily accessible.[1] He was a Swiss theologian who taught in Germany until the Nazis forced him out. Decades after his death, he remains the dominant figure in modern Protestant theology. A recent study likened his work to the Chartres Cathedral: "Once one's eyes get used to the light, one discovers that one is inside an awesome and many-splendored structure."[2] There is a monumental, architectural quality to his work, but to me it is not remote, dark, static, or cold. I hear in it a vital, engaging voice.[3]

Thirty years ago, I sought out Barth in Basel, Switzerland. I had come to know a little of his work in college and then read him extensively in divinity school, under the guidance chiefly of Paul Lehmann but also of Richard R. Niebuhr. By the time I graduated, Barth had profoundly shaped my thinking. I made my way to Europe and participated in a seminar he offered. (We convened in a large common room on the second floor of a neighborhood restaurant/pub. The management was glad to reserve the space; there was honor in receiving Barth and a good

73

return on orders for refreshment.) The seminar was working its way through Barth's multivolume *Church Dogmatics*.

When my turn came to lead one of the evening discussions, I scheduled an appointment with Barth several days in advance. In the seminar presentation, I planned to raise critical questions about the pages assigned to me and wanted him to understand that my argumentative stance in the event did not mean I was an enemy. I had been greatly, positively influenced by him; my criticism would be a kind of lover's quarrel and a way of paying serious tribute. When I was ushered into the study in his home, I delivered very little of the speech I had memorized. He grasped my meaning quickly, put me at ease, and devoted the remainder of the appointment to close, lively questions about various Civil War battlefields in areas of the South where I had lived. His knowledge of that war, like many other subjects, was encyclopedic, but he had never been to the United States and was eager for firsthand information from a person who had walked the land.

His eyes were small, the eyebrows raised as though in an effort to see through the substantial lenses of his glasses. He drew constantly and happily on a pipe whether or not there was fire in the bowl. When he spoke his mouth curled around the words. His congenial look conveyed a hint of surprise, as though he had been momentarily recalled from deep concentration on something or someone elsewhere. He was rigorous in thought, capable of powerful criticism, imaginative, and sometimes puckish. The general impression was one of immense goodwill.

When class time arrived, I was so charged with anxiety as to be nearly speechless. For me it was Job's appointment with God, in which I was cast in the role of Job: "Then the Lord answered Job out of the whirlwind: 'Who is this that darkens counsel by words without knowledge? Gird up your loins like a man, I will question you, and you shall declare to me" (Job 38:1–3). The subject for the evening mattered to me, and it mattered to Barth.[4] We argued, seminar fashion, for a couple of hours. At the end I was too thankful to have survived with enjoyment and credibility to appreciate immediately the significance of Barth's generosity of mind and the correspondent pedagogical vulnerability he mounted for that occasion.

Fresh out of the academy, I was an innocent. Barth had stood up to the Nazis, was acknowledged to be the leading theologian of the twentieth century, and, as far as I could tell, had read everything and enjoyed instant recall of each page. Who was I to be arguing theology with this man? More important, who was he to be arguing theology with me?

He did not speak from an Olympian height of claimed authority. He handed down no pronouncements. He took no refuge in his fame, accomplishments, advanced age, learning, or intellect. He shared laughter. He was both demanding and freely approachable, in the manner of a teacher who cares passionately about both his subject matter and his students. He also had a strength of humility that I have come to associate with faithfulness.

Barth founded no school and did not invite a following of disciples. He was always in the process of reevaluation, ready to rethink everything and start all over again from the beginning. The beginning, God's self-revelation, remained constant. I shall return to this central emphasis of his later in this chapter and briefly again in the next.

My use of his writings here is a borrowing and is not an exposition of his thought. His deployment of theological categories is as usefully necessary to my understanding of secular law now as it was to other subjects years ago.

A DISTINCTION BETWEEN RELIGION AND BIBLICAL FAITH

Barth at last visited the United States, and several Civil War battlefields, shortly after my encounter with him. One of the people he met was William Stringfellow, a lawyer whose theological acumen won particular praise from Barth. Stringfellow, like Barth, drew a distinction between religion and the biblical faith, and the distinction made an essential difference for Stringfellow's practice of law in New York's East Harlem. "The central idea about religion in America," he once remarked, "is that religion has only to do with religion, not with life."[5] This segregating idea arose from Americans' hope to avoid the religious controversies and persecutions that had bedeviled Europeans and others.[6] For many, religion has come to be a subject of personal, private, individual choice, with each person expected to be tolerant of others' selections of beliefs. The significant factor has then become not what a person believes but the sincerity with which she believes it, not the contentious content but the benign heartiness of belief. So understood, religious belief is then supposedly protected from the state, and the state supposedly protected from religious belief, by the Constitution's free exercise and establishment clauses.

But if religion has mainly to do with religion, it has little immediate bearing on a law practice like Stringfellow's, deeply engaged in life, a law practice that "does not often permit the luxury of hypothetical and speculative matters."[7] To close the gap between religion and the lawyer's daily work, "some application of the propositions of religion is required to make them relevant to secular issues."[8] Such applications, however, further entrench the fundamental assumption that religion and life are strangely different and require the operations of specialists to achieve a match between them.

Stringfellow was not much diverted by religion, but he was thoroughly captivated by the Word of God. His was the nonreligious understanding that God is present in the world caring decisively for human life. No special applications are needed as a bridge between the Word of God and the world, for the chasm between them has been closed by God. The believer's role is to discern, rely on, and celebrate the Word present in the common, actual life of the world. The believer's role is theological but not religious, simple but not easy, and I shall have more to say on the subject later (although, now and later, the primary emphasis is on the action of the Word rather than believer response).

First, I must work at the distinction, drawn by Stringfellow and Barth as well as others, between religion and the Word. My understanding of the people and practices described in chapter 1 derives from my understanding of the Word and is not religious. I must find ways to make the distinction sensible—to me as well as to you—and shall try to do so with descriptive experiments rather than hard-driving, irresistible arguments, for I covet your understanding more than your agreement. In any event, the important subject is less the distinction between religion and the biblical Word than the context that is the matrix of the distinction. Like Stringfellow, I do not have time for idle religious speculation and argument. I do have time to attempt discernment of the structures and dynamics of law practices like those I have described and many others like them.

THE RELIGIOUS PROBLEM AND THE SELF

Not all of the many uses and impacts of religion are beneficial, as witness religion's service of established power and the acute example of the chaplain on board the warship *Bellipotent* in Herman Melville's short novel *Billy Budd.* Such a chaplain is "the minister of the Prince of Peace serving in the host of the God of War—Mars. . . . He lends the sanction of the religion of the meek to that which practically is the abrogation of everything but brute Force."[9] When the sailors are provoked to an ominous unease, the chaplain is summoned to conduct worship service. "That done, the drum beat the retreat; and toned by music and religious rites subserving the discipline and purposes of war, the men in their wonted orderly manner dispersed to the places allotted them when not at the guns."[10]

This ability of religion to legitimate established power and to tranquilize its subjects was harnessed to slavery. For example, Harriet Jacobs, in her *Incidents in the Life of a Slave Girl*, tells how, after Nat Turner's insurrection, fearful slaveholders decided to "give the slaves enough of religious instruction to keep them from murdering their masters."[11] The clergyman who volunteered to instruct Jacobs and her fellow slaves is named in her account "the Rev. Mr. Pike." (He was John Avery, D.D., product of Williams College and Yale University, rector of St. Paul's Church, Edenton, N.C.)[12] As the text for the first instructional session he chose Ephesians 6:5: "Servants, be obedient to them that are your masters according to the flesh, with fear and trembling, in single-ness of your heart, as unto Christ."[13] He proceeded to inform his audience that they were rebellious sinners. He promised that God was angry and would punish them if they did not forsake their idleness and serve their masters faithfully. Jacobs reports: "We went home, highly amused at brother Pike's gospel teaching."[14]

Less amusing was the effect of religion on those in power. Dr. James Norcom, Jacobs's master and sexual harasser ("Dr. Flint"), joined the church because, as he told her, "my position in society requires it."[15] On him, as a wielder rather than victim of force, religion acted as a stimulant rather than sedative. Jacobs recounts: "The worst persecutions I endured from him were after he was a communicant."[16]

The ongoing war against Indian tribes is another instance of religion overtly placed in the service of power. The United States has deployed as much religion as weaponry in its attempts to tone—to "Americanize and Christianize"—Native Americans. For many years, for example, the federal government paid Christian missionaries to be the agents of its Indian policy.[17]

The alignment of religion with established power is certainly not novel. It is as ancient, in Christendom, as the accommodation reached between the Church and Constantine and as contemporary as the support of the Church for the white South that earned Martin Luther King's censure: "Is organized religion too inextricably bound to the status quo to save our nation and the world?"[18]

If not religion gone wrong, religion in the service of established power is religion at its lowest, and it has long been recognized and criticized as such. Less often noted, however, and far more resistant to familiar forms of critique, are the noxious possibilities of religion at its *best*.

Some experience of these possibilities is available in a page or two of William Faulkner's *Light in August*.[19] In that novel, an old, discredited, lost minister, the Reverend Gail Hightower, hears the sounds of approaching Sunday evening service in the Presbyterian church that had been his parish years ago. He does not himself attend the service, but his memory re-creates the action, and in that form the reader participates in it. From his living room window, Hightower sees members of the congregation exchange greetings as they approach from the streets. Then in his memory he hears their low-toned talking as they enter the church for the Sunday evening prayer meeting: "It has seemed to him always that at that hour man approaches nearest of all to God, nearer than at any other hour of all the seven days. Then alone, of all church gatherings, is there something of that peace which is the promise and the end of the Church" (p. 321). There, in "the cool soft blowing of faith and hope" (ibid.), religion achieves its apex. Pressed forward by the rich strains of the organ, the congregation raises its voice in songs of praise. And yet.

> Yet even then the music has still a quality stern and implacable, deliberate and without passion so much as immolation, pleading, asking, for not love, not life, forbidding it to others, demanding in sonorous tones death as though death were the boon, like all Protestant music. . . . Pleasure, ecstasy, they cannot seem to bear: their escape from it is in violence. . . . *And so why should not their religion drive them to crucifixion of themselves and one another?* he thinks. (Pp. 321–22)

On the following day, the town lynches Joe Christmas.

At the very moment when their religion carried those Presbyterians as close to God as it could, at that same point of highest reach, it also drove its practitioners away from God toward death. "It was as though they who accepted it and raised voices to praise it within praise, having been made what they were by that which the music praised and symbolized, they took revenge upon that which made them so by means of the praise itself" (p. 322). This is religion at its highest, not its lowest.

It was when Martin Luther King saw southern churches' "lofty spires pointing heavenward"—the architecture embodying their aspirational striving—that he was driven to ask, "What kind of people worship here? Who is their God?" The answer to his question is: ordinary white American religious people worshiping the customary gods of their religion; at the moment of their religious best, religious people may also be at their most moribund.

This phenomenon is the subject of a substantial but not widely known inside—that is, theologically grounded—critique of religion that originates in the biblical texts. In Exodus 32, already at Mt. Sinai immediately following the making of the covenant and the giving of the law, God tells Moses: "Let me alone, that my wrath may burn hot against [the people of Israel]" (32:10). The cause of his anger is a religious exercise, described by Karl Barth as "Israel, the congregation of Yahweh, the people of the revelation, under the leadership of Aaron, the head of the priestly class, in the full panoply of its religion," celebrating a feast of Yahweh, but "in adoration and sacrifice before the molten image of a calf. With a sacrificial zeal which cannot be denied they all gave of their best toward it. Aaron himself designed and made it."[20]

Later, the prophet Amos's condemnation of northern Israel was sharpest when directed against the people's worship of Yahweh. "The truth," Barth observed, "was that the whole inhumanity and injustice of Samarian society allied itself, not with a worship of gods or idols, but quite decorously with the worship of Yahweh."[21]

The New Testament is equally hard on religion. Jesus' disciples are religious, but disbelievers to the extent of their religion. Peter is the exemplary religious figure, and it is he who denies Jesus in the hour of betrayal. Moreover, in that fantastic scene, on a high mountain, when Jesus is transfigured and Elijah and Moses appear, it is also Peter who proposes building three commemorative booths, a bit of religious inspiration whose obnoxious irrelevance is immediately and mercifully drowned in the voice of God.[22]

The characteristic of religion that draws theological criticism is less its weakness than its strength: its attempt to reach beyond the present world toward a god whom it postulates and whose help and protection its adherents invoke.[23] This attempt at self-transcendence is worthy and noble. Its worthiness and nobility are no small part of the difficulty encountered in criticizing it.

The question is whether, by inviting self-transcendence, religion is not a misdirection. In the biblical stories God gives himself and makes himself known. This self-revelation does not correspond to religion, to human striving toward God.

I am a survivor of Daily Vacation Bible School, a summer phenomenon perfected in southern Protestant churches and visited upon small children. Fixed in my memory is the felt board that, like lemonade, was standard equipment in the church basement, cool and smelling of concrete. Felt was stretched across a board, and cut-out felt figures were applied to it. It was a poor precursor of Velcro, but the felt on felt usually held for the duration of a lesson. One of the regular demonstrations began with a felt earth applied to the left center of the felt board, a heaven placed in the upper right, and a hell below spread across the bottom (orange and red flames against the light blue background; in between the flames, occasional small human figures in suggestions of torment).

How to get from the world to heaven without falling into hell? Build a bridge. If you obeyed your parents, that would constitute one section. A small piece of bridge would be placed on the board and start to cover the blue distance from earth to heaven. But obedience to parents, although necessary, was insufficient, a conclusion that was illustrated by the teacher: A little felt figure runs up the first installment of bridge, tries to leap off the end to heaven, fails, and drops to hell. Regular attendance at Sunday school would add another section. But neither was that enough. (Pause, little figure, same result.) The bridge progressed in stages (obey teachers, say prayers, be good, etc.). Lots of little figures fell to the flames. After every bridge-building section-act had been thought of and added, an open space remained. Still no way to make it all the way to heaven. Every running jump added to the pile in hell. Despair. Enter Jesus. You had to have Jesus. Accomplish all the hard acts of obedience to authority and then believe in Him, and He would become the last, gap-closing section to heaven.

In addition to the trivialization, the attempted manipulation of children, the flight from the world, and the deus ex machina at the end, this little, unintentionally comic exercise in religious propaganda is unrepresentative only in its relative lack of sophistication. It is at odds with the biblical accounts of God's activity.

The revealed Word does not fill in our various attempts to make our way to God. In the received language for talking about these matters: Grace does not perfect nature, revelation does not complete reason, and mercy does not make up the deficit of good works.[24] God makes his own way to humans, and his self-revelation bears its own possibilities for being known or not known. Jacob's ladder extended from heaven to earth, not the other way around.

If we try to grasp at God, we do not believe. If we did believe we would listen, but in religion, as Barth noted, we talk; consequently, "because it is a grasping, religion is the contradiction of revelation [and is] the concentrated expression of unbelief. . . . Revelation does not link up with a human religion which is already present and practiced. It contradicts it."[25]

Religion expands the believing self from which it cannot at last break free. This self-limiting fixation was brought home to me in the aftermath of an extended religious experience in late winter Alaska. My wife and I, a guide, and two teams of sled dogs ventured into the back-country of Denali National Park. The expanse, the beauty, Mt. McKinley looming in the distance, the extremes of weather, the great quiet, the aurora borealis, the wildlife, and the journey itself daily challenged the senses of wonder and mystery and made for profound religious experience.

Still thankful and euphoric afterwards, I talked to a Georgia friend, Coleman Barks, about that riveting territory and how it had demanded total concentration. His immediate and accurate response, offered as an encouraging, positive assessment, was that the Alaskan backcountry had constituted an "interior landscape" for me and that I had been exploring myself. Until then I had supposed—as I have about other worthy religious experiences—that I had been drawn beyond myself. That was a false impression.[26] The Alaska adventure, like the triathlons that I also do, was an elaborate form of enlarged narcissism disguised as challenge.[27]*

Many of my religious experiences have occurred in interaction with natural settings and phenomena. Equally many have been responses to art, theater, and music. Also politics. For example, as delegates from Georgia to the 1984 Democratic Convention in San Francisco, my wife and I were members of the congregation when, as a fellow member put it, "Jesse Jackson held Church in the Democratic National Convention."[28]

Whatever their occasion, sophistication, and affecting power to exalt, these experiences were essentially affairs of the self. I do not deny or denigrate my own or others' religious impulses, but neither do I now mistake their import. Barth correctly observed that "not even a Spanish mystic, has ever really looked away from himself and beyond himself, let alone transcended himself in a purely formal negation. If we try to do this, looking into an empty beyond, we are really looking quite cheerfully at ourselves again, however solemnly we may pretend that it is otherwise."[29]

So from the biblical perspective, religion is unbelief. It is a fruitless effort to justify ourselves before our imagination's capricious picture of a highest being, a God described by Barth as "the tedious magnitude known as transcendence, not as a genuine counterpart, nor a true other . . . but as an illusory reflection of human freedom, as its projection into the vacuum of utter abstraction."[30] Strive though we may after God, we end up cheerfully or solemnly exploring ourselves.

So understood, religion is not necessarily the antithesis to science. Paul Davies believes that science provides a surer path to God than does religion, now "that the biblical perspective of the world . . . seems largely irrelevant."[31] People like Davies, who seems to have a good grasp of science, should not be allowed to broadcast their picture of God ("the supreme holistic concept")[32] as though it is either related to the God of the biblical stories or unrelated to religion. Science does not provide a surer way to God, but a way to a different god. When modern philosophers and scientists like Davies conclude that the larger patterns they discern are the traces of a God who, as a minimum datum, does not throw dice, their movement from the natural order to the larger scheme of things to a God is the treading of the path of religion. At the end of the path is a greater or lesser abstraction of ourselves.

The religious try to prove the existence of God, but as Barth pointed

*An asterisk signals a substantive discussion in a note.

out, we, rather than God, are the text in need of establishment and interpretation: "It is primarily the creature and not the Creator of whom we are not certain, and in order to be certain of him we need proof or revelation."[33] Needing to find ourselves, we try to find God and discover uncertainty about both.

RELIGION AND THE WORD

A "No" is pronounced upon religion. This profound negative judgment, however, is penultimate. The ultimate judgment about religion is a "Yes." God does embrace religion.[34]

Again William Faulkner provides the experience for reference and orientation. Contrast to the Sunday evening religious service remembered by the Reverend Gail Hightower in *Light in August* the very different Easter service that constitutes the climax of *The Sound and the Fury*. (My reading of this service owes much to Thomas Merton.)[35]

The world Faulkner created in *The Sound and the Fury* is largely that of white Compsons, but at its center is the black Dilsey. The father of the Compsons is Jason III, a lawyer who sits all day at his office with a decanter of whiskey and copies of Horace, Livy, and Catullus. He is present in the story through the eyes of others and mostly as a memory after his death. His widow is put-upon, hypochondriacal, inadequate. One son, Quentin III, kills himself after completing a year at Harvard. Daughter Caddy flees, leaving her illegitimate daughter, Quentin, behind. Son Benjamin is an idiot whose sole medium of speech is a howl. The other son, Jason IV, is a scheming, cruel, avaricious liar. He is described as "the first sane Compson" (p. 16).

Dilsey raises not only her own children, Frony and Luster, but also those of the Compsons, for whom she works in close quarters. She cooks, serves, repairs such threads as bind the Compsons together, and suffers their abuse. It is bitterly ironic when the widow, "Miss Cahline," in her incessant complaining, says to Dilsey, who daily bears the Compson burdens: "You're not the one who has to bear it. . . . It's not your responsibility. You can go away. You don't have to bear the brunt of it day in and day out" (p. 288).

The sound and fury of the Compson world tumble toward Easter when Jason discovers that his niece Quentin has run off with a circus showman. She has taken from Jason's hidden lock box three thousand dollars that he had squeezed out of his store clerk's income plus four thousand that he had either squeezed out of Quentin's mother as blackmail or embezzled from Quentin. He rages off in vain pursuit of Quentin and the showman. Mrs. Compson, reeking of camphor and defeat, now has more complaints. Benjamin bellows. Dilsey has her hands full.

In the midst of this uproar, after breakfast has been served to the whites, Dilsey and the members of her community emerge from their cabins and struggle up the road, forming a procession. They are summoned to a weathered church set in a scene that is "flat and without perspective as a painted cardboard set upon the edge of the flat earth, against the windy sunlight of space and April and a midmorning filled with bells" (p. 308). Benjamin, unwelcome in the white churches, accompanies Dilsey.

There is promise of an unburdening. A visiting clergyman, Reverend Shegog, is to preach. He is unnoticed by the gathered congregation when he enters and, when seen, evokes disappointment: "The visitor was undersized, in a shabby alpaca coat. He had a wizened black face. . . . They watched the insignificant looking man . . . with something like consternation and unbelief. . . .

"'En dey brung dat all de way fum Saint Looey,' Frony whispered.

"'I've knowed de Lawd to use cuiser tools dan dat,' Dilsey said" (p. 309).

When Reverend Shegog rose to preach, he began in the level, cold voice of a white man. His insignificance was soon forgotten in the first virtuoso display of his voice. And then a further transformation began to take place. His voice took on the quality of "an alto horn, sinking into their hearts" (p. 310). The meager, stooped figure is overtaken:

> "I got the recollection and the blood of the Lamb!" He tramped steadily back and forth . . . hunched, his hands clasped behind him. He was like a worn small rock whelmed by the successive waves of his voice. With his body he seemed to feed the voice that, succubus like, had fleshed its teeth in him. And the congregation seemed to watch with its own eyes while the voice consumed him, until he was nothing and they were nothing and there was not even a voice but instead their hearts were speaking to one another in chanting measures beyond the need for words, so that when he came to rest against the reading desk, his . . . face lifted and his whole attitude that of a serene tortured crucifix that transcended its shabbiness and insignificance and made it of no moment, a long moaning expulsion of breath arose from them, and a woman's single soprano: "Yes, Jesus!" (P. 310)

The unburdening had begun. "Two tears slid down [Dilsey's] fallen cheeks, in and out of the myriad coruscations of immolation and abnegation and time" (p. 311).

The voice took yet another turn: "'I got de ricklickshun en de blood of de Lamb!' They did not mark just when his intonation, his pronunciation, became negroid, they just sat swaying a little in their seats as the voice took them into itself" (ibid.).

He "sees de light en . . . sees de word" (ibid.). And, borne up by the punctuation of the congregational response "Yes, Jesus!" what he reports on and elaborates are biblical stories: the enslavement in Egypt, Mary and the baby Jesus, the crucifixion, and at last:

> "I sees de resurrection en de light; sees de meek Jesus sayin Dey kilt Me dat ye shall live again; I died dat dem whut sees en believes shall never die. Breddren, O breddren! I sees de doom crack en hears de golden horns shoutin down de glory, en de arisen dead whut got de blood en de ricklickshun of de Lamb!"
>
> In the midst of the voices and the hands Ben sat, rapt in his sweet blue gaze. Dilsey sat bolt upright beside, crying rigidly and quietly in the annealment and the blood of the remembered Lamb. (Pp. 312–13)

It is a beautiful, affecting scene. It is also richly instructive theologically. The Word is proclaimed. Religion, the contradiction of the Word, is made the medium of the Word. Religion, which misdirects by deflecting the search for God back upon the self, becomes occasion for the self-revelation of God and the self-forgetfulness of the unburdened congregation.

Barth observed that "the abolishing of religion by revelation need not mean only its negation: the judgment that religion is unbelief. Religion can just as well be exalted in revelation, even though the judgment still stands. It can be upheld and concealed in it. . . . Revelation can adopt religion."[36] The religion of Dilsey's community offers clues about—is indicative or parabolic of—religion adopted by revelation.

The operative power is in the Word. Reverend Shegog "seed de power en de glory," and Dilsey "seed de first en de last," "de beginnin, en now I sees de endin" (p. 313). The recollection and the blood of the Lamb given to Shegog and the congregation are the acts of the God of the biblical stories.

This type of proclamation about and from the Word in the context of religion is found also in Zora Neale Hurston's *Jonah's Gourd Vine*, when John Pearson preaches a sermon (pp. 174ff.) reciting the creation, the incarnation, and then the crucifixion ("I see Jesus," p. 177):

> He died until the great belt in the wheel of time
> And de geological strata fell aloose
> And a thousand angels rushed to de canopy of heben

With flamin' swords in their hands
And placed their feet upon blue ether's bosom, and
    looked back at de dazzlin' throne
And de arc angels had veiled their faces
And de throne was draped in mournin'
And de orchestra had struck silence for the space of half an hour
Angels had lifted their harps to de weepin' willows
And God looked off to-wards immensity
And blazin' worlds fell off his teeth
And about that time Jesus groaned on de cross, and
Dropped His head in the locks of His shoulder and said,
"It is finished, it is finished." (P. 180)

The biblical events in such representation have affective power. In Reverend Shegog's sermon before Dilsey's congregation, the mighty acts are proclaimed and in the proclamation claim both the figure who announces them and the congregation whose response is called forth. This is a communal event and, unlike normal religion, is nondivisive because it is lacking in privilege: Reverend Shegog is unremarkable save for his lack of remarkable features and of hierarchical authority; his disappointing insignificance is transcended and made of no moment in the event of his preaching. And the voice takes the congregation of unprivileged black servants and laborers—and Benjamin—into itself until Reverend Shegog "was nothing and they were nothing and there was not even a voice but instead their hearts were speaking to one another in chanting measures beyond the need for words" (p. 310). Thereby raised to affirmation—"Yes, Jesus!"—the congregation is made participant in the action: "I sees, O Jesus! Oh I sees!" (p. 312).

There is nothing here about human fulfillment, or human flourishing, or ethical values, or the power of positive thinking, or what one must do to be saved, or the believing self and its work of belief, or of applications of biblical teachings to daily life. Instead, there is the Word. And there is belief, but belief happens, is enacted, is generated by the communal proclamation.

In the religion it thus adopts, the Word, although incorrespondent, becomes nonetheless accessible—in words and in hearts speaking beyond the need for words. The otherness of the Word is expressed in the sermons of John Pearson and Reverend Shegog by the odd, striking images on which it rides. In Pearson's sermon the orchestra "struck silence for the space of half an hour," and "God looked off to-wards immensity / And blazin' worlds fell off his teeth." In Shegog's sermon, after he "hears de weepin en de cryin en de turnt-away face of God: dey done kilt Jesus; dey done kilt my Son!" he "can see de widowed God shet His do'"

(p. 312). Blazing worlds falling off teeth and a widowed God. But the more other it is revealed to be, the more the Word proclaimed becomes particular and available to those to whom it is announced. So does Reverend Shegog's intonation shift from that of an alien white voice to that of the black congregation. The foreign tongue rises to the familiar and, like a horn, sinks into their hearts. The incorrespondent Word, the wholly other, is contextually, particularly human.[37]

This is critical. Religion adopted by the Word is not about religion or the self but about the world and humans, about what Paul Lehmann calls the struggle "to make and to keep human life human in the world."[38] Those who are addressed are addressed as humans and so are constituted human. Harriet Jacobs reported that not all the white clergy sent to the slaves came with an unalloyed message of obedience to slaveholders. Blacks went to hear one white minister gladly: "It was the first time they had ever been addressed as human beings."[39]

Dilsey recognizes this phenomenon of being humanly addressed and constituted as the essentially responsive, authenticating act of being named. In *The Sound and the Fury* when Benjamin was discovered to be an idiot, his name had been changed from that of a family member, an uncle, Maury. Dilsey objects:

> His name's Benjy now, Caddy said.
> How come it is, Dilsey said. He ain't wore out the name he was born with yet, is he.
> Benjamin come out of the bible, Caddy said. It's a better name for him than Maury was.
> How come it is, Dilsey said.
> Mother says it is, Caddy said.
> Huh, Dilsey said. Name ain't going to help him. Hurt him, neither. Folks dont have no luck, changing names. My name been Dilsey since fore I could remember and it be Dilsey when they's long forgot me.
> How will they know it's Dilsey, when it's long forgot, Dilsey, Caddy said.
> It'll be in the Book, honey, Dilsey said. Writ out.
> Can you read it, Caddy said.
> Wont have to, Dilsey said. They'll read it for me. All I got to do is say Ise here. (P. 77)

Her religion—religion adopted by the Word—is determinative of who she is as a human and of how she is human. It cannot occupy an isolated sphere either metaphysical or private. It gives her humanity and life instead of rescuing her from either.

Like other members of the congregation, she is returned to the world. For her and her family, this means the Compson place: After the service "they reached the gate and entered. Immediately Ben began to whimper again, and for a while all of them looked up the drive at the square, paintless house with its rotting portico" (p. 313).

Dilsey had been unburdened, really unburdened, but in order to return to the burdening world and not in order to escape from it. Dietrich Bonhoeffer correctly observed that, although "redemption" is now taken to mean "redemption from cares, distress, fears, and longings, from sin and death, in a better world beyond the grave," this is not its essential character. "The difference between the Christian hope of resurrection and the mythological hope is that the former sends a person back to life on earth in a wholly new way."[40]

Dilsey returns to the Compson place, but in what way is she or it new? Everything remains the same, but everything is also different, a tension realized in part in the experience of time. Time figures prominently in *The Sound and the Fury*. For example, Benjamin's experience of time is only the immediate now. For Mrs. Compson, time is an endless procession of grievances. For Jason, time is money. Dilsey lives in their times as well as in her own, and also in another.

The Compsons are haunted by time and determined by it, but the house clock is oddly out of joint. After Easter church, Dilsey returns to the Compson kitchen and its now cold stove. "While she stood there the clock above the cupboard struck ten times. 'One oclock,' she said aloud" (p. 316). Ten is one. Dilsey lives in broken time, in the meantime.

On the afternoon of Easter Sunday, Benjamin renews his wail, the wail that is "hopeless and prolonged. It was nothing. Just sound. It might have been all time and injustice and sorrow become vocal for an instant by a conjunction of planets" (pp. 303–4). Dilsey leads him to a bed and draws him down beside her "and she held him, rocking back and forth, wiping his drooling mouth upon the hem of her skirt. . . . 'Dis long time, O Jesus,' she said, 'Dis long time'" (p. 332). Dilsey's post-Easter has been alleviated of none of its ordinariness, suffering, or tedium.

Also in the Gospel stories there is no amelioration of world conditions even in the instance of the miracles performed by Jesus. The miracles, as Barth pointed out, lack continuation: "There must have been many other storms on the sea of Galilee after the calming of the tempest, and more than one boatload must have perished. The five thousand and four thousand fed in the wilderness knew what it was to be hungry again, and sooner or later those who were healed died either of the same or of a different disease. Even those who were raised from the dead had to die eventually."[41] Existence does continue to be finite, or, as W. H. Auden put it,

> . . . for the time being, here we all are
> Back in the moderate Aristotelian city
> Of darning and the Eight-Fifteen, where Euclid's geometry
> And Newton's mechanics would account for our experience,
> And the kitchen table exists because I scrub it.
>
> . . .
>
> The Time Being is, in a sense, the most trying time of all.[42]

Dilsey's post-Easter world is unalleviated of ordinariness, but that is not to say it remains the same. Its ground has been fundamentally, radically revised. When she had returned to the Compson kitchen from the Easter celebration and heard the clock strike ten, and therefore one, she realized that she lived in the midst of broken time but also in the fullness of time: "'Ise seed de first en de last,' she said, looking at the cold stove, 'I seed de first en de last.' She set out some cold food on a table. As she moved back and forth she sang a hymn" (p. 316).

What is to be said about Dilsey's life after Easter? Barth notes about "the deadly and incommensurable power of the Resurrection" that it is singular: It is "not an event in history elongated so as still to remain an event in the midst of other events," but

> is the non-historical . . . relating of the whole historical life of Jesus to its origin in God. It follows therefore that the pressure of the power of the Resurrection into my existence, which of necessity involves a real walking in newness of life, cannot be an event among other events in my present, past, or future life. My new life is . . . *hid with Christ in God* (Col. iii. 3): it is the invisible point of observation and of relationship, the judgment exercised by my infinite upon my finite existence.[43]

The Compson place continues along its customary trajectory. But its foundations have been shaken. Dilsey's infinite existence intersects her finite existence, judging the sound and fury of the Compson household. The intersection is both radical and unremarked (and in that sense secret).

Her continuing life in the Compson household may be read together with Jesus' passive conservatism in the face of Roman imperialism and militarism. In Barth's terms, "the declaration and irruption of the kingdom of God had swept away the ground from under" the existing economic, social, and political order and precipitated "a questioning of the very presuppositions which is all the more powerful in its lack of any direct aggressiveness."[44] Similarly, Martin Luther King's nonviolence and subsequent assassination only highlight the fact that his dream of a racially reconciled South undercut the old racist premises. The continuing—and growing—oppression of African-Americans does nothing to restore those premises.

Animated by Easter, Dilsey was no more acquiescent than revolutionary, although she might appropriately have been either or both. Her alternatives and her preparation for them is indicated at the beginning of Easter day. The day had "dawned bleak and chill, a moving wall of grey light out of the northeast" (p. 281). She opened the door of her cabin. Her "collapsed face that gave the impression of the bones themselves being outside the flesh, lifted into the driving day with an expression at once fatalistic and of a child's astonished disappointment" (p. 282). She went back in.

> The earth immediately about the door was bare. It had a patina, as though from the soles of bare feet in generations, like old silver or the walls of Mexican houses which have been plastered by hand. Beside the house, shading it in summer, stood three mulberry trees, the fledged leaves that would later be broad and placid as the palms of hands streaming flatly undulant upon the driving air. A pair of jaybirds came up from nowhere, whirled up on the blast like gaudy scraps of cloth or paper and lodged in the mulberries, where they swung in raucous tilt and recover, screaming into the wind that ripped their harsh cries onward and away like scraps of paper or of cloth in turn. Then three more joined them and they swung and tilted in the wrung branches for a time, screaming. The door of the cabin opened and Dilsey emerged once more, this time in a man's felt hat and an army overcoat, beneath the frayed skirts of which her blue gingham dress fell in uneven balloonings, streaming too about her as she crossed the yard and mounted the steps to the kitchen door. (P. 282)

She is ready for what lies ahead. Without romanticism or sentimentality, Dilsey mounts to the kitchen clothed as both female servant and male soldier. She could bear the abuse and the burdens of the Compsons, but her life was also a remonstrance against them. She was capable of rebuking as well as of accepting, of war as well as of peace. Jason is afraid of her:

> Logical rational contained and even a philosopher in the old stoic tradition, thinking nothing whatever of God one way or the other and simply considering the police and so fearing and respecting only the Negro woman, [Jason's] sworn enemy since his birth and his mortal one since that day in 1911 when she too divined by sim-

ple clairvoyance that he was somehow using his infant niece's il-
legitimacy to blackmail its mother, who cooked the food he ate.
(P. 16)

She uses Jason's fear against him to protect his niece Quentin when
Jason threatens a beating: "'Jason,' she says, 'You, Jason! Ain't you
shamed of yourself.'" He flings her aside, but she manages to put herself
between them. "'Hit me, den,' she says, 'ef nothin else but hittin somebody wont do you. Hit me,' she says" (p. 203). He backs down and withdraws.

The nature and complexity of her life are highlighted immediately
at the conclusion of this episode when Dilsey turns and puts her comforting hand on Quentin, whom she has just rescued. Quentin knocks
her hand away: "'You damn old nigger,' she says" (p. 203). She is repudi-
ated, like Jesus, by her friend.

Post-Easter life for Dilsey is not a question about the status or being
or ethics of the religious person but about the nature of human life. "To
be a Christian," Bonhoeffer recognized, "does not mean to be religious
in a particular way, to make something of oneself . . . on the basis of
some method or other, but to be human—not a type of human, but the
human that Christ creates in us. It is not the religious act that makes the
Christian, but participation in the sufferings of God in the secular
life."[45]

Dilsey recollects the Lamb in the midst of the kitchen. She sings
hymns there not as a religious interlude but in the midst of her life and
in support of it. Unburdened, she becomes burdened again: comforting
the afflicted Benjamin, protecting Dilsey, rebuking Jason.

She has seen the first and the last, the beginning and the end. She
lives from the one and toward the other, in the meantime. The end, the
new coming of the kingdom, is the work of God and is no more a human
accomplishment than was the beginning, the first coming of the kingdom. Between them the believer participates in the suffering of God in
the world. Because the suffering is that of *God,* and the believer is only a
participant, she is not called to bear the burdens of the world stoically,
joylessly alone.

There is here something of both acceptance and rejection, of the
joyfulness companion to suffering, of the affirmation of life in the face
of its negation, something neither cheap nor sentimental. Something
like Baby Suggs's celebration in Toni Morrison's *Beloved,* the story of former slaves set in post–Civil War Ohio.[46] Sethe, who lost a husband,
risked death to escape the hell of slavery with her children and to join
her mother-in-law, Baby Suggs.

Baby Suggs had been redeemed from slavery, her freedom painfully purchased by a son forced to stay behind. Slavery had stripped her of everything but her heart, and that is what she offered. Baby Suggs, holy, became a kind of apostle. "Accepting no title of honor before her name, but allowing a small caress after it, she became an unchurched preacher, one who visited pulpits and opened her great heart to those who could use it" (p. 87). In the winter and fall, she paid visits to the AMEs and Baptists, Holiness and Sanctified, the Church of the Redeemer and the Redeemed. In the summer, every Saturday afternoon, she led the community to a clearing in the woods where her heart "pumped out love" and her mouth "spoke the Word" (p. 180). She called the children to laugh, and the men to dance and the women to cry until the dancing and laughing and crying were all mixed up and exhausting, and then:

> She did not tell them to clean up their lives or to go and sin no more. She did not tell them they were the blessed of the earth, its inheriting meek or its glorybound pure.
>
> She told them that the only grace they could have was the grace they could imagine. That if they could not see it, they would not have it.
>
> "Here," she said, "in this here place, we flesh; flesh that weeps, laughs; flesh that dances on bare feet in grass. Love it. Love it hard. Yonder they do not love your flesh. They despise it. They don't love your eyes; they'd just as soon pick em out. No more do they love the skin on your back. Yonder they flay it. . . . *You* got to love it, *you!* . . . More than eyes or feet. More than lungs that have yet to draw free air. More than your life-holding womb and your life-giving private parts, hear me now, love your heart. For this is the prize." Saying no more, she stood up then and danced with her twisted hip the rest of what her heart had to say while the others opened their mouths and gave her the music. (Pp. 88–89)

"Love your flesh" might be thought antibiblical. It is not. It is anti-religious. Although religion opposes nature to grace, the biblical stories oppose nature to the unnatural.[47]

("Love your flesh" is also anti-Calvinistic to the extent of Calvinism's religiosity. Religion is the "misfortune which takes fatal hold upon some men, and is by them passed on to others," Barth noted. "It is the misfortune . . . which laid upon Calvin's face that look which he bore at the end of his life."[48] Had Calvin pressed beyond religiosity and more fully understood the implications of God's humanity, "his Geneva would then not have become such a gloomy affair. His letters would then not have contained so much bitterness.")[49]

God's deity includes his humanity. God decides to exist together with humans, and, as Barth says, "in this divinely free volition and election, in this sovereign decision. . . , God is *human*."[50] God is allied with the natural, with the human, against the unnatural. "Love your flesh" in the Clearing is a celebration of this alliance. No recitation of the mighty works of God is necessary, for the participants are in the midst of one.

Beloved points up the destruction of the black self as one of the consequences or implements of slavery. "Anybody white could take your whole self for anything that came to mind. Not just work, kill, or maim you, but dirty you. Dirty you so bad you couldn't like yourself anymore. Dirty you so bad you forgot who you were and couldn't think it up" (p. 251). Consequently, when Baby Suggs crossed the river into Ohio and freedom, she did not know and did not care what she looked like. As Barth said, it is primarily ourselves and not God of whom we are uncertain. It is primarily ourselves, our flesh, our world that are in need of establishment and acceptance. In order to be certain of humanity, our humanity, we need proof or revelation.

"Suddenly [Baby Suggs] saw her hands and thought with a clarity as simple as it was dazzling. 'These hands belong to me. These *my* hands.' Next she felt a knocking in her chest and discovered something else new: her own heartbeat. Had it been there all along? This pounding thing?" (p. 141).

"Freeing yourself was one thing; claiming ownership of that freed self was another" (p. 95). The Clearing is where the claiming took place, where release was proclaimed to the captives. It was the place for unburdening and celebration. Here, as in the Easter service in *The Sound and the Fury*, the proclamation of the Word does not issue in any form of triumphalism or miraculous alteration in the circumstances of its black addressees. In fact Baby Suggs is finally overwhelmed by the white world.

Her daughter-in-law Sethe—abused, violated, beaten—escapes slavery and joins Baby Suggs. Too soon whites come to recapture the fugitive and her children and return them to bondage. To preserve her children from that fate, Sethe sets about killing them. Before she can be stopped, she slits the throat of the youngest, a baby girl. It is too much for Baby Suggs. She withdraws from the world, stops preaching, and finally lies down to die: "The heart that pumped out love, the mouth that spoke the Word, didn't count. [The whites] came in her yard anyway and she could not approve or condemn Sethe's rough choice. One or the other might have saved her, but beaten up by the claims of both, she went to bed. The whitefolks had tired her out at last" (p. 180).

Her last word is not that of the Clearing but another: "There's more of us they drowned than there is all of them ever lived from the start of time. Lay down your sword. This ain't a battle; it's a rout" (p. 244). Baby

Suggs, holy, is defeated. She is no less defeated outside of slavery than in it. The world of the present is too much.

Baby Suggs's granddaughter, Sethe's surviving daughter, Denver, takes Baby Suggs's word of defeat to heart. She fears the present. She refuses to leave the house and yard. But at long last she does. She ventures into the world. She is empowered to do so in a scene in which her memory of the dead Baby Suggs, or the voice of Baby Suggs, visits her. At first all she remembers is her grandmother's last and final words about defeat, and she "stood on the porch and couldn't leave it." But then her grandmother's ultimate word—not her last but her ultimate word—comes to Denver. It is the word about her forebears' living struggle against the death of slavery:

> Her throat itched; her heart kicked—and then Baby Suggs laughed, clear as anything. "You mean I never told you nothing about Carolina? About your daddy? You don't remember nothing about how come I walk the way I do and about your mother's feet, not to speak of her back? I never told you all that? Is that why you can't walk down the steps? My Jesus my."
> But you said there was no defense.
> "There ain't."
> Then what I do?
> "Know it, and go on out the yard. Go on." (P. 244)

Perhaps Sethe, too, is finally enabled to reenter the world—to "go on out the yard"—without promise of victory or success. She has been visited by Beloved. Beloved is and is not the slain child, is and is not an apparition. Beloved consumes more and more of Sethe's attention, time, and life, until all else is forgotten. In this sense Beloved is and is not also religion. She becomes at the end the perfection of beauty, attraction, and fecundity: "It had taken the shape of a pregnant woman, naked and smiling in the heat of the afternoon sun. Thunderblack and glistening, she stood on long straight legs, her belly big and tight. Vines of hair twisted all over her head. Jesus. Her smile was dazzling" (p. 261).

Beloved's hold over Sethe is broken at last by a group of women who gather outside the house to which Sethe has retired with Beloved. They make music. They "took a step back to the beginning. In the beginning there were no words. In the beginning was the sound, and they all knew what that sound sounded like" (p. 259). For Sethe that sound is "as though the Clearing had come to her with all its heat and simmering leaves, where the voices of women searched for the right combination, the key, the code, the sound that broke the back of words. Building voice upon voice until they found it, and when they did it was a wave of sound wide enough to sound deep water and knock the pods off chestnut trees. It broke over Sethe and she trembled like the baptized in its wash" (p. 261).

Beloved disappears. And with that disappearance, Sethe, like Baby Suggs before her, may be lost, defeated. But the ultimate word from the Clearing may yet have created the possibility of affirmation for her as well as Denver. Paul D., her old friend-lover from slavery days, returns. At the end, when last we see Sethe, Paul D. tells her a version of the Clearing proclamation.

"'You your best thing, Sethe. You are.' His holding fingers are holding hers.

"'Me? Me?'" (p. 273).

It is a tentative, tortured step toward loving her tortured black flesh, a redemptive step toward acceptance of her humanity, the humanity, the flesh, embraced by God. God, said Dietrich Bonhoeffer, "calls people, not to a new religion, but to life."[51]

Sethe, Denver, and Baby Suggs, like Dilsey in *The Sound and the Fury*, are our informants: The affirmation of the world empowered and authorized by the Word is hard won. Death is always, everywhere too close at hand in the personal forms of despair, hopelessness, anxiety; in the institutional, systemic forms of slavery, poverty, racism, sexism, enforced silence, bombast. It may seem to dominate.

Even or especially the biblical stories bear witness that the "beast" is "allowed to exercise authority. . . . Also it [is] allowed to make war on the saints and to conquer them" (Rev. 13:5, 7). Grace and its consequent affirmation of life are not cheap. A juxtaposition at the beginning of Morrison's book makes the point. One page bears a dedication, the next an epigraph. The dedication reads: "Sixty Million / and more." The epigraph is Romans 9:25:

> I will call them my people,
> which were not my people;
> and her beloved,
> which was not beloved.

The suffering of the sixty million is proximate to their being called the beloved people. In Dilsey's universe, "de darkness en de death everlastin upon de generations" is hard by "de resurrection en de light" (p. 312). The affirmation of the human is ultimate, but it does not deny that negation has penultimate force.

Such affirmation is particular, contextual, dependent on circumstances. God's deity includes his humanity. Jesus Christ is true God and true human. "He is the Word," Barth wrote, "spoken from the loftiest, most luminous transcendence and likewise the Word heard in the deepest, darkest immanence."[52] In the course of Reverend Shegog's sermon in *The Sound and the Fury,* the wholly other Word adopted the intimate, black voice of the congregation. In the Clearing in *Beloved,* the Word took form in black flesh. In this way, among these people in this time and place, "the Word became flesh and dwelt among us" (1 John 1:14). In this way, the Word establishes the world, certifies humanity, and celebrates life.

THREE

What of Ethics, Faith, Christian Religion?

CHAPTER TWO RAISES MORE questions than I can answer. Several of them warrant trailing a little further for the help they may yield in identifying the nonreligious Word.

RESPONSIVE ACTION OR ETHICS

This book does not address the question of ethics. Ethics is an important subject, especially for lawyers, but it can only be taken up after the kind of description that I am attempting here. However, some provisional comment on ethics may serve to distinguish my subject and help clarify its content and limits.

I must begin by noting a radical variance between my understanding of ethics and that of the State Bar of Georgia, to which I belong. In order to remain an active member of the bar, I am required to take twelve hours of continuing legal education every year. One (formerly two) of those hours must be in ethics. What is taught under the rubric of ethics seems to me a gross distortion. At my first session years ago, the lecturer began by stating that his assignment was to teach us "how to keep the money you earn in your own pocket"—that is, how to avoid being successfully sued for malpractice. Every session since has been devoted to the same subject, malpractice avoidance. I do not recall the word *ethics* being used during that first session or during any other since.

When I use the word *ethics*, I do not adopt the bar's definition. I do not mean hints about staying out of trouble with the bar and clients: "How can I avoid malpractice?" Like Thomas Shaffer, when I use the word *ethics* I mean ethics, reflection on the question "what am I to do?"[1] For me, this is a question about response to the Word.

The wholly other Word is human and therefore specific. It addresses us in its and our particularity. The particularity is important. "Love your flesh" is never a universally valid injunction or principle. Not in every circumstance is it the command of God and would not have been if uttered in white churches to comfortable slaveholders. (Although if whites had truly loved their flesh, they might not have so despised that of others; so even there it might have been appropriate.) It is such a command in the Clearing in *Beloved* because of the immediate circumstance. It is the particular address of the Word among those whose flesh had been hated and abused.

The response of people to the Word, the response engendered by the Word, is no less particular. Accordingly, it is tentative, episodic, and heavily dependent on the factual context, and is not to be confused with conventional charity, whether religiously motivated or not. We may well not know whether our course of action is good, for the actor cannot preempt God's judgment.

Then, too, as William Stringfellow pointed out, there is "the further peril of tyrannizing the one of whom it is said that he is being helped."[2] The danger is that the reason for doing good to another may be the justification of the doer, so that the issue is not the other's welfare but the doer's own. And the criterion becomes not the good of the other, but "how far the one who is being helped becomes like the one who is helping him."[3]

The nature of response to the presence of the Word is contained in a story Stringfellow tells of one of his early East Harlem clients, whom he calls Ramon.[4] Ramon was wanted by the police for questioning about a crime. He was shrewd enough to move from his parents' tenement to the apartment of relatives in another police precinct. He had not been apprehended. He came to Stringfellow: "You're a lawyer—tell me what to do. The police are looking for me and I want to go into the Marines and I want to know what will happen if I turn myself in to the police."[5]

A seminarian doing fieldwork in the area with the gang to which Ramon belonged heard some street talk about the request for advice and proposed that Stringfellow should counsel Ramon so "that there would be precipitated, out of his anxiety about whether to give himself up, a personal crisis, a repentance for what he had done, and, hopefully, a traumatic conversion."[6] Stringfellow thought the proposal manipulative and morbid but nonetheless found in it a serious issue: a concern for the evangelization of all, including Ramon. (Careful note should be taken of Stringfellow's understanding of evangelism: "Evangelism is not essentially verbal, even though it seems commonly to be believed that the recitation of certain words constitutes efficacious evangelism. Evangelism consists of loving another human being in a way which represents to him the care of God for his particular life."[7] Evangelism takes the form of genuine friendship.)

In addition to the seminarian, a minister from the neighborhood also came to talk about Ramon, whom the minister regarded as a menace. "'For the good of society, for the good of the neighborhood,' the minister proposed, 'we should get him to turn himself in.'"[8] Stringfellow thought this approach was too little concerned with protecting the innocent until they are proved guilty, but again credited it with raising a significant concern: "the welfare and order of society as a whole."[9]

Stringfellow's own advice to Ramon was to join the Marines. Between the Marines and East Harlem, there was not much choice. The Marines might at least teach him something useful for later employment, and there was no legal impediment to his joining. He had not been indicted for, charged with, or convicted of a crime. The three approaches to Ramon's situation, Stringfellow points out, highlight "the fact that there is never an abstract, single 'Christian answer' to an issue to which all Christians are bound to adhere or conform."[10] The positions of both the seminarian and the minister were creditable. So was Stringfellow's. His advice arose from the fact that the Word is directed caringly to people "in a radically individual sense." In response, Stringfellow was "free to advocate the cause of one, as in this case of Ramon, as over against everyone and everything else in the world."[11] The Word so divests people "of their own individual self-interest," Stringfellow concludes, "that they may intercede—stand in the place of, represent, advocate—the cause of another, any other at all."[12]

Like the Word, those addressed and constituted by it are concerned with people. They are, as Barth says, humanists. They are not interested in any cause save the cause of humans. Nor are they slaves of their own decisions or of sacrosanct consistency, for "the people about whom they are concerned cannot be helped . . . by principles that are enunciated and venerated as divine, that these are rather the works and products of human perversion which can only increase the evil which suppresses and oppresses people."[13] Principles warrant "only a relative Yes or No" and are always to be resisted when they claim to be irrefutable.[14] One serves the neighbor rather than a cause or principle, howsoever lofty.

This is the difference that the distinction between religion and the Word makes for responsive action. Religion is finally centered on the self. The Word directs to the other. "God," Dietrich Bonhoeffer observed, "is beyond in the midst of our life."[15] It follows that our relation to him is "not a 'religious' relationship to the highest, most powerful, and best Being imaginable—that is not authentic transcendence—but our relation to God is a new life in 'existence for others,' through participation in the being of Jesus. The transcendental is not infinite and unattainable tasks, but the neighbour who is within reach in any given situation."[16]

For Dilsey, the transcendent is Luster and Frony, whom she nurtures; Benjamin, whom she consoles; Quentin, whom she protects; and Jason, whom she rebukes. For Baby Suggs, the transcendent is her black-skinned neighbors. For William Stringfellow, the transcendent is Ramon.

These are examples. In my citation of them there is a possibility for misunderstanding, because each is focused on care for individuals. The response—the form assumed by the Word in our action—is always specific in this way, but must always also contend with systems. It is not institutionally and politically sentimental. Those freed for others may repeatedly look like suckers because they are incautious and imprudent about preserving their lives, but they are not romantically naive about the opposition. Stringfellow kept pointing out that institutions, or what the biblical stories refer to as "principalities and powers," are as fallen and in need of redemption as are individuals, that they in fact are the aggressive embodiment of death.[17] Dietrich Bonhoeffer's life—and his death at the hands of the Nazis—bore witness that responsible service to the neighbor requires taking account of the institutions that shape thought and life. Or, as Martha Minow puts it in a tribute to her grandmother, who taught her the lesson: "People can make a difference for one another by remaking the institutions that surround them."[18]

Although they concern individual action on behalf of individual neighbors, the examples I have given should not be construed as exempting concern for systems and institutions. Outwardly they are a remonstrance against systems, and inwardly they are examples of community rather than individualism. Dilsey and Baby Suggs, like Bonhoeffer and Stringfellow, are members of communities, and their community membership is fundamental, essential, decisive. The central biblical image of responsibility and humanity is the formation of a community—a people or kingdom. Like other important images in the biblical stories—the coming of a messiah, for example—it is political. God is seen to be doing politics.[19] The discernible outcome of this political activity is a redeeming community.

It needs only to be added that this community is repeatedly formed among the poor. Dilsey, Baby Suggs, and Sethe are types of its members. In the biblical stories, Barth points out, "almost to the point of prejudice—[God] ignored all those who are high and mighty and wealthy in the world in favour of the weak and meek and lowly."[20]

A book on ethics would be composed of an elaboration of the stories and examples I have offered and many others like them that are types of specific, episodic service of the neighbor, including service of the neighbor by remaking dehumanizing institutions. These would be stories and examples of the Word taking form—action that is the responsibility and choice of humans, but action that is responsive to and engendered by the Word. Paul Lehmann observes that "the *environment* of decision, not the *rules* of decision, gives to behavior its ethical significance."[21] In this book, I am attempting a description of the environment of decision in a given field of activity: the Word active and present in the practice of law. I view it as the kind of description that is necessary to ethics and precedes it.

FAITH AND RELIGION

Norman McLean opened his novel *A River Runs through It* with the observation: "In our family, there was no clear line between religion and fly fishing."[22] And Sanford Levinson writes about constitutional law as though it is constitutional faith.[23] Because it is part of life, religion is bound to have importance as a subject and as an experienced phenomenon, and therefore as a theological concern. As I have tried carefully to say, religion may be adopted by the Word. For that reason religion does bear on faith.

I follow Barth's views on the question. He pointed out that faith rather than religion corresponds to God's self-revelation,[24] and he insisted that faith is the work of the Word. The Word "reveals and discloses itself. It gives itself to be known. It creates the possibility of a seeing and hearing and understanding of it. Or rather, it creates eyes to see it and ears to hear it and a mind to understand it."[25]

The Word generates faith rather than religion. However, faith is not necessarily inseparable from religion. "Faith," Barth said, "is neither religion nor irreligion, neither sacred nor profane; it is always both together."[26] Religion is not to be discarded. For one thing, it cannot be discarded, but "must be borne as a yoke which cannot be removed."[27] For another, antireligious negation has no advantage over religious affirmation; to destroy temples "is not better than to build them."[28]

Religion is the attempt to know God. God's self-revelation does not correspond to religion but contradicts it. Nevertheless, revelation can and does adopt religion. This is so not because religion is privileged or especially apt to revelation, but because religion belongs to the human condition. "Nothing in true human nature can ever be alien or irrelevant."[29] In embracing humanity, the Word embraces religion.

CHRISTIAN RELIGION

Our faith is our faith, but as it is the faithfulness of God, it cannot be restricted by formulas or definitions or anything applied from without, as though in some way, unauthorized by the Word, faith were declared to belong exclusively to those who count themselves Christians. Or as though the present, active power of the Word should be restricted to performance in history only through faith, and then only through Christian faith. There is no biblical warrant for such restrictions and abundant biblical basis for repudiating them. It would be wrong, as Hans Küng says, to "go about dogmatically with that Protestant claim to truth" by which world religions are dogmatically condemned or simply ignored.[30]

What then is to be said about Christian religion—as in John Calvin's *Institutes of the Christian Religion*—the faith generated by the Word that is entwined with Christian religion? Again, I follow Barth.

After noting that revelation intersects the Church, Barth adds that this "does not mean that the Christian religion is the true religion, fundamentally superior to all other religions. . . . We cannot differentiate and separate the Church from other religions on the basis of a general concept of the nature of religion."[31] Christian religion can only apply first to itself the judgment that religion is unbelief.[32] It cannot claim superiority over other religions; it can only claim solidarity with them. To the extent that it is a religion, and in comparison with others, Christian religion "is in a position of greater danger and defencelessness and impotence than any other."[33]

Nor should the Christian religion ever expect to be in the majority. It is critical and singular exactly as a minority that exists for the sake of the majority. Membership in it is certainly not to be disparaged, but neither is it to be envied: "After all, the active life has other less burdensome and in their own way no less worthy forms. We can be genuinely in the hands and under the protection of God, and we can truly participate in human freedom, in other forms than that of real Christianity."[34] Moreover, true Christians can only "remember that the first might also be last, so that at the very best [they] can only believe that [they] believe."[35]

Any conjunction of the Word with the Christian religion is an activity of the Word that affirms humanity and not Christian superiority.

MODES OF THINKING THEOLOGICALLY

Several years ago, following a public lecture, Paul Lehmann was asked if he opposed abortion. He gave a long, complex answer. When he was done, the questioner, in exasperation, demanded: "Dr. Lehmann, are you opposed to abortion, yes or no?" His answer was: "Yes . . . and no. In that order." There is similar tension and maybe ambiguity, too, in my comments on religion. I both critique religion and affirm its value. I refer to the Word as both judging and adopting religion. This is my version of a form of theological analysis undertaken by Barth. As his *Church Dogmatics* unfolds, Barth characteristically brings to first one subject and then another the careful dialectics of a penultimate No and an ultimate Yes. In doing so, he allows the form of his thought to follow his substantive emphasis on the centrality of the revealed Word.

Barth believed that "what we find in the case of the man Jesus is a valid model for the general relationship of man to the will of God."[36] This was not for him a distant abstraction, but a source for his forms of understanding, among other things. Theology, as Barth did it, was not only thinking about Jesus Christ but also thinking drawn from and reflective of Jesus Christ. This is what is meant when his theology is described as thoroughly Christocentric.

The dialectic of a penultimate No and an ultimate Yes—adopted as an analytical approach—is one of the ways in which Barth translated the relationship of God and man in Jesus into a form of thinking. It constitutes an attempt to reflect that relationship in a method of analysis. It is an attempt to repeat the Word in other words.

The same is true as well of the recurring, specific patterns followed by Barth in carrying his dialectics forward. For example, George Hunsinger points to one pattern or thought form of Barth's—affirmation, negation, and reconstitution—that is reflective of the incarnation, crucifixion, and resurrection. As Hunsinger notes about Barth's exposition of the doctrine of salvation, "human beings (and all else with them) are . . . affirmed, negated, and reconstituted on a higher plane in Christ."[37] And, in Barth's account of the natural, "nature has no autonomous or independent freedom alongside or over against the freedom of grace. Instead . . . nature is affirmed, negated, and then reconstituted on a higher plane."[38] This Barthian pattern is distinguishable from the Hegelian pattern of thesis-antithesis-synthesis because it yields no synthesis. Instead, the human and the natural are presented as reconstituted (resurrected) in a free relatedness to God.[39]

This relatedness may be identified by reference to another Christocentric pattern of thought adopted by Barth and described by Hunsinger as "the Chalcedonian pattern."[40] The Council of Chalcedon, held in 451, laid down the basic orthodox groundwork for affirming that Jesus is both divine and human. According to the Chalcedonian formula, the relation of the two natures of Christ is one of "unity ('without separation or division'), differentiation ('without confusion or change'), and asymmetry (the unqualified conceptual precedence of the divine over the human nature . . .)."[41] The relation is said to be asymmetrical—in contrast to hierarchical—because it embodies "a mutual ordering in freedom" rather than a domination of the human by the divine.[42] In the Barthian pattern corresponding to the Chalcedonian formula, the human and the natural are understood to be reconstituted and restored, not synthesized, by the divine.[43]

The affirmation-negation-reconstitution pattern and the Chalcedonian pattern inform my critique-affirmation of religion. The Word affirms, negates, and reconstitutes the religion of Dilsey and Baby Suggs (incarnation-crucifixion-resurrection). Their religion is adopted, not swallowed up, by the Word (their religion is related to the Word as the human is related to the divine in the Chalcedonian formula).

No matter what the pattern of analysis and exposition, Barth always insisted that theology must reflect the central Christological priority: In the relationship between God and us, God is radically precedent. This insistence placed Barth at odds with adherents of both Roman Catholicism and liberal Protestantism.[44]

On the Roman Catholic side, in Thomas Aquinas's theology, arguably, the divine and the human are interdependent. For example, the soul is open to grace; or divine grace perfects human freedom, and human freedom cooperates with and supplements divine grace.[45] Barth believed it profoundly wrong to think that personal encounter with God is somehow a given of human nature, as though grace actuates an inherent human possibility. This approach is wrong because it attempts to save some room at the center for the self, which eventually usurps priority. As Hunsinger summarizes: "Rather than understanding ourselves from him, we would come to understand him from ourselves."[46] The order is irreversible: God and us. God is love; not love is God.

This asymmetrical priority also distinguishes Barth from a Protestant like Reinhold Niebuhr. Niebuhr believed love to be an ideal. In the real, sinful world, humans strive for love but never fully attain it. Love is thus an impossible possibility.[47] Barth held such an approach to be a reversal of priority. It renders reality anthropocentric. To Barth, reality is theocentric. God, not humans, determines what is real and sets its terms.[48] God's love in Christ establishes the real; sin is the impossible possibility.[49] Hunsinger notes that "Barth and Niebuhr both used the term 'impossible possibility,' but in diametrically opposite ways."[50] Love is Barth's reality and Niebuhr's ideal; sin is Niebuhr's reality and Barth's unreality.

Barth's distinguishing insistence on the priority of God can be misread or taken in the wrong direction. It does not entail rejection of persons, culture, or human agency. Quite the opposite is true. God has priority, but the world has its place. Indeed, God creates and ensures that place.[51] If Barth were a misanthropist or theomonist or revelation positivist, he would corruptly betray the relation between God and man in Jesus, the self-revelation of God's humanity.

A coincidence and distinction of human and divine agency—an "I, yet not I"—follows upon the relation of God to humanity in the person of Jesus.[52] This coincidence, like the relation of the divine and the human in Jesus which is its ground, cannot be explained. That God, the prior, omnipotent, and wholly other, engenders a relationship with humans in which he is mightily sovereign, and yet humans find themselves liberated and their integrity established, is the mystery of His self-revelation.[53] Barth was not befuddled, burdened, or stupefied by this mystery. He could not explain the mystery, but he could describe it. And then continually redescribe it all over again from the beginning, because no description could finally contain it. That is why he wrote and why he was always in the process of reevaluation.

The description of the Word that follows in the next chapter emphasizes its priority and otherness. This emphasis should be read together with the focus on responsible human actors in secular law that has gone before and will come after—the focus on Henry, John, Margaret, David, Tim, Steve, and Carla (also Dilsey and Baby Suggs). Enactment of appreciation for them and of respect for their integrity is a performance of the fact that the wholly other Word is intimately, supportively present to women and men to whom it draws us.

If this were a piece of music instead of a book, different voices could express multiple, even contradictory, views simultaneously. As it is, I must take up matters *seriatim*. The linear is not easily accommodated to a No borne by a concurrent, greater Yes. A sense of this constraint in writing books may partially explain why Barth daily turned with such relish to Mozart's music, with its "wise confrontation and mix of the elements," in which Barth found that

> the sun shines, but it does not blind, consume or burn. Heaven arches over the earth, but it does not weigh down upon it, it does not crush or swallow it up. And so the earth is and remains the earth, but without having to assert itself in a titanic revolt against heaven. Thus darkness, chaos, death, and hell show themselves, but not for a moment are they allowed to prevail. Mozart plays his music, aware of everything, from within a mysterious center; and so he knows and defends the boundaries right and left, up and down. He maintains proportions. . . . There is no light here that

does not also know the darkness, no joy that does not also contain suffering, but conversely too, no terror, no rage, no lament that does not have peace standing by, whether close up or far off. Thus there is no laughter without tears, but also no tears without laughter.[54]

FOUR

⌒⌒⌒

Mark, Isaiah, and the Empty Place

I HAVE BEEN EMPLOYING *Word* as though the meaning were self-evident. Of course it is not. This chapter is intended to give the usage some locating content.

Law is not constituted by abstractions but by texts like the Constitution and by people like those presented in chapter 1. The same is true of theology. It begins and ends with particulars. That is why I turned to people like Dilsey, Baby Suggs, William Stringfellow, Dietrich Bonhoeffer, and Karl Barth. And that is why I now give expression to *Word* with particular texts.

The central text is Mark 4:10–12. I have been engaged by it for a long time and have grown confident enough to realize that what I know now is tentative, incomplete, and likely to undergo significant change. In the course of describing his beliefs to a group of us, a medicine man of the Navajo, two weeks before his ninety-fifth birthday, said that long life was good. And then he said that, if you lived long enough, you could begin to understand the prayers. Given another forty years, I may begin to understand Mark and the other texts. This chapter is no more than an interim field report. Its function is not to give conclusive statements about the texts considered but to indicate what is meant by *Word* when I say that the Word may be discerned in the practices of Henry Schwarzschild, John Rosenberg, Margaret Taylor, David Harding, Tim Coulter, Steve Wizner, and Carla Ingersoll.

MARK 4:10–12

And when he was alone, those who were about him with the twelve asked concerning the parables. And he said to them, "To you has been given the secret of the kingdom of God, but for the others everything is in parables; in order that they may indeed see but not perceive, and may indeed hear but not understand; lest they should turn again, and be discharged."

In the text, Jesus had been telling parables, and his followers had asked for their meaning. Jesus' response is the statement quoted.

Frank Kermode brings contemporary, secular literary criticism to bear upon Mark 4:10–12 in his book *The Genesis of Secrecy* (1979). He compares Jesus' statement to one made by the doorkeeper in the well-known parable from Kafka's *The Trial.* In Kafka's story, a man comes and begs admittance to the Law. He assumes the Law to be open to all, but is kept out by the doorkeeper, who makes him wait outside on a stool, year after year. At last, near death, he sees a radiance within. Shut out, wondering why he alone has come to this entrance, he is told by the doorkeeper: "This door was intended only for you. Now I am going to shut it."[1]

Kermode finds Jesus' statement equally perverse—telling parables so that the hearer will be sure to miss the point. Mark writes that everything is in parables *in order that—hina* in the Greek—the hearer may not understand and not be forgiven. That does seem repellent.

In Matthew the statement appears far more tolerable. The author of Matthew employed the Gospel of Mark as a principal source. However, Matthew renders Jesus' response with a small but crucial difference: "I speak to them in parables *because* they see without perceiving" (Matthew 13:13). "In order that" *(hina)* is changed to "because" *(hoti).* In this version, the parables are more Jesus' accommodation of the hearers' weakness than his exclusion of them.[2]

Kermode makes much of the change from *hina* to *hoti.* He draws from it a general proposition about the nature of narrative: "The desire to change *hina* to *hoti* is a measure of the dismay we feel at our arbitrary and total exclusion from the kingdom, or from the secret sense of the story. . . . Mark is a strong witness to the enigmatic and exclusive character of narrative, to its property of banishing interpreters from its secret places."[3]

Narrative is opaque, he says. It requires and frustrates interpretation; it makes interpretation necessary and virtually impossible. He concludes: "Hot for secrets, our only conversation may be with guardians who know less and see less than we can; and our sole hope and pleasure is in the perception of a momentary radiance, before the door of disappointment is finally shut on us."[4]

Kermode is right to maintain that story can always be reinterpreted and that history can always be revised, but I think he is wrong to find the Markan passage peculiar testimony to the notion. Jesus' saying *is* deeply disturbing. The question is whether that makes it a "witness to the enigmatic and exclusive character of narrative." I think it is a witness to the power of the Word. I shall take the long way around to saying why. My primary purpose is not to disagree with Kermode but to give content to *Word,* and for that the short way is less fruitful. The starting place is another text. When Jesus explained that he told parables "in order that they may indeed see but not perceive," he was alluding to Isaiah 6:9–10.

ISAIAH 6:9–10 (1–13)

And he said, "Go and say to this people:
'Hear and hear, but do not understand;
see and see, but do not perceive.'
Make the heart of this people fat,
and their ears heavy,
and shut their eyes;
lest they see with their eyes,
and hear with their ears,
and understand with their hearts,
and turn and be healed."

Here God commissions Isaiah. He speaks, and gives Isaiah to speak, words that will do what they say. When spoken, the words will prevent understanding and forestall the possibility of redemption. It is another difficult text. Such texts invite tempering. This one is no exception, as a second look at Matthew discloses.

According to Matthew, when Jesus was asked by his disciples why he spoke in parables and he responded that he did so "because seeing they do not see, and hearing they do not hear, nor do they understand," he then added: "With them indeed is fulfilled the prophecy of Isaiah which says:

You shall indeed hear but never understand,
and you shall indeed see but never perceive.
For this people's heart has grown dull,
and their ears are heavy of hearing,
and their eyes have closed,
lest they should perceive with their eyes,
and hear with their ears,
and understand with their heart,
and turn for me to heal them." (Matthew 13:13–15)

Kermode says these lines "retain a trace of their original [Isaianic] tone of slightly disgusted irony at the failure of the people to perceive and understand. The sense is now something like: As Isaiah remarked, their stupidity is extremely tiresome; [telling parables] seems the best way to get through to them."[5]

There is a discrepancy, however, between the words of Isaiah as I have reproduced them at the beginning of this section and as they appear in Matthew. In Isaiah, God says: "Make the heart of this people fat." In the quotation of Isaiah in Matthew, God says: "For this people's heart has grown dull."

In Matthew's version, responsibility for the failure of understanding and its results has been shifted from the action of God and prophet to the dullness of the people, from speaker to hearer. The bite of the text is replaced by "slightly disgusted irony." The difference between the two versions of Isaiah is about the same as that between *hina* and *hoti*, and may be traced to the point at which Isaiah was translated from Hebrew to Greek in what is called the Septuagint.[6] Matthew's quotation of Isaiah appears to be taken from the Septuagint version.[7]

The critical line as it appears in the Septuagint and then in Matthew reads in the Greek: *Epachunthe gar he kardia tou laou toutou* ("for this people's heart has grown dull"). *Epacunthe* (has grown dull or fat) is a passive form of the verb *pachuno* (to thicken or fatten). But the Hebrew word being translated was *hashmen* (*make* dull or fat). It is a form of imperative (causative active). The Hebrew text employed by the translator was unpointed—that is, it was composed of consonants without vowels. The points (or signs) that indicate vowels were added much later. The vowels are determinative of the intended form of the word. Showing only consonants in the text to be translated, the critical verb could have been read as passive if it stood alone. The translator chose the passive when he rendered it in Greek in the Septuagint ("for this people's heart *has grown* dull").

But the verb did not stand alone. It had a context. Absent vowels, context provides the information about the form of a word. The context here should have directed the translator away from the passive. The immediately preceding verbs in the text are all clearly imperatives ("Go and say to this people: 'Hear and hear, but do not understand; see and see, but do not perceive'"). The translator should have seen the next verb as belonging to the series and therefore to the imperative rather than the passive ("Make the heart of this people dull" rather than "for this people's heart has grown dull").

The Isaianic text in the Hebrew trails no slightly disgusted irony. Instead and dismayingly, the prophet is given a terrible word to utter. We are confronted here by the *dabar* (pronounced "davar," translated "word") spoken by God. What is said is done. ("God said, 'Let there be light'; and there was light." Gen. 1:3) Thus:

as the rain and the snow come down from heaven,
>   and return not thither but water the earth,
making it bring forth and sprout
>   giving seed to the sower and bread to the eater,
so shall my *dabar* be that goes forth from my mouth;
>   it shall not return to me empty,
but it shall accomplish that which I purpose,
>   and prosper in the thing for which I sent it. (Isaiah 55:10–11)

When Isaiah is directed to say "Hear and hear but do not understand; see and see but do not perceive," he is given *dabar* to utter.[8] He unleashes words that will do what they say. The words will make the heart of the people dull and their ears heavy, and will shut their eyes. The people will not understand and will not perceive and will therefore not turn and be healed—because of those operative words. This will take place on God's motion and not that of the people. Understandably Isaiah asks: "How long, O Lord?" only to be told: "Until cities lie waste without inhabitant, and houses without men, and the land is utterly desolate" (6:11).

Incorporated in Isaiah's prophetic charter was a shutting down of the possibilities for understanding and transformation that might produce repentance and so avert punishment. This potency of the prophetic word—certain doom in the instance of Isaiah 6—is not an isolated anomaly. It is a central theme of Isaiah and is characteristic as well of other classic eighth-century prophecy.[9] (The Isaiah referred to here is the Isaiah of chapters 1–39, designated by biblical scholars as the "first Isaiah" and dated roughly in the fifty-year period from 742 to 690 B.C.E.. The other classic eighth-century prophets are Amos, Micah, and Hosea.)

PROPHECY AND LAW

The eighth-century prophets employed various rhetorical forms. One of the more frequent and typical was the divine lawsuit, often associated with the term *rib* (pronounced "reev," translated "controversy"). The text in Isaiah is set in this rhetoric of law.

The Lawsuit

The notion of God's lawsuit[10] may be summarized, according to the account I find persuasive, in the following terms: God rules over a heavenly assembly *(sodh)* composed of the old gods (Heaven and Earth,

Mountains, Rivers, etc.). The assembly convenes as a court of law wherein God as judge and prosecutor summons, indicts, and sentences various nations, but especially his own people, who have broken their covenant with him through idolatry and injustice.[11] In the legal-rhetorical tradition of the lawsuit, the prophet is designated to be the messenger of the assembly/court. He is admitted to the assembly at some point in the lawsuit process to hear or see what God speaks, and is then commissioned to deliver to the people the words spoken by God.[12]

Isaiah 6:1–13 fits within this lawsuit tradition.[13] According to 3:13, "the Lord has taken his place to contend *[nissab larib]*, he stands to judge his people." The lawsuit proceeds much as it does in other prophetic accounts. An initial statement of God's love in electing Israel is followed by a charge of rebellion (1:2ff.) and religiosity (1:10ff.). The poor are robbed of justice (10:1ff.). Destruction of Israel has been decreed (10:5, 23; 2:12ff; 13:9ff.).

The cosmic setting of Isaiah's vision is laid out in 6:1–13. God is high and lifted up, surrounded by seraphim. (The temple reproduces the scene of the heavenly assembly.) Isaiah, cleansed for the office by the symbolic cauterization of his lips, is sent as messenger from the court to report its action. The text ("Hear and hear but do not understand. . .") is the word he is commissioned to deliver. The people have broken their covenant. God has brought a lawsuit against them. A verdict has been handed down. The land is to be made desolate. The judgment will be carried out. The people's heart is to be hardened. There will be no option of repentance. This pronouncement, the biblical scholar Gerhard von Rad observed, "sounds as if it shut the door on everyone, and it was intended to be understood this way."[14]

I am brought back again to my observation that this is a difficult text.

Possible Qualifications

In what I have said so far about Isaiah, there are two latent ambiguities that may seriously qualify the tenability of my reading of the text and open the way to easier, more moderate approaches.

Hope. The text is a proclamation of doom and is not in context hortatory. It is an announcement, not an exhortation to the end of transformation; a hardening, not a changing of hearts.[15] However, both in Isaiah and in the other classic prophets, there are texts of promise that are difficult to interpret except as expressions aimed at repentance, at changing hearts, at keeping hope alive, at placing effective choice in human hands.

These texts may have been later additions (e.g., Amos 9:11: "In that day I will raise up the booth of David that is fallen"). In other instances, they are likely original. The latter fall into two groups. One is illustrated by Amos 5:15:

> Hate evil, and love good,
>> and establish justice in the gate;
> It may be that the Lord, the God of Hosts,
>> will be gracious to the remnant of Joseph.

In such cases the faint hope is arguably an editorial or personal addition to the commissioned message (the prophet speculates: "It may be. . ."). Other expressions of hope, however, belong to the *dabar* and are neither later additions nor personal sentiments (e.g., Amos 5:4: "Thus says the Lord to the House of Israel: 'Seek me and live'"). In this event, God issues active words of unalterable doom in one circumstance and of saving repentance in another.[16]

The dominant texts in classic prophecy—the dominant burden—seem to me the announcement of punishment as destruction that will surely take place. But there are as well, undeniably, descriptions of an impossible, miraculous salvation. What is true in both is that the unavoidable doom and the inexplicable redemption are the work of the free *dabar* of God. It is not in human hands one way or the other.

The particular verses from Isaiah 6 are a prophecy of unqualified, unqualifiable doom. The outcome is guaranteed by the word's hardening of hearts. The inescapable foreclosure of understanding and its consequence of destruction is the work of God's word, as would be so also were salvation the end.

Law and prophets. The second ambiguity that may undercut my reading has to do with the possible conflict between law and doom-saying prophecy. According to Isaiah, God will punish Israel. The message takes the rhetorical form of a lawsuit. The people have been tried and found guilty of idolatry and injustice. A sentence has been handed down and will be executed. Violent punishment—including the foreclosure of understanding and repentance—is forthcoming. But if this is so, how explain the form, the *rib* rhetoric?

The form and familiarity of lawsuit rhetoric may have arisen from secular courts, cultic ceremonies, international law, or a general concern with law characteristic of the time.[17] Whatever its matrix, however, lawsuit rhetoric is drawn from a universe of legal discourse. Prophetic employment of the *rib* depends to that extent on the rhetoric of law and its associations.

Law, however, appears to compose a very different universe of discourse than that of doom-saying prophecy like Isaiah 6. Is law not preservative rather than destructive of a future? Is it not exactly intended for human action? Is it not addressed animatingly to the heart? Is it not a bridge from this world to another, better one, as Robert Cover argued persuasively?[18]

The prophets could scarcely employ lawsuit rhetoric shorn of the promissory quality of law that invites meaningful human response. The language of law evokes human possibility and aspiration materially at odds with performative utterances that harden hearts and guarantee doom. Could prophecy have been delivered in a hope-invoking, human-empowering form that ran counter to its doom-announcing, predestinating substance?

I do not think so, for the reason that the legal discourse available to the prophets was not exclusively characterized by sanguine expectancy and conditional human choice for the future. Law did not always evoke hope and empower choice. To the extent it did not, prophetic substance and legal rhetoric were not in conflict. Consider the Deuteronomic history, and particularly the story of Josiah in 2 Kings 22–23.

2 KINGS 22–23

Josiah, at the age of eight, ascended the throne of Judah, the southern kingdom. (The land, earlier united under David, had been divided.) His rule continued from 640 to 609, overlapping the early years of the prophecy of Jeremiah. In 621, while Josiah was still in his early twenties, the Book of the Law was discovered during restoration of the temple. Upon hearing the book read, the king rent his clothes and set about reforming the nation "that he might establish the words of the law which were written in the book" (2 Kings 23:24).

The discovered book was some portion of Deuteronomy.[19] Although its discovery took place after the period of classic prophecy had ended and it is not the only code of law extant in the Bible,[20] the Deuteronomic collection of legal material is representative, embodies sources that antedate its discovery, and is likely reflective of law and attitudes about law that would have been typical of the world of Isaiah.[21] In brief, I think it justifiable to rely on Deuteronomy in exploring the compatibility of legal rhetoric and prophetic discourse.

At first glance Deuteronomy appears to contrast radically with classic prophecy and to support the sense of law as a bridge to a better, future world. Deuteronomy is utopian, hortatory, programmatic. The choice of blessing and curse, life and death is set before the people, and they are urged to choose life (11:26; 24:17; 28). The law is accessible and can be done by the faithful, who are exhorted to wholehearted obedience.[22] Here, it has been observed, "much that the prophets announced as Yahweh's work becomes the task of man."[23] Law is a bridging gift, the covenant partner's enabling means of expression.[24] Grounded in the past, it posits a future.[25] Whether law holds off or brings in the Messiah, it makes room for human initiative and seems thereby to be disqualified as a rhetorical resource for prophecy commissioned to exclude human action and future possibility.

For my reading of Isaiah to stand, it must be supported by establishing a compatibility between prophetic substance and legal-rhetorical form not immediately apparent from the surface of Deuteronomy.[26] A closer look reveals, I believe, that law could be more foreclosing and less bridging than might be supposed. Prophetic substance can then be reconciled with juridical form insofar as pre-exilic law is preclusive. This side of law is turned up by the story of Josiah and the discovery of the Book of the Law.

Second Kings is part of the Deuteronomic corpus that includes the several books from Deuteronomy through 2 Kings.[27] This larger Deuteronomistic work presents a theological history of Israel from the conquest of Canaan to the fall of the state. It is composed of edited, revised writings selected from diverse sources, some very early. The compiler or school of compilers had before them some form of Deuteronomy to which chapters 1–4 were appended as an introduction to the story of Israel in Palestine. The history as a whole was completed during the exile and may be described as an attempt to understand the calamity that had befallen this people.[28]

The original core material comes from the covenant tradition of the northern kingdom[29] (and is framed in the conditional "if . . . then . . ." style). The collection was removed to the south when the northern kingdom fell. The Deuteronomist editors belong to the southern kingdom's royal theological tradition and its unconditional expectation of a successor to David who would be the messiah. Their first edition may have been produced during Josiah's day and may have portrayed Israel's past as leading up to his illustrious reign. This positive fulfillment of history was disappointingly disrupted by his death. The final edition might then have revised and closed the account after the fall of Jerusalem in 587.[30]

The story of Josiah is a critical episode in the larger history. He was a young reformer. With appropriate piety he both rent his clothes upon hearing the Book of the Law and sent for advice from the seeress Huldah.[31] After reading the law to the people, he led them in renewal of the covenant and set about giving effect to its injunctions by destroying alien worship, centralizing religious practice in Jerusalem, and keeping the Passover.

All of this faithfully obedient, sweeping, and effective reform, however, did not forestall punishment for the faithlessness of the prior generation and the offenses of Manasseh. "Still the Lord did not turn from the fierceness of his great wrath, by which his anger was kindled against Judah, because of the provocations with which Manasseh had provoked him" (23:26). In the story of Josiah, the *dabar* of the Book of the Law performs like the *dabar* pronounced by the classic prophets. (*Dabar* in reference to the Book of the Law occurs eight times directly and once indirectly in 2 Kings 22–23.)

The word of law performs like the prophetic word also in the larger story told by the Deuteronomist. (*Dabar* is featured right from the start: The title of Deuteronomy in the Hebrew Bible, "These Are the Words," is taken from the book's first line: "These are the words that Moses addressed to all Israel on the other side of the Jordan.")[32] Israel's history in Palestine is set out in the series of books from Joshua through 2 Kings. The whole is prefaced with Deuteronomy. The Book of the Law is offered as the introductory guide to understanding the story that unfolds in the succeeding installments. The Deuteronomist structured his materials so that the exile could be comprehended in the light of the law. The reader is invited to begin with the law and to discern its word at work in Israel's history.

The discovery of the Book of the Law in Josiah's reign is the Deuteronomist's discovery of an explanation for what happened to Israel.[33] Confronted by the recovered book, Josiah sent to Huldah. She reported: "Thus says the Lord, 'Behold, I will bring evil upon this place and upon its inhabitants, all the words of the book which the king has read'" (22:16). This utterance becomes a statement—the central *dabar*—of the Deuteronomistic history.[34] The word of the law unleashed here performs like the active word proclaimed in Isaiah 6. As much so as prophetic words, the words of the Book of the Law are potent, prevenient, predetermining.

Several observations are in order.

Blameworthiness and Community

The violence visited upon Israel by God had been preceded by the violence done by Israel to the covenant. The default of idolatry was an offense to God, and the default of injustice was an offense to the poor and the faithful as well as to God.[35]

For modern readers the difficult question is less whether punishment was legitimate than whether punishment of later, nonoffending generations was warranted. If hearts were hardened by the prophetic word commissioned by God, so that repentance became impossible, who was the active, responsible party? If reform and renewal took hold under the impact of the Book of the Law on Josiah, why punish the repentant for their predecessors' sins?

An argument can be made that the people of Israel were an intergenerational community and that dividing it temporally would be false or artificial. Israel was a single community across time. This fact does not alleviate the alienating effect on the modern reader's sense of fairness, however. Familiarly enough, the law offers curse as well as blessing: "the curse, if you do not obey the commandments" (Deuteronomy 11:26). But what of the second commandment's gloss that God is a "jealous God, visiting the iniquity of the fathers upon the children" (5:8)? Why do the sins of Manasseh and his generation outweigh the reform of Josiah and his generation? How measure the comparative weights of sin and obedience? Why would the faithfulness of one generation count for less than the faithlessness of an earlier generation?

Correspondence, Not Fate

The doom that fell upon Israel in fulfillment of the curse is not an inexorable turning of a wheel of fate. It is not unalterable once set in motion. There is correspondence between wrong and punishment, a certain symmetry, even if it does not square with modern readers' notions of justice. Nevertheless, this correspondence is not to be understood as the product of implacable necessity.[36] It arises from the will and action of God. God could decide against punishment. He could change his mind. Indeed, the prophetic word foreclosing the people's repentance may remove a critical stimulus to God's repentance of the punishment.[37]

The Practicability and Reward of Law

The Josianic interlude might be said to vindicate God and the law insofar as it demonstrated that the law was possible of fulfillment, that it was not merely utopian, that it could and should have been obeyed all along.[38] Left unexplained, however, is why the positive consequences of obedience were so spare for Josiah and his repentant generation. If they demonstrated the practicability of the law, why would they not also reap the rewards of obedience to it?

Isaiah proclaims what God is doing in the historical moment. The outcome cannot be affected by the disclosure, cannot be affected by human intervention, cannot be altered by human response to the announcement. His prophetic commission is a word to harden hearts, preclude understanding, and remove the ground for repentance and forgiveness. Response is deactivated in the face of and by revelation.

There is a distinction in this respect between Isaiah 6 and 2 Kings 22–23. In the story of Josiah, the Book of the Law stirred the king and nation to action. It spoke to the heart (22:19). This is a distinction without a difference. The law contained and had become curse; there was to be no alteration of the decreed destruction.[39]

Huldah had announced that Josiah would be rewarded: "I will gather you to your fathers, and you shall be gathered to your grave in peace, and your eyes shall not see all the evil which I will bring upon this place" (22:20). Even this bleak promise was not to be fully kept. At the age of forty-one, Josiah was slain in battle with Neco, Pharaoh of Egypt. He was granted the "favor" of dying before the exile. The reform he successfully led did not alter the outcome for Jerusalem. As Huldah had also announced at the start: "Thus says the Lord, Behold I will bring evil upon this place and upon its inhabitants, all the words of the book which the king of Judah has read" (22:16).

If readers are concerned with theodicy, which do they judge to be the more violently perverse: the hardening of hearts that prevents repentance or the stimulation of repentance barren of reward?

Revealed Mystery

Isaiah and the Deuteronomist make declarations about events past, present, or in the making: the work of the active *dabar* of God in history. This presence is mysterious but not secret. It is announced.[40] The announcements of doom made by Isaiah and Huldah may be thought by the reader fair or unfair, just or unjust, but they can scarcely be thought secret. The offense and difficulty of the texts are their plain meaning, not some hidden or elusive sense.[41]

The single, limited conclusion to be drawn for present emphasis is that, in the Josiah story in particular and the Deuteronomic history as a whole, law functions as active word. It is a word that does not return empty, a form in human speech of the *dabar* of God. To this extent there is affinity between law and prophecy. And to this extent the potent declaration of doom in Isaiah 6, as a report from the lawsuit of God, is cast in a sympathetic rather than a foreign or countermanding idiom. There is no absolute conflict between the substance of prophecy and the rhetorical form it takes as *rib*.

Dabar: Prophecy, Law, and Other Mighty Acts

Amos wrote:

> The lion has roared;
>   who will not fear?
> The Lord God has spoken;
>   who can but prophesy? (3:8)

A similar formula is found in Jeremiah:

> If I say, "I will not mention him,
>   or speak any more in his name,"
> there is in my heart as it were a burning fire
>   shut up in my bones,
> and I am weary with holding it in,
>   and I cannot. (20:9)

God roars. It is impossible not to prophesy. When God utters his word, prophetic speech—like hardened hearts or silence—is one of the possible, irresistible consequences. Josiah's action is another. When the Book of the Law was read, he established its words. No more than the prophets were he and Israel drawn by reward. Josiah acted as he did for the same reason that the prophets spoke: He could not do otherwise.

As in other instances of prophecy and law, so in Isaiah 6: The *dabar* that exerts pressure on people and events erupts in speech.[42] There is a tremor, in verbal form, of events in the process of taking place. Although the hardening of hearts is itself a mighty act, it is not a discrete moment but an opening to further acts of God in the making.[43] In Isaiah 6 it is the prelude to God's devastation of Israel.

In the best-known story of the phenomenon, hardening of hearts has a very different consequence for Israel: It precedes and leads to the exodus. Chapters 7–14 of the Book of Exodus contain multiple references to the hardening of Pharaoh's heart. Moses is repeatedly sent to Pharaoh with the demand: "Let my people go." Each time Pharaoh refuses because his "heart was hardened." And each refusal is punished by a plague sent upon the Egyptians by God, until at last the Israelites cross the Red Sea. But even then God hardens Pharaoh's heart and the hearts of the Egyptian people in order that they may pursue the escapees and so be drowned when the sea closes over the dry path made for the Israelites.

At the beginning of the story of encounters between Moses (and Aaron) and Pharaoh, God explains to Moses that the petition for the release of the people should be presented although it will be denied because "I will harden Pharaoh's heart." Because of the refusals, God will "multiply my signs and wonders in the land of Egypt" (7:3).

According to the story, after plagues of blood, frogs, gnats, flies, livestock disease, and boils, Moses is once again sent to Pharaoh to repeat the demand for his people's freedom with the forecast of a further, greater torment that will flow from another refusal. And he is instructed to inform Pharaoh that all these things are being done "that you may know that there is none like me in all the earth. For by now I could have put forth my hand and struck you and your people with pestilence and you would have been cut off from the earth; but for this purpose have I let you live, to show you my power, so that my name may be declared throughout all the earth" (9:14–16).

Pharaoh and the Egyptians are kept alive with hardened hearts in order that God's power can be demonstrated and his name universally declared.[44] Pharaoh's refusal of immigration to the Israelites was produced by words that would then work signs and wonders.

In Isaiah 6, as in the exodus story, there is a foreclosure of understanding and perception which renders the prophecy's audience participants in the declared events shorn of their capacities to interpret and to alter outcomes. It is a hardening of the heart, like that before the exodus, preliminary to further mighty acts.

The difference between the two events is instructive. Pharaoh was an outsider. Isaiah's audience were insiders. No special interpretive privilege devolves upon insiders. Understanding is not a function of the inside status of the hearer. The word bears its own possibilities for being known or not known by insiders or outsiders. This theme is repeated and subsequently developed in Isaiah. Isaiah 29:9–12 is an example:

> Stupefy yourselves and be in a stupor,
> blind yourselves and be blind!
> Be drunk, but not with wine;
> stagger, but not with strong drink!
> For the Lord has poured out upon you
> a spirit of deep sleep,
> and has closed your eyes . . .
> and covered your heads . . .

And the vision of all this has become to you like the words of a book that is sealed. When men give it to one who can read, saying, "Read this," he says, "I cannot, for it is sealed." And when they give the book to one who cannot read, saying "Read this," he says, "I cannot read."

For both reader and nonreader, both insider and outsider, there is no hermeneutical potential, no latent sense, no role for interpreters privileged or unprivileged. There is the word. The word does what it says as God performs mighty acts.

And that is the context in which Mark 4:10–12 may be read.

PARABLES

The Greek for *word* is *logos*. *Logos* means that by which inward thought is expressed. But it also means the inward thought itself, and so could be translated into Latin as *ratio,* "reason." In the Greek tradition, *logos* bore the sense of rationality and so made its way directly into the English language as "logic."

The Hebrew for "word," *dabar,* has the sense of power: the word that accomplishes what it says, be it doom or redemption, interpretation or the foreclosure of interpretation. The Hebraic *dabar* is different from the Greek *logos.* Something of the difference may be captured this way: If I speak logically, I speak with correct reasoning; but if I speak *dabar*ly, I speak with effective power. I would associate the Hebrew *dabar* with the Greek *dunamis,* which gives us the English words *dynamite* and *dynamics.*

In Order That They See But Not Perceive

By quoting Isaiah, Mark's Jesus locates himself and his statement within the Hebraic tradition of the dynamic word. The Word of God takes form in speech in Isaiah's prophecy, and also in Jesus' parables.[45] To say that "everything is in parables; in order that they may indeed see but not perceive, and may indeed hear but not understand," is to say that the parables function like Isaiah's prophecy. They have the power of the *dabar* uttered by Isaiah. They are a form taken by the Word in the process of accomplishing signs and wonders.

In the Markan text, the parable which precipitated the disciples' question about parables had to do with a sower of seeds. Some seeds fall along the path, some on rocky ground, some among thorns, and some on fertile soil. Jesus explains that it is word of the Kingdom which is being sown. In some instances Satan immediately takes it away; in others its recipients fall away or allow it to be choked by diversions; but "those that were sown upon the good soil are the ones who hear and accept it" (4:14–20).[46]

Although the parable may be read several ways, one possibility is that it describes a type of the Word's historically effective action. I read it this way. So does the biblical scholar Joel Marcus, who notes: "There is no suggestion that one can alter the sort of soil one is; God's will, it must be assumed, determines that"; it is a parable about "the mystery of God's will whereby he causes some to bear fruit for him while he hardens others by the mediation of Satan and Satan's agents."[47]

The Word that creates faith in some, hardens the hearts of others, and, in any event, produces a harvest. The content of the parable is thus consistent with Jesus' explanation for his speaking in parables.

The parable, Jesus' explanation of the parable, and his explanation of the use of parables have to do not with secrets and knowledge but with the mysterious power of God in human affairs. They are preface to and part of the events that gather to a climax in the text.[48]

The hearts of those outside are hardened by the *dabar* of parables. Their turning and forgiveness are foreclosed. Therefore the crucifixion will be carried out "as it is written" (Mark 9:12). After Jesus entered Jerusalem, nearing the end, he again told parables. In response, the authorities "tried to arrest him, but feared the multitude, for they perceived that he had told the parable against them" (12:12). The effect of parable-telling is to spur the powers that be toward the crucifixion.

Neither the Pharaoh addressed by Moses nor the audience for Isaiah's proclamation could turn, be forgiven, and avert the forthcoming doom. Just so, those whose hearts were hardened by Jesus' words could not repent. The doom would not be averted. The infinite qualitative distinction between the instances of Moses and Isaiah on the one hand and Jesus on the other is that, in the latter, the punishment is borne by the speaker.

Just as the disciples are made party to the meaning of the parables, so are they made party to the events as they develop—in both cases in spite of their recalcitrance and weakness. This is the work of the Word. As the story proceeds, they exhibit hardness of heart (6:52, 8:17) and fail to understand the meaning of either parables (7:18) or events (8:21) until their failure issues in total abandonment of Jesus (14:50) and, in the case of Peter, overt denial (14:66–72). No disciples remain at the last, and the text leaves to a total stranger, a Roman soldier, the declaration at the moment of Jesus' death: "Truly this man was a son of God!" (15:39).

The disciples are not in better case than outsiders. But neither are they in worse case. The power of the Word is inclusive of both. The Roman soldier is one example. Pilate is another. Careful note should be taken of Pilate in Mark's story. After his arrest, Jesus was brought before Pilate, who found no grounds for the capital charge (15:2–5; 14). Pilate would release a prisoner at the feast of Passover. The crowd asked for Barabbas. "So Pilate, wishing to satisfy the crowd, released for them Barabbas; and having scourged Jesus, he delivered him to be crucified" (15:15).

Karl Barth observes that Pilate was committing injustice and violating law as well as duty: Pilate recognized Jesus' innocence but delivered Jesus to the political process instead of granting him release. Pilate's hardness of heart, however, does not place him outside the power of the Word. "Where would the Church be if this released Barabbas were in the place of the guiltless Jesus?" Barth asks, and then adds:

> Even at the moment when Pilate . . . allowed injustice to run its course, he was the human created instrument of that justification of sinful man that was completed once for all time through that very crucifixion. . . . What would be the worth of all the legal pro-

tection which the State could and should have granted the Church at that moment, compared with this act in which humanly speaking, the Roman governor became the virtual founder of the Church?[49]

Pilate and the state are biblically understood as principalities and powers under the jurisdiction of angels. As Barth notes, they are "invisible, spiritual and heavenly powers, which exercise . . . a certain independence. . . . An angelic power may indeed become wild, degenerate, perverted, and so become a 'demonic' power. That, clearly, had happened with the State, represented by Pilate, which crucified Jesus."[50] Importantly, however, the "destiny of the rebellious angelic powers . . . is not that they will be annihilated, but that they will be forced into the service and the glorification of Christ, and, through Him, of God."[51]

Outsiders no less than insiders are drawn into the service of the Word; Pilate no less than Peter. Like Amos, Josiah, and Isaiah, they cannot do otherwise. The story does not move them about like pieces on a game board. Pilate and Peter have minds and wills of their own. It is they who act. And yet not they. The story presents, but does not—because it cannot—explain, the coincidence of divine and human agency; this is a mystery. First and last, the story presents the power of the Word that, even in the crucifixion, acts on outsiders as much as insiders and acts on behalf of the one as much as the other.

To You the Mystery

When Jesus says, "To you [insiders] is given the secret of the Kingdom of God, but for those outside everything is in parables," he is not creating a distinction of privilege. Nor is he imparting secret knowledge to some while concealing it from others.

The action is not that of concealment. Isaiah, like the Deuteronomist, makes declarations about events past, present, or in the making: the work of the active *dabar* of God in history. There is announcement. The textual action is that of disclosure. Also in Mark 4 there is announcement rather than concealment.

The parables Jesus tells are specifically parables about the coming of the kingdom of God. The parable about the sowing of seed that immediately precedes the explanation for speaking in parables concerns the prospering of the Word among some and its rejection among others. Two more "seed" parables follow the explanation, and they also have to do with the growth of the kingdom (4:26–32). Another parable is about the divided kingdom of Satan that is ending (3:24–26), and yet another about a strong man entering a house (3:27). The other parable in this same collection is the one about putting a lamp under a bushel or on a stand: "There is nothing hid, except to be made manifest; nor is anything secret, except to come to light" (4:22). The parables of the kingdom declare the coming of the kingdom of God in and with Jesus. No more than words of prophecy are they performances of concealment.

Nor is the thing disclosed and imparted to the disciples a secret sense or interpretive key. The doom prophesied by Isaiah and announced in the 2 Kings story of Josiah may be thought outrageously unfair, but can scarcely be thought secretive. There is revealed mystery—a terrible mystery—rather than concealed secret. The difficulty and offense of the texts are their plain meaning. Similarly, in Mark the subject matter is not arcane rites or esoteric knowledge but the coming of the kingdom.[52] This is certainly mysterious, but it is not partially or completely hidden. The parables do not let out coded bits and pieces, leaving much or all enticingly unknown. The whole is revealed. But it is revealed to be a mystery: illuminating for some, darkening for others; redeeming of both.

In Mark, as in Isaiah, God's activity in the midst of history is announced and is mysterious. There is no key to interpretation and understanding offered to insiders. God's word bears its own possibilities for being understood or not.[53] Nor do the disciple-insiders acquire the ability to interpret. They remain uncomprehending (4:41). The teller must continue to interpret for them (4:34). There is no institution of interpretation and no enticement to the hermeneutic impulse. Their incomprehension is repeated both in their response to the transfiguration (9:2–8) and in the inability to understand that accompanies their fearful reluctance to ask for help (9:30–32). An insider, Judas, is the betrayer (14:17–21), and his treachery is matched by that of Peter, *the* insider (14:30, 66–72). Jesus himself becomes the rejected outsider. There are no privileged, certainly no interpretively privileged, insiders.

The Greek word translated as "secret" in the Revised Standard Version is *musterion,* "mystery." The mystery of the kingdom given the disciples is the mystery of God's action in bringing his kingdom.[54] The disciples are not given data. They are given the mystery of God's action in the person of Jesus. The biblical scholar Joachim Jeremias concluded "that Jesus not only proclaimed the message of the parables, but that he lived it and embodied it in his own person. Jesus not only utters the message of the Kingdom of God, he himself is the message."[55] The mystery is God's action in the world bringing the kingdom in the person of Jesus. He is the Word given to the disciples.[56]

Matthew makes this point explicit. After Matthew's Jesus quotes the Isaiah 6 passage, he says: "But blessed are your eyes, for they see, and your ears, for they hear. Truly, I say to you, many prophets and righteous men longed to see what you see, and did not see it, and to hear what you hear, and did not hear it" (13:16–17).

The disciples have the Word in the person of Jesus. He is with them. The others have the Word in parables. They remain outsiders. In both cases the Word is powerful. The parables are as plain and their content as mysterious as Jesus. Outsiders' hearts are hardened. The same is said later of the insiders, who do not understand and, in the end, flee. The insiders, like the outsiders, fail to realize their confrontation by the Word.

In the instance of Isaiah, violence is visited upon Jerusalem; in Mark, upon Jesus. The thing announced is done. Antagonistic outsiders and betraying insiders are made participants. Jesus, the insider, becomes the rejected outsider. Darkness falls on him. He dies for all.[57]

THE EMPTY PLACE

By locating Jesus' comment in its Isaianic context, I give Mark 4 a very different reading than does Kermode. Kermode says Jesus' parables expressly conceal secret senses understood only by insiders. The Isaiah connection renders this interpretation less apt. I disagree with Kermode but find his reading instructive, especially in one of its aspects. He directs attention to the structure of Mark as a text. Many interpreters find Mark stylistically coarse and unsophisticated; it is to be read in spite of its style. Kermode says Mark is artfully constructed; by attending to the text as text, the reader will find it revealing. I think Kermode makes the correct judgment about this gospel's structure.

Structure

Kermode points out that Mark is built with the device of intercalation, or interleaving: One story is cut into another. There are numerous examples. The story of Salome is placed in the middle of the story about the sending of the twelve disciples and their report back to Jesus (6:12–30). The story of the healing of the woman with a hemorrhage is dropped into the story about the raising of Jairus' daughter (5:21–43). These are not lapses but artful narrative devices that enrich the meaning of one story by placing it against another.[58]

The cultivation of structural opposition is a clue to Mark's gospel as a whole. It establishes, says Kermode, "a continuity which makes sense only in terms of that which interrupts it. All Mark's minor intercalations reflect the image of a greater intervention represented by the whole book. And all such lesser interventions deepen and complicate the sense of the narrative; or they are indications that more story is needed, as a supplement, if the story is to make sense."[59]

What Comes After

Kermode is right to suggest that "Mark's interest is in the space between two concurrent events" and wrong to suggest that "it is for interpretation to fill the gap."[60] In his view, the gaps in Mark or in other texts or in life require interpretive filling, but, because they are empty, they make interpretation impossible. We catch a glimpse of radiance within, but then the door is shut. So, he says, Mark is a "witness to the enigmatic and exclusive character of narrative."

Mark, as I understand it, instructs us in a very different kind of reading of texts and world. There are gaps, but they do not require what Kermode refers to as "our own bewilderment projected into the text."[61] This self-projection into a text replicates the religious impulse and is subject to the same kind of judgment. The bewilderment in Mark is in the text, already expressly there and highlighted at the end.

I have related the text about parables, Mark 4:10–12, to Mark's concluding text about the crucifixion. I now want to make explicit the implicit assumption that the two texts are to be read together. Mark 4:10–12 is a preliminary text of the power of the Word that will come to fruition in Mark 16. Mark concludes with these words:

> And when the sabbath was past, Mary Magdalene, and Mary the mother of James, and Salome, brought spices, so that they might go and anoint him. And very early on the first day of the week they went to the tomb when the sun had risen. And they were saying to one another, "Who will roll away the stone for us from the door of the tomb?" And looking up, they saw that the stone was rolled back, for it was very large. And entering the tomb, they saw a young man sitting on the right side, dressed in a white robe; and they were amazed. And he said to them, "Do not be amazed; you seek Jesus of Nazareth, who was crucified. He has risen, he is not here; see the place where they laid him. But go, tell his disciples and Peter that he is going before you to Galilee; there you will see him, as he told you." And they went out and fled from the tomb; for trembling and astonishment had come upon them; and they said nothing to anyone, for they were afraid. (16:1–8)

This is a singular ending for the story. Kermode notes that to end a sentence this way in Greek is a violation of accepted grammar, and that to end a whole book in this fashion is a striking abnormality.[62] He adds: "The scandal is, of course, much more than merely philological. Omitting any post-Easter appearance of Jesus, Mark has only the empty tomb

and the terrified women. The final mention of Peter . . . can only remind us that our last view of him was not as a champion of the faith but
as the image of denial."[63]

The effect of the ending is very like that achieved by the telling and
explaining of parables, but even more arresting. It, like Mark 4, may be
read as an invocation of the power of the Word if the text is taken seriously as a text.

Readers who treat the text as merely an indicator of some other reality behind or beyond the page miss the experience the text offers. They
look through the words to something else and try to see the physical reality of an empty tomb—there is a place in Jerusalem marked as the
spot—which requires explanation: What did or did not happen to the
body of Jesus? What proof is there of a resurrection? Was there a historical Jesus? Is Mark a report about him and, if so, is it factual? Provable?

This is the way the disciples took the parables, looking for a hidden
meaning. But the parables were a presentation of Jesus. By disregarding
the text of the parables—a failure of good listening—the disciples, as
much as outsiders, missed the experience they offered of the power and
person of the Word.

The reader of Mark 4 can miss the experience in the same way that
the disciples did. Note that the reader is not asked to solve riddles. The
possibility of secret senses is emptied out in the text. Mark publishes
Jesus' explanation. The reader is made as much an insider, and as much
an outsider, as the disciples and outsiders in the text.[64] Jesus' statement
about his use of parables disturbs our expectations. It is meant to disturb
our expectations, to break the surface and thereby strike an opening
that allows us, like its audience in the text, to be confronted by the powerful mystery of the Word.

In the instance of the conclusion of Mark, if you look through the
text, you will see an empty place that must be filled by your own
exertions—as though if you believed energetically enough, if you really
worked at it, you could raise Jesus from the dead, at least in your own
mind. But then you would have supplied what the text deliberately
omits. You would project your own labor of belief into the gap. And you
would foreclose the experience the text offers.

Mark's interest lies in what happens in the space not between text
and tomb behind, but between text and reader. There is the space for
the power of the Word.

Where I would have placed sightings of the risen Jesus and exhortations and a hallelujah chorus, Mark ends with flight and silence. The
words walk us up to a textually empty, silent place and leave us there.

Well, not exactly empty or silent. There is a strange figure. It is possible endlessly to speculate on his identity if you look for something or

someone beyond the text, as though this were a news report and as though the real object of interest were the people and events reported rather than the report. In the text, this white-robed young man is simply inexplicable. He disturbs the surface of the narrative as Mark would disturb the surface of the reader's life.[65]

In the story, three women come expecting a corpse and are confronted instead by this strange figure and his words saying Jesus has gone ahead to Galilee, where he will be seen "as he told you." (Throughout Mark's gospel, from 1:2 to 16:17, events take place "as it is written" and "as he told you." The Deuteronomic history describes the power of the Word in Israel's history. Mark describes Jesus' history as the power of the Word.) The young man and his message break into the concluding story about the empty tomb and the resurrection. There is no closure. The story is never completed. It stops at the verge of the resurrection and never gets to sightings in Galilee. We are left with an inexplicable figure, terrified women, and an empty tomb. Or are we?

Are we not left, rather, with a question: After that, what happened? If there were only fear and silence, how and why did Mark come to be written? That is to ask: Are we not confronted by an empty place between the ending and the beginning of Mark? I think so. And I think that in this negative space the Word works its power in the experience of reading. It is Mark's testimony to that power. It is an invocation of the Word rather than an invitation to the reader's filling interpretation.

Follow the trajectory along which the story is proceeding before it seems to be cut down. What happens after the flight from the tomb? At some point afterward, the Gospel of Mark was written. On its own terms, after an interlude, it follows the silence about which it does not speak. What is said to us after the empty tomb and about it is the Gospel of Mark, the story. Sometime after the end, it began. Between the end and the beginning is a silence. The fact and structure of Mark are Mark's testimony to the Word breaking in to give us the Gospel of Mark.

The tomb in the text, like a parable, contains the Word. This is not the genesis of secrecy. It is the genesis of revelation, the power of the Word.

Mark has done all that words can do. A negative space irrupts. The text does not fill it and does not invite us to fill it. Either the resurrection has purchase there, or it does not. The first word in Mark is the Greek for beginning, and the first word in Genesis is the Hebrew for beginning. The beginning begins. After the end, there is either a beginning, or there is not.[66]

I have heard the conclusion of Mark read as the lesson for the day in an Easter service of worship. (This is its proper situs now, as it probably was shortly after it was written.) The church was packed. The congregation was dressed in its finest. The children were restless. A brass choir had been brought in for the occasion. And then Mark 16 was read, concluding: "And they went out and fled from the tomb; for trembling and astonishment had come upon them; and they said nothing to anyone, for they were afraid." That was it. No more. Is that a text for celebration? It certainly disturbed the expectations and needs I had brought to church. Is this not its function? To break the surface of things for openings in which the Word works or does not?—the way bread is broken in the eucharistic sacrament, and the body of Christ is discerned, or is not?[67]

WORD

At the start of this exploration of Mark and Isaiah, I said that its purpose was not to make a conclusive statement about the texts but to clarify my usage of *Word*. *Word* has for me the primary, specific content given it by the texts of the prophetic *dabar* that accomplishes what it says and the Gospel texts of the Word become flesh.

In the Christian tradition, *Word* refers to the biblical texts, to the proclamation or preaching arising from those texts, and to the subject of those texts and proclamation. I adhere to that tradition. Although wooden distinctions may not be made between the three, a priority is to be established according to which the subject is foremost. Proclamation depends on the biblical texts and repeats them in a kind of continual translation. The biblical texts point beyond themselves to their subject and are dependent on it.

There is no identity between words of the Bible or proclamation and the Word of God. The former serve the latter—like parables, as Barth suggests, so that "the New Testament parables are . . . the prototype of the order in which there can be other true words alongside the one Word of God, created and determined by it, exactly corresponding to it, fully serving it and therefore enjoying its power and authority."[68*]

FIVE

〜〜〜

Aesthetic Meaning and Political Freedom

BARTH COMMENDED "a wide reading of contemporary secular literature—especially of newspapers," for "if thinking is not to be pseudo-thinking, we must think about life; for such a thinking is a thinking about God. And if we are to think about life, we must penetrate its hidden corners, and steadily refuse to treat anything . . . as irrelevant."[1] Anticipation is instinct in wide reading because the Word which makes true witnesses of the words of proclamation and Bible is free to wrest similar service from other words as well.[2]

The Sound and the Fury and *Beloved* have subject matter that is religious or theological, or nearly so. Barth had in mind texts more fully secular. This chapter's brief "eavesdrop in the world at large"[3] is guided by the education offered in Mark. I read in expectation of surprise by parables of the kingdom. This is not to cast about for little moral or religious or theological lessons; in secular parables also, the consuming lion may be heard to roar. (I construe "reading texts" broadly and include attention to music, art, and the art of politics as well as attention to literature.)

THE WORD IN ART, LITERATURE, AND MUSIC

Frank Kermode thinks Mark is a primary witness to the enigmatic character of narrative that makes interpretation necessary but impossible, thereby condemning us to endless disappointment. I think Mark is a primary witness to the possibility of reading with hope. I venture the proposition that aesthetic meaning—the understanding that occurs between reader and narrative—is a secular parable.

Texts are incomplete. Interpretation is endlessly possible. But Mark encourages the reader to approach texts with expectant regard for what is unsaid as well as for what is said—for their open-endedness, silences, negative spaces, inexplicable disturbances, and omissions as well as for their plain statement. There the Word may be at work.

To explore the point, I shall follow George Steiner's path to the presence of what he calls "otherness" in literature, art, and music. (His "otherness" is very like my "Word.")[4] He believes the open-endedness of literature, art, and music—the spaces that are the source for discordant responses, findings, interpretations—is exactly the access they provide to the insuring presence of otherness. I follow Steiner but shall finally strike off in a different direction.

Think of Shakespeare's *King Lear*. You will recall—can reperform in your mind—the critical early scene when Lear takes a map and would divest himself of territory and cares of state and divide his kingdom among his three daughters. It is his giving up, his dying before the end of his life. I want to focus your attention not so much on him, however, as on Cordelia. In Lear's proposed division of the kingdom, the bounty of each part is to be determined by the bounty of each daughter's profession of love.

Goneril and Regan make effusive declarations and are rewarded. Lear turns last to Cordelia:

> ". . . what can you say to draw A third more opulent than your sisters? Speak."
> "Nothing, my lord."
> "Nothing?"
> "Nothing."
> "Nothing will come of nothing. Speak again."
> "Unhappy that I am, I cannot heave
> My heart into my mouth. . . ."[5]

Cordelia's "nothing," in a Steinerian reading,[6] is an opening.

First, Cordelia says "nothing," and yet we hear much more. Lear misses it, but we do not. She utters that word, and in it, through it, beyond it, we feel much more. We have here what Steiner recognizes as an "excess of wholly present but unsayable meanings."[7] Within the text of *The Sound and the Fury*, the phenomenon occurs when "all time and injustice and sorrow become vocal for an instant" in Benjy's wail, and in the Easter service, when Rev. Shegog's "voice consumed him, until he was nothing and [the congregation] were nothing and there was not even a voice but instead their hearts were speaking to one another beyond the need for words."[8] Within the text of *Beloved* it takes place in the Clearing, when Baby Suggs, saying no more, stood up "and danced with her twisted hip the rest of what her heart had to say," and when the women, come to free Sethe of Beloved with their music, "took a step back to the beginning" and made "the sound that broke the back of words."[9]

Second, there is no Cordelia. No one says anything. No one is there. We create Cordelia—and Lear, like Rev. Shegog and Baby Suggs—in our minds. What we are given is marks on a page. We see them as a string of letters. And from this assemblage we create something—someone. From the characters on the page we create the character Cordelia. She is *our* creation—and yet she is not. There is something other than me in the Cordelia I create. From the dead letters there springs up a Cordelia. And this Cordelia says "nothing," and much more than nothing is communicated.[10]

Third, this creative act—this act whereby marks on a page become Cordelia—this wonderful event, says Steiner, is a kind of reenactment of the first creation. It is our experience of our and the world's origin. Steiner writes: "The analogy I have in mind would be that of 'background radiation,' of 'background noise' in which astrophysicists and cosmologists see . . . vestiges of the origins of our universe."[11]

Steiner suggests that the creative act of the writer, painter, or musician, and our creative response to it—the response of the good reader or viewer or listener—is like the background radiation that remains in the universe in the aftermath of the big bang. In Steiner's view, we have in our experience of literature, art, and music a remaining experience, a reenactment, of God's creation of the heavens and the earth. And more.

Steiner says: "There is in the art-act and its reception, . . . a presumption of presence, . . . of 'otherness.'"[12] He proposes that this assumption of God the Creator's presence underwrites the meaning we experience in literature, art, and music. Cordelia says nothing and, in the silence, we hear much more because we wager on this presence, on this making alive.

Markings on a page, pigments on a canvas, notes sung or played on an instrument may enlist "the proposal that we move among orders of pragmatic substance themselves permeable to that which lies on the other side."[13] When "nothing" is said, we may be struck by everything.

I propose a revision of this conclusion. Steiner holds that aesthetic meaning is underwritten by an assumption: We take the risk that God is present. I think it works the other way around: Aesthetic meaning is underwritten by the risk God takes with us. It is His venture of trust in us that empowers. Steiner says "grammar lives and generates worlds because there is a wager on God."[14] I think grammar lives and generates worlds because there is a wager on us: We speak and understand because and as the Word is given us. According to Steiner an author's creation of a character and a good reader's re-creation of her are reverberations of the original creation. I think the event is attributable not so much to creation as to revelation; is not so much the fading afterglow of the creation as the undimmed radiance of the incarnation, crucifixion, and resurrection. The Word became flesh, accepted the risk of rejection, and was made triumphant over its consequences. The Word which foreclosed understanding becomes the giver of understanding. (Understanding was foreclosed to this end.)

When Cordelia emerges from within marks on a page, when nothing is said and much is heard within, the Markan not-exactly-empty tomb is replayed. No guarantee of meaning comes with text or reader. But meaning happens and is a gift, by grace.

W. H. Auden is an aid here:

> From the beginning until now God spoke through his prophets. The Word aroused the uncomprehending depths of their flesh to a witnessing fury, and their witness was this: that the Word should be made Flesh. . . .
>
> But here and now the Word which is implicit in the Beginning and in the End is become immediately explicit. . . .
>
> By the event of this birth the true significance of all other events is defined. . . .
>
> Because in Him the Flesh is united to the Word without magical transformation, Imagination is redeemed from promiscuous fornication with her own images. . . .
>
> Because in Him the Word is united to the Flesh without loss of perfection, Reason is redeemed from incestuous fixation on her own Logic, for the One and the Many are simultaneously revealed as real. . . .
>
> And because of His visitation, we may no longer desire God as if He were lacking: our redemption is no longer a question of pursuit but of surrender.[15]

I am trying to conjure here a fugitive truth in language heavily freighted with potential for writer mistake and reader misunderstanding. Perhaps it will help if I summon the aid of a suggestion made by James Boyd White that literary texts are "invitational: they offer an experience, not a message, and an experience that will not merely add to one's stock of information but change one's way of seeing and being, of talking and acting."[16]

The first part of his statement is critical: Literary texts are *invitational.* They cannot be more. They do not compel us to open their covers or to give them a good reading if we do. They cannot of themselves change our way of seeing and being. First must come willingness to accept the invitation, the will to welcome the work of art and the stranger.

We must be inspired to be vulnerable to transforming change. This capacity for courtesy, for welcoming the stranger and listening, comes as a gift. Neither the text nor we ourselves generate it. In the biblical formula, "we love, because [God] first loved us."[17] We risk trust in art, because God first trusts us. We speak because we have been addressed by the Word.

Texts are partly given, partly created in the writing and in the reading. That we express and receive meaning in literature, art, and music, that there is open-endedness and yet understanding, that there is meaning and the possibility of multiple other meanings—this is the opening within which we are grasped as Mark would have us to be.

Nor is the phenomenon esoteric or limited to the privileged few who read books, visit museums, and attend orchestral performances. If the Word is free to make parables in the sermons of Rev. Shegog or Baby Suggs and in the daily newspaper, how can I say it is not free to do the same in folk art and subway art, in rap music and rock and roll? Even there, cannot the unsayable be spoken and heard together with the sayable? And is that not, when it happens, a gift of the Word and a sign of his presence?

That there is meaning in a wide reading of contemporary texts I take to be itself a parable.

THE WORD IN POLITICS

We are speaking animals perhaps for the reason that we are first political animals. There is offered in Mark an education in politics as well as in aesthetics. We are taught to read disturbances of the surface of politics and its open-endedness as no less subject to the promise of the Word than those in literature, art, and music. This is so notwithstanding the huge difference between poetry and politics, in the quantity and directness of force if in nothing else.

An example emerges in a recent book, *As I Saw It* (1990), that is a kind of dialogue between former secretary of state Dean Rusk and his son, Richard. Richard was taping talks with his father to produce the material for the book. He brought the conversation to its most difficult, loaded subject: the war in Vietnam. Dean had been deeply engaged in its conduct, and Richard had grown to oppose it. Richard pressed his father on the subject of Viet Cong commitment to continue fighting notwithstanding the huge loss of life:

"Why did they keep coming?" I asked him. "Who were those people? Why did they fight so hard?"
These were questions for which he had no answers.

"I really don't have much to offer on that, Rich," he finally said. Both of us were emotionally drained.

I turned off the tape recorder. . . . Inadvertently I was asking my father to do what I had done in the late 1960's. As a Marine reservist whose Syracuse, New York, tank battalion was never activated for Vietnam, and as a student at Cornell University, I tried doggedly to believe in American policy until the war's relentless illogic made this impossible. Not wanting to volunteer for Vietnam, unwilling to embarrass my father by joining an antiwar movement that was appearing all around me, unable to stop the war, unable to take part, caught between love for my father and the growing horror of Vietnam, I had begun to question the premise and assumptions that underlay my dad's thinking. All this led to an emotional and psychological journey that ended, one year after he left office, in psychological collapse.

"You had your father's nervous breakdown," a psychologist told me seventeen years later.[18]

The difference between the Rusks, father and son, was the particular, personal version of the chasm that opened in the nation's politics. And Richard's breakdown was also his share of the nation's breakdown. Between the desire to believe the policy and the devastating illogic of the war, between love for the father and horror of the war, between loyalty to the people with their democratic government and despair over the unaccountable suffering they can inflict—in that gap breakdowns may well occur. Crucifixion is always possible.[19]

But there, in the same place, supplication is also always possible. In fact, breakdowns and crucifixions may themselves be types of supplication and constitute the political equivalent to Cordelia's "nothing" in which much is heard. Suppliants initiate a relationship to the strong, who are thereby cast in the role of recipients. The powerful are put to the test by the powerless in an ironic reversal. Paul Vallière explains that the supplicated one is more powerful in terms of established power and speaks for himself or in the name of that power; suppliants, however, do not speak mainly for themselves, and instead invoke a higher reality: "It is this prophetic power of supplication that establishes the dialectic of power and powerlessness, thus putting the whole question of power into a new perspective. *Supplication is historical action which bears witness to social and political theonomy.*"[20]

In Cordelia's "nothing" there is an excess of wholly present but unsayable meaning. In supplication there is an excess of wholly present but unrealized justice. Dilsey's life among the Compsons, a remonstrance in the face of their sound and fury, is a form of supplication, as is the suffering and endurance of Baby Suggs and Sethe, which invokes judgment on the oppressing world of whites. Martin Luther King's nonviolence was a form of supplication summoning a power that changed the South.

So was Robert Moses' strategy. Moses was deeply engaged in the struggle for the rights of black people in Mississippi in the 1960s. In *Parting the Waters,* Taylor Branch relates how, on one of the occasions when he had been jailed for his work, Moses "finally glimpsed an opening in the large paradox: how Negroes could obtain freedom without power and power without freedom."[21] They could fill the jails. "By the next morning, . . . Moses had shed his usual reticence to rejoice out loud in his cell. . . . Urged on by the regular prisoners, Moses began a chant: 'Do you want your freedom? Are you ready to go to jail?' and even the thieves and vagrants around him understood the chant to be a revelation of hope."[22]

I believe that finding freedom in jail, like finding meaning in "nothing," is to have been found by the Word. It is a sign or clue of the presence of the Word in our midst creating human community and keeping human life human. It is a secular parable of the Kingdom.

SIX

❧❧❧

Morbidity and Viability in Law

LAW LOCKS UP DEALS and people and wants to leave no openings. Far more than either literature or politics—it is a form of both—law appears bluntly resistant to a reading expectant of surprise. George Steiner suggests that remembrance safeguards the core of our individuality; what we commit to memory—the poem, the image, the musical score—"is the ballast of the self."[1] I have not seen the contract, statute, brief, or judicial opinion that I should want to memorize. The legal texts are deadening rather than stabilizing and are best not had by heart. This concluding chapter addresses the formidable, sprawling mortality of law and comes to an end which returns to the beginning and the people in whose performances with the dead letter of law may be discovered enlivening parables of the Word.

DEATH IN LAW

Death is not merely a physical event that occurs only at the end of our lives. It takes shape already before the end in many forms, including poverty, enforced silence, despair, fear, hate, anxiety. James O'Fallon and Cheney Ryan elaborate on Hegel's observation that one person's exploitation of another "inflicts a sort of death of both parties insofar as it denies the humanity of both";[2] whenever we close ourselves off to others, as the master refuses to listen to the slave, "we are dead as human beings, though we may remain alive physically."[3]

Death intrudes upon our lives before the end.

Nor is this a phenomenon of individual experience only. It is also social, political, cultural. And juridical. It takes form in law. Death is integral to American law.

In *McCulloch v. Maryland,* Chief Justice John Marshall wrote that "the power to tax involves the power to destroy."[4] More recently, William Stringfellow pressed Marshall's insight further, noting that "every sanction the State commands embodies the meaning of death: . . . imprisonment, . . . conscription; impeachment, regulation of production. . . ; confiscation, surveillance, execution, war. Whenever the authority of the State is exercised in such ways . . . the moral basis of that authority remains the same: death. That is the final sanction of the State and it is the *only* one."[5]

So capital punishment may be more telling of American law than we customarily suppose. Capital punishment means death plain and simple for the person killed, but more than that it is a statement, too, of the death of the society, an expression of our despair and fear. A yielding to hopelessness. Our giving up.

There are subtler forms of death in the law, textual forms that are discernible when we fix a careful eye on what lawyers think and write. Take as an example the 1947 Supreme Court opinion in *Francis v. Resweber.*[6] Willie Francis had been convicted of murder and sentenced to die. He was electrocuted, but there was insufficient current to kill him. The case came before the Supreme Court when the state set the date for another attempt. The vote on the Court was four to four, with Justice Felix Frankfurter casting the decisive ballot. He, and therefore the Court, decided to let the state proceed, and Francis was successfully killed.

Frankfurter knew very well that his was the decisive vote. His explanation of it opens with a magisterial review of the Constitution's great clauses on the privileges and immunities of citizens, cruel and unusual punishment, due process, and equal protection, which together, he said, "summarize the meaning of the struggle for freedom"[7] and enunciate "a decent respect for the dignity of man."[8] But recitation of stirring constitutional clauses would be of no avail to Willie Francis.

Frankfurter said these clauses did not readily answer the question whether Willie Francis could be electrocuted a second time. The answer to that question required, said Frankfurter, "not the application of merely personal standards but the impersonal standards of society which alone judges, as the organs of Law, are empowered to enforce."[9]

In that statement, or so I ask you to consider, in that turn of mind, death takes textual form: Judges as organs of law, as instruments, as mere channels of impersonal standards of society, as powerless to do otherwise, as lifeless. It is the judicial cannot, the resignation of responsibility couched as a theory of judicial restraint.[10]

Frankfurter concluded: "I cannot bring myself to believe that [to carry out] . . . a sentence of death . . . because a first attempt to carry it out was an innocent misadventure, offends a principle of justice 'rooted in the traditions and conscience of our people.' Short of the compulsion of such a principle, this Court must abstain from interference with State action no matter how strong one's personal feeling of revulsion."[11]

The judge is portrayed as powerless, as acting only under the "compulsion" of principle. But principles do not compel. As Ronald Dworkin puts it, they have weight—not compulsion, but weight.[12] They belong to the way we persuade and are persuaded. They figure in the arguments we make to each other. They are our arguments. We are responsible for them.

Moreover, the contrast Frankfurter draws between personal, private standards and impersonal standards of society is an artifact. He added: "I cannot rid myself of the conviction that were I to hold that Louisiana . . . [may not] carry out the death sentence, I would be enforcing my private view rather than [the] consensus of society's opinion."[13] But the two are mutually dependent: Social standards fundamentally shape personal standards, and, in turn, personal standards may influence those of society. Think of the effect of Nelson Mandela's standards on his world.

What a justice of the Supreme Court stands for and endorses with the quality of his character and the quality of the arguments he addresses to us influences what we hold to be right. If Frankfurter believed electrocuting Willie Francis a second time was wrong, then, as a justice of the Supreme Court, he was bound to say so in the language of constitutional law.

That is the difficult work of translation.[14] It is not easy and never ends. But the attempt, the trying ever and again, is the calling of Article III judges and their vocational responsibility. They are not to follow the example of Pontius Pilate, whose washing of his hands has, for two thousand years, held central place as the condemnable paradigm of terminal leave from judgment.

Frankfurter speaks of principles as though they exist apart from and above him. He invests them falsely with power and then surrenders to them his responsibility for judgment, as though, like caskets, they could receive the intellectual remains of his giving up. It is a way of thinking that is a form of dying, or so I think if we look closely.[15]

During the period of internal negotiation when the Court was framing its opinion in the *Francis* case, Frankfurter wrote a note to one of his colleagues. In it, he quoted approvingly Justice Oliver Wendell Holmes, who "used to express the relationship between the Supreme Court and the States by saying he would not strike down State action unless the action of the State made him 'puke.'"[16] The second execution of Francis, in Frankfurter's view, failed to meet this test.

Here is a rare, revealing version of the image of the judge as organ through which higher principle is communicated. In this version the judge is the anatomical tract through which overwhelming nausea courses: the judge as one overcome by illness; judgment as involuntary disgorgement. The metaphors are those of passivity, sickness, and death.

It is not my purpose to pillory Felix Frankfurter. To do so would run counter to my proposal and undermine it. I could have employed other, current examples: the present Court giving up on affirmative action,[17] or finding that a state has no obligation to a child beaten into permanent senselessness by his father,[18] or referring Native Americans to the luck of the political process instead of the Constitution and the Court for protection of their religion.[19] The point I am pursuing is not so much personal as systemic, not so much past as present.[20] The phenomenon is deeply, currently, institutionally entrenched in law—in us—as it takes overt form in the electric chair. I am asking you to consider whether death does not take subtle form in legal texts and turns of mind.[21]

Judicial texts are not its only locus. Death is to be read, too, in leases, deeds, and contracts. Just as some people spread their butter all the way to the edges of a slice of bread, so do lawyers draft all the way to the edges of the permissible. If there is not enough space on the page, we use fine print. We want everything covered.

We draft to the edges also in statutes. If something is omitted the first time around, it will be added in a later session. That is why almost the only occasion for new legislation in Congress is prior legislation: amendments, revisions, expansions, reauthorizations, reforms, and midcourse corrections of statutes already on the books.

The Clean Air Act is the benumbing product of frequent, wholesale amendment, vast political maneuvering, and little clarity. It is massive. And none of it can be set to music. There is no life in it. Instead there is a bureaucratic voice from on high.[22] It is like Lyndon Johnson's campaign for the Senate in 1948, when he flew over towns in a helicopter with an external loudspeaker fixed to the strut, blanketing the landscape below with his disembodied voice.

The purpose of all this flattening wordiness in ordinary legal texts is to forestall creative alternatives. In fact, a will or contract or statute that leaves much to the imagination will be void. There is little or nothing for the reader to do but to obey or disobey, to accept or reject. Innovative response is discouraged.

Patricia Williams says that contract law exerts "a certain deadening power . . . by reducing the parties to the passive. It constrains the lively involvement of its signatories by positioning enforcement in such a way that parties find themselves in a passive relationship to a document: it is the contract that governs, that 'does' everything, that absorbs all responsibility and deflects all other recourse."[23]

This is what I mean by saying that death takes shape in the thought forms and rhetoric—in the texts—of law as in its system. The force of death in the force of law.

LAW TOWARD ART

Steiner says we are "close neighbors to the transcendent. Poetry, art, music are the medium of that neighborhood."[24] Law is omitted from the list. Joseph Vining may well be right in saying that in law, too, "there is always something behind the texts."[25] But can law be a medium of transcendence?

When we open a copy of *The Sound and the Fury,* or *Beloved* or *King Lear,* the marks on their pages prompt us to engage in the creation of Dilsey, Baby Suggs, and Cordelia. But open a copy of the statutes of a state or of the federal government, or unfold an insurance policy or a deed, and marks on their pages, I think, prompt a different response.

Legal texts appear to discourage otherness and creative responsibility. Lawyers' language seems fortresslike and impermeable to transcendence. This is so because such writing is done and received on a wager of the absence of God, not His presence. As though God were dead. It is assumed that there is no real presence to reinsure meaning, so everything has to be set out on the page.

This may be appropriate, and necessary. Should not legal documents be drafted as if God were absent? Do we not want a Bill of Rights and a Clean Air Act with teeth and bite rather than poetry? A close friend of mine, a fine lawyer, represents a musical group. Negotiations with a recording company, covering every contingency, produced a document of eighty-nine close pages. Both sides wanted music, but they were right not to want it in their contract.

There is a dilemma here, and no resolution. When we try to say and to settle everything, as often we must, we embark upon the impossible, for the most complete legal drafting cannot eliminate options, either politically or hermeneutically. What is true of literary and biblical texts—what leads Frank Kermode to disappointment and almost despair—is true also of legal texts and leads lawyers to great wealth: Interpretation is always possible, always necessary.

Stanley Fish gives this example:

"As a frequent flyer," he writes, "I have been amused by the efforts of airlines to police their lavatories. [Toilet law, we might call it.] In particular, I've noticed the now almost desperate search for a sign whose wording will make absolutely and explicitly clear what should and should not be flushed down the toilet. The latest (and doomed) effort goes something like this: 'Only toilet paper and tissue should be deposited in the toilet.' How long," Fish asks, "before flight attendants . . . begin to find bodily waste . . . deposited in the most inconvenient places."[26] Only toilet paper and tissue in the toilet. "Language cannot be made so explicit as to preclude interpretation."[27]

Law cannot impose the language of command or principle or theory on life. It can neither foreclose nor constrain interpretation with its wordiness. As Fish instructs us, any rule for interpretation of a text is itself a text requiring interpretation.

We live in a time in which it becomes daily clearer that anything can be said about anything. The aging rulers of China said nothing happened in Tiananmen Square. Ronald Reagan said nothing happened in the White House. There is no necessary correspondence between any word and any real thing, between our words and realities external to us. The word *peacemaker* may refer equally to Jesus or Jimmy Carter or the MX missile system. Nihilism is a distinct possibility. If any text can be deconstructed, if self-interest can be read in any statement of values, if anything can be said about anything, perhaps nothing meaningful can be said at all. And then Lear would be right: Nothing will come of nothing.

In literature, art, and music, however, there is that other possibility Steiner directs us to, the possibility to which he clings: a creative presence who reinsures meaning and holds us against the void. It is a possibility impossible of proof. But it does happen in art, this miracle of meaning and transcendence and therefore of life rather than nothingness and death.

What limits this possibility in law is that we write and read law on the very different assumption of absence. That is why we try to get everything on the page and to leave nothing to the imagination. And, as I say, this may be an appropriate and necessary—if finally impossible—undertaking.

There is afoot just now an attempt to nudge law toward art, to open its language to the possibility of transcendence and creative vitality found in literature, art, and music. It is an attempt to do law on the assumption of a real presence.

The most recent move in this direction can be dated to 1973 and the publication of James Boyd White's *The Legal Imagination*. What gained some acceptance from White's performance, and from subsequent performances by others as well as White, is that law as a form of rhetoric may be an art, that a lawyer may make something new out of the existing language of the law by the power of imagination, that a lawyer may be a writer, really a writer.

That idea and practice—if it needs a label, call it the law and literature movement—helped prepare the way for, or is coming to fruition in, or is properly being overtaken by, recent work of minority legal scholars, feminists, and people of color, whose medium is stories.[28] They write chronicles, parables, myths, and autobiographies.

Their stories expose readers to the felt effects of law and therefore to something of the nature of law: on being, as a black woman, an object of property;[29] on being, as a Japanese-American, hurt by constitutionally protected speech;[30] on being a minority member of a white law faculty;[31] on being a member of an Indian tribe ground down by the individualism that has overtaken equal protection jurisprudence.[32]

These stories fix for the reader much that law and law school have left out. They give expression to the experience of exclusion and give voice to those on the bottom who have not been heard. I do not mean that these stories are tools of access to information as though they are language-instruments that convey to a reader certain objects from a real world that exists outside of or apart from language. I do not mean that they are illustrations of universal truths. I do mean that they are real stories, that they create worlds, characters, and experiences to be re-created in good readings in response. They are literature, and, wonderful to say, they are appearing in law reviews and law books.

They challenge the law and the legal academy as presently constituted. Their authors are engaged in a new form of legal scholarship.[33] The presently dominant form of legal argument in the academy is that of social science. It is linear and coercive. It strings together propositions that lead to a conclusion that must be either accepted or rejected.[34] Something on the order of "just say no," but folded in upon itself and elaborated many times over. It is the form death takes in academic legal discourse.

The arguments of stories told by feminists and scholars of color are of a different order. They do not coerce us into agreement. They lead to recognition, the way Hamlet's play caught the conscience of the king. They do not try to say everything. They leave much to the imagination. They are deliberately open-ended. They "generate a pressure toward the inexpressible."[35] They invite the King Lears of the academy to hear the Cordelias and to attend to the heart that cannot be heaved into the mouth.

They justly claim that they are examples of legal scholarship, but scholarship that invites us, with their authors, to wager on a real presence underwriting their meaning. They would have life read in law.

RESISTANCE OF LAW

I greet this new departure with hope and good wishes for success. But also with reservations.

The development I have described is taking place in the *legal academy*. I am uncertain about how it will continue to play there. I am more uncertain about how it will play outside the little world of law school in the bigger worlds of law practice and litigation and legislation.

One of the strengths of the movement is that it returns to a central element of law. Lawyers have customarily been storytellers. More important, law depends fundamentally on story for its meaning and legitimacy. But there are limits.

O'Fallon and Ryan believe that, in the abortion cases, the voices of many women—their stories—are not heard: "If the experiences of women were articulated in court as they are now being heard in the streets, they would reflect the realities of poverty, abuse, isolation, and ignorance, as well as the aspiration for accomplishment and independence."[36]

But then they add a qualification: Telling in court the stories of embattled women may be a waste of time, because, in order for those stories "to be meaningful, the court must possess the capacity to hear [them]. . . . The crucial question . . . is whether the court is capable of opening itself in this sort of way."[37] About that, O'Fallon and Ryan are uncertain, and so am I.

Let me illustrate by returning to Willie Francis and Felix Frankfurter. The story of Willie Francis was eventually told to the justice.

Here are the essential elements of that story:[38] Willie was fifteen years old at the time when he was accused of murder. He was the child of an impoverished black family in Louisiana. The year was 1945. The victim was a locally popular white man. The jury was all white and male. Trial began on the morning of September 12. The temperature was ninety-eight degrees. By September 14, the jury had reached its verdict, and the judge had imposed sentence. Willie Francis had no counsel until six days before the hasty trial began. His attorneys' performance was, at best, perfunctory. The trial took place close by the murder scene in a racially and emotionally charged context, but counsel made no motion for change of venue. No attack was made on the questionable indictment. No evidence of any sort was introduced on the defendant's behalf. There was no motion for a new trial. No appeal was taken. Willie Francis was never informed he had a right to appeal.

When the state tried but failed to kill him and set the date for a second attempt, he then received the help of different and able lawyers, Bertrand DeBlanc and, before the Supreme Court, Skelly Wright, who would later become a federal judge.[39] They told his story to the Supreme Court. It was well told. But it was not well heard.

In his opinion Felix Frankfurter wrote that the botched first execution had been an "innocent misadventure."[40] In light of that statement, Wright and DeBlanc filed a *habeas corpus* petition that brought the case and the story before the Court one last time. (They had already filed a petition for rehearing that had failed.) DeBlanc had discovered additional circumstances about that innocent misadventure and a witness. The witness said the executioners were so drunk it was impossible for them to know what they were doing. The story about that first attempt at electrocution was supplemented. What the Supreme Court was now told ran in essence as follows.[41]

When the drunken executioners threw the switch and tried to generate more power, Willie Francis's nose began to flatten on his face, and in a short while was so flat it was impossible to detect he had a nose. His lips began to swell until they were several times larger than normal. The current was left on for about three minutes, during which time he was conscious and suffering pain so great that it caused him to jump and kick, lifting the entire 250-pound electric chair as much as six inches off the floor. The chair finally came to rest a quarter turn from its original position. The witness said it was the most disgraceful and inhumane exhibition he had ever seen.

That was the retold story of the innocent misadventure. Still Frankfurter did not hear and did not puke.

My point—and O'Fallon and Ryan's—is that stories may nudge law toward art and transformation, but stories require good listeners as well as good tellers if they are to have effect. Willie Francis's story did not find a good audience in the majority of the Supreme Court. Stories cannot gather willing hearers among us if we do not have ears to hear. Stories cannot entice nongamblers to wager on a real presence.

This is the limit to the power of stories in law and is the cause for my reservation about the potency of current story-telling in the legal academy. I do not disparage my profession or the office of storyteller by recognizing this limit, which I construe as counseling realism when we assess the origin and extent of our craft's power.[42]*

POSSIBILITIES FOR OTHERNESS IN LAW

But if the worlds words generate and the freedom acts yield are parables of the Word, if aesthetic meaning and political justice witness God's venture with us, there must be hope for law. For if the Word is initiating presence, our predication of absence in the wordiness of law cannot be controlling. The giving up and resignation we express in legal thought forms and texts are not dispositive. The presence who contends with us in art and politics is transcendent and cannot be excluded from law, resistant though law may be. The question is what to look for and where.

Judicial Review

The received wisdom suggests judicial review as promising evidence of a transcendent other, Justice Frankfurter to the contrary notwithstanding. However, I have grown uncertain about the potential of judicial review as a site of research for encounters with the Word.

Contracts, statutes, codes, constitutions, and common law precedent may be invitations from their authors to litigants and judges to join in deciding what they mean. This may be generally true; for example, common law precedents are less a limit on judges than they are a representation of possibilities for decision. It may also be particularly true; for example, the Uniform Commercial Code Section 2-302 provides courts with flexibility in the enforcement or nonenforcement of a contract if they find it "to have been unconscionable."

This is to leave the subject deliberately open to judicial development. Such invitations to join in creating law may constitute the same kind of open-endedness that in literature provides access to otherness. In this event, courts may represent an inherent openness of law to transcendence.

I belong to a generation particularly susceptible to the investment of courts with inherent capacity for transcendence. My young adulthood was spent in the years of the Warren Court. The Supreme Court, federal district courts, and a few state courts in the South were—sometimes— places where law was viable, where people new to the experience were addressed as human beings, where the voiceless were given a voice, where truth was spoken to power. I assumed courts were naturally, necessarily theaters for performance of the American commitment to human dignity. For this reason, I, like many others, became enamored of theories of judicial review that supplied a rationale for viewing courts as the protectors of discrete and insular minorities. I believed in these theories and wanted to believe in them so deeply that it required a long time for the bleak education of the Burger and finally the Rehnquist courts to teach me the error of such beliefs. As the Court now increasingly understands itself—returning to the lawyerlike and conventional that has dominated its history—the judiciary in a democracy leaves protection of the dissentient and the oppressed to the political process. We may catch occasional glimpses of otherness in the judiciary, but not because courts are its natural, necessary habitation.

Judicial review belongs to an institutionally closed loop. It is a complement to the legislature's power to amend or repeal its statutes. Judicial review may tighten or expand the loop, but has the office of keeping it politically and substantively closed. As one metaphor would have it, the law is to be kept a seamless web. Or, in another, law is a chain novel for which judges write successive chapters; the story is to remain internally coherent, is to remain a chain.[43] New departures, when they occur, represent either the failure of the office or the exception. The institutionalization of interpretation in the judicial branch of government establishes an enforced monopoly not found in literature, art, and music. It ensures that the state is the final arbiter, that the loop remains closed. We tend to want it that way. It is designed to keep anarchy at bay and violence off the streets.

The Other Than the Case

There are times when otherness breaks in, but not because of a native capacity of law. *Brown v. Board of Education,* the Court's great case beginning school desegregation, was part of a transcendent moment. The story of African-Americans was heard, and first the Court, and then the Congress and the president, responded. But to think equality for African-Americans is the consequence of American law's disposition to justice, to think it the natural, inevitable outgrowth of a "living" Constitution, is to embrace a civil religion in which the Constitution is a sacred document ("the supreme law of the land" in every sense), the Supreme Court justices are chief priests, and academic lawyers like me are staff theologians. This religion, too, can be adopted by the Word. And has been. The point is that adoption has to take place.

Brown is a particular instance of the mighty achievement and animating goal of equality. But it is critical to remember its circumstances and how recent and fragile a phenomenon it is. Not until almost a century after its adoption did the Constitution include provision for equal protection. After equality entered the Constitution, almost another century passed before the nation became effectively committed to it. More recently the commitment has been losing purchase in the Court and the society before it has been sufficiently realized to prevent regression. To whatever extent the commitment has been realized, extragovernmental intervention has been necessary. Only by selective revision can the story be made a congratulatory tale about the power of American law to work itself pure.

Constitutional equality depends on a history that includes the lives and extraordinary labors of many people. One is Frederick Douglass. Douglass's break with the Garrisonians followed from his conversion to the view, as historian William McFeely describes it, "that moral suasion was clearly not enough and that politics was precisely the arena in which slavery should be fought."[44] The Union's dissolution would allow slavery to continue unimpeded in the southern states. Because abolition required the Union, he would have to affirm the Constitution. To affirm the Constitution, he would have to construe it as an antislavery document promising equality. To do that, he would have to tell an American constitutional story that embraced African-Americans. The solution to this political-rhetorical problem lay in a language that would register with his audience and allow him both to embrace and to reject the constitutional facts.

The Declaration of Independence was a means to this end. By beginning with the Declaration and its commitment to equality, Douglass could characterize the black freedom movement as placing no "new consideration upon the public" and as no more than an "endeavor to carry out the great fundamental principles of American government."[45] So, in his famous speech of 1852, "What to the Slave is the Fourth of July?" he applauded that day's celebration—the celebration of freedom and of the Declaration with its "saving principle."[46] Then he juxtaposed the story of slaves in the United States: Next to the Declaration's words on equality he placed the fact that Americans held in "bondage . . . a *seventh part* of the inhabitants of your country."[47] The irony was judgmental and supplicative. Douglass's conclusion that the "Fourth of July is *yours, not mine*" was a searing plea to make it his as well.[48]

However commonplace this might seem to us now, now that we have grown accustomed to talk of constitutional equality, at the time it was surely quixotic, as *Dred Scott v. Sandford*[49] soon made clear. The Supreme Court would not give the Constitution a Douglass-like reading. Taney agreed with Garrison to this extent: The Constitution was a slavery document.

Lincoln's Gettysburg Address may have helped as much as anything to make the Douglass version of the American constitutional story eventually canonical. The method of that address is instructive.[50] Like Douglass, Lincoln returned to the Declaration of Independence and bypassed the Constitution. His opening, "Fourscore and seven years ago," is a type of the fairy tale's introductory "once upon a time." It is also a reference, not to 1789 and the adoption of the Constitution, but to 1776 and the Declaration of Independence. In that beginning the nation had been dedicated to the "proposition" about equality.

Lincoln distinguished the nation he said was begun in the Declaration and dedicated to equality ("that nation") from the presently existing one ("this nation"). There was a gap between them, realized in the field at Gettysburg, where the struggle for their meaning took place. Faith was necessary. Lincoln's word was "dedication." He used it five times. The nation was "dedicated" to equality; he had come to "dedicate" the cemetery; the living are to be "dedicated" to the great task remaining. Dedication is a way of trying to make sense of discrepancy by both setting apart and committing oneself, by giving up and binding. With dedication, from the cemetery there would come a "new birth of freedom." The method and movement are those of Mark.

The Address, like some of Lincoln's actions, made it clear that, instead of attempting to make the Constitution cover the gap, as it could not, the Constitution would be set aside. U. S. Grant straightforwardly noted that the Constitution had not been allowed to impede or restrain the government and was "in abeyance for the time being, so far as it in any way affected the progress of the war."[51]

The Constitution brought back into play after the war was a different Constitution, changed by the Fourteenth Amendment's addition of equality to the text. Although the text had changed, the oppressive reality faced by African-Americans was not radically different from what had gone before. And then *The Civil Rights Cases* of 1883[52] and *Plessy v. Ferguson* in 1896[53] raised questions about how much the text had been changed.

Eventually the Court did come around to the view that the equality added to the Constitution was to be introduced into the society as well. The judicial stance taken by the Taney Court was abandoned and from 1938 "until the 1960's, when a political consensus favoring civil rights again emerged, the courts stood virtually alone in articulating and enforcing the law of race discrimination."[54]

In 1922, Charles Garland, a Harvard undergraduate who chose not to accept his share of the estate left by his millionaire father, announced: "'I am placing my life on a Christian basis,' and gave $800,000 to establish a foundation."[55] The Garland Fund made a grant of $100,000 to the NAACP to undertake a legal campaign to gain the rights of blacks in the South. The NAACP's first Supreme Court victory came in 1938 in *Missouri ex rel. Gaines v. Canada*,[56] in which the Court held that a state's refusal to admit blacks to its law school was not saved from an equal protection challenge by the state's provision of financial support to blacks to attend out-of-state law schools. The path thus opened led to *Brown* in 1954.

Some had doubted the efficacy of mounting such a campaign. It was certainly not clear in the 1920s that equal protection arguments would have much effect. As late as 1927, Justice Oliver Wendell Holmes referred to the Equal Protection Clause as "the last resort of constitutional arguments."[57] Attorneys arguing equal protection to the Court would have been admitting the abject weakness of their cases. Moreover, the NAACP attorneys who eventually prevailed with the arguments did not pursue and could not have pursued a single, grand equal protection strategy. Instead they seized upon targets of opportunity and conducted their campaign "on terrain that repeatedly required changes in maneuvers."[58] The role of African-Americans in World War II and the altered demands of foreign relations lent support to their cause.

Brown was a watershed for the Court and the country. But more than the decision and the Court and the law and school desegregation is required to leap from Constitutionally supported slavery to the Fourteenth Amendment's equal protection to a society in which African-Americans are full participants. The Civil War was needed for the entry of equality into the Constitution, and political action in the streets was needed for its entry into society.

In the 1960s blacks did not seek and could not have found room in the white world as it was still constituted. The white world, like that of blacks, had to be transformed. Blacks did not simply march into the white world. They remade the white world and their own with their marches. In the process they reconstituted the streets, the D.C. Mall, and Mississippi jails as public, political forums.

Human dignity for African-Americans is no more the product of the original Constitution or the originally constituted legal system than the Exodus was the expected outcome of Pharaoh's law. From Frederick Douglass and Harriet Jacobs to Gettysburg and Abraham Lincoln to Martin Luther King, Jr., Robert Moses, and Rosa Parks, such equality as blacks enjoy—and it is far from assured—has come about because equality was discerned where it was not, and justice intervened through supplication. Such events are indications of the Word breathing the life and hope into law that the dead letter of law does not bear within itself.

It is to be expected that the unfinished work of justice for African-Americans—like the justice for women, poor people, and Native American tribes that has yet to be begun in earnest—will be a theater for further signs and wonders. Perhaps litigants, attorneys, and courts will discover new instruments for renewal if equal protection jurisprudence has reached the limits imposed by its association with individualism and assimilation.[59] Fresh departures are to be anticipated.

THE BEGINNING

Steiner observes that "the best readings of art are art."[60] The authoritative readings of Homer are Virgil's *Aenead* and James Joyce's *Ulysses*. The most telling interpretations of plays are performances of them on stage: "In respect of meaning and of valuation in the arts, our master intelligencers are the performers."[61] This is so because, unlike vivisecting reviewers, literary critics, and academic commentators, "the executant invests his own being in the process of interpretation."[62]

Steiner's point is to be extended: Telling enactments do not take place only in theaters or subsequent works of art but also, richly, in encounters with others, in the art of politics, including law. That is why my own research has been shifting from exclusive reliance on the law library and from too-great fascination with theories of judicial review to the lived lives of lawyers, legislators, judges, and others laboring in law. They are the master intelligencers from whom to learn: Henry Schwarzschild in the struggle for human rights, John Rosenberg in eastern Kentucky, Margaret Taylor in landlord-tenant court in New York, David Harding on the Warm Springs Reservation, Tim Coulter directing the Indian Law Resource Center, Steve Wizner in the clinical program at the Yale Law School, Carla Ingersoll in the New Haven train station, and many others like them. Those most deeply engaged in life are most likely to be engaged by the Word present in the midst of life; among them are parables most likely.

IN PERFORMANCE

The life given law may be found in the lives of its performers. Their stories say how and why. There is no substitute for attention to the particulars in discerning the Word taking form. Simply repeating the stories with which I began would therefore be a fitting way to end. What I have said in the meantime supports, if nothing else, sympathetic appreciation for practitioners—for who they individually are and what they independently do. They speak for themselves. That is why I placed them first. They have priority.

Moreover, it should be apparent that they are likely to disagree, in some cases fundamentally, with what I have said in the intervening chapters and with what I read in their work in the law. I cannot make them lie down neatly together with each other or with my way of thinking about them. I cannot perform an intellectual equivalent to sardine canning. There are too many heads, fins, and tails that do not fit. And, because they are very much alive, the subjects keep jumping out whole.

If I have not given my depictions as illustrations or allegories, neither are they intended as models, as though these practices are exact patterns to be copied line for line with no room for doubt and disagreement. Neither individually nor corporately do they make a statement about the necessary and sufficient conditions for the power of the Word in law.

To be found here are analogies, types, clues, possibilities, rather than illustrations or models. Discernment of the Word in the lives of women and men does not deny their individual integrity but affirms it. I would not look through them, as through the words of a text, for some other, higher reality, as religion would have us do. Participants in the Eucharist are not exhorted to believe their way *through* the elements and action of that sacrament but to discern the body *in* them.

I conclude, then, with only a few notations of the commonalities which, together with the individual diversity of these people, suggest the Word taking form as I have been schooled for such nonreligious discernment by Isaiah, Mark, Barth, Bonhoeffer, Stringfellow, Faulkner, Morrison, Steiner, Moses: meaning from nothing, freedom from bondage, power from weakness, justice from injustice, a beloved people from those who were neither beloved nor a people, a presence from absence, life from death.

The following are simple observations about the obvious. It is important that they be so. There is not something hidden to be uncovered by special insiders' knowledge. You, like some of these people, may disagree with me. Our disagreement, however, should not be about the arcane but about what to make of the obvious and easily available. I intend my reflections to be indicative, with the hope that they will be openings rather than closings.

Poverty

The tribal members David Harding worked and played with and judged on Warm Springs Reservation, the clients who find Steve Wizner and Carla Ingersoll through Yale's clinical program, the tenants who make their way to Margaret Taylor's court in lower Manhattan, the tribes advised by Tim Coulter, the people of Appalachia joined by John Rosenberg—all are poor.

What these clients do not bring to law, the practitioners do not take from it. None makes much money from doing law. (Tim Coulter even raises money elsewhere in order to be able to practice.) Some are financially pressed. If there is reward in their labor, it is primarily that of satisfaction or joy: John Rosenberg's pride in the people around him and his thankfulness for the alignment of his principles with his life; Margaret Taylor's "you sleep well at night." Henry Schwarzschild has been worn out more than once. He would never don one of those buttons with a smiley face. The happiness of these people in their engagement with law is not shallow, cheap, or sentimental. It is not a question of feeling good about themselves. Their exuberance is that of self-giving, as with Baby Suggs in *Beloved* and Robert Moses in a Mississippi jail. They go to work, as did Dilsey in *The Sound and the Fury*, with resolution and expectancy but without anticipation of wealth.

Karl Barth drew from the biblical stories one of their plainest testimonies: "Almost to the point of prejudice [God] ignored all those who are high and mighty and wealthy in the world in favour of the weak and meek and lowly."[63] Contemporary secular literature and the newspaper give no reason to suppose that this almost-prejudice has been shed. Poverty and self-giving rather than power, wealth, and self-aggrandizement still constitute the likely sites for gathering evidence of the Word taking positive form.

Poverty does not guarantee the presence of the Word. The qualities of God rather than the characteristics of the poor account for God's favor of them. "God loves the poor by preference," Gustavo Gutierrez says, "not because the poor are good persons, better than others, or good believers, better than other believers, but because God is God."[64] God chooses to make the poor bearers of His presence. Advocacy of their cause is the likeliest place to look for signs of the Word in action.

Much current law practice will therefore present itself as an unpromising field for research. Graduating law students with the proper credentials may be offered starting salaries, as I have noted, of $72,000 and up (add an inflation factor by the time this is published). Senior partners in large law firms make many times more. Their offices are decorated with lavish ostentation. No cathedral is so richly appointed as the offices of a typical, successful, large law firm I recently visited. The elevator opens onto a two-story reception area. Visitors find themselves before a painting that stretches up most of the height of the two stories. Basically white and gold and dramatically lighted, it is an abstract work that conveys the feeling of—symbolizing the firm's self-image?—gold pouring down from heaven. The receptionist's desk at the foot of the painting, forward of the base a few feet, is fixed in the position of an altar. The aura is that of power and religion in conjunction, not of the Word in law.

The possibility of signs and wonders, however, cannot be categorically excluded from such venues. Although I have not written about the exceptions, they do exist. An example—Harry Wachtel—is to be found in Taylor Branch's book *Parting the Waters*. Wachtel was the lawyer for a conglomerate built by perfecting leveraged buy-outs. He heard Martin Luther King, Jr., speak and asked for a meeting with him. Branch reports that "Wachtel's reputation as a business predator made him an unlikely sympathizer for King, but he disgorged a capsule life history in a confessional tone. He was a Jewish shopkeeper's son, he said, and as a college radical in the late 1930's had vowed to use his law degree for the downtrodden. But things had not turned out that way, and he had worked, as he put it, 'not on the side of the angels.' The cruelest irony for him was that his conglomerate . . . owned several of the chains whose segregated lunch counters still were the targets of sit-ins in the South." Wachtel said he "was resolved to recapture the idealism of his youth"; he would resign and "make a splash." But King advised against leaving "a spot like that for a flare" and proposed instead that "Wachtel could help the civil rights movement more where he was than out on the street."[65] Wachtel took the advice, became an important legal adviser to Dr. King, and created a foundation to support the movement's work. It was Wachtel who "knew how to get high government officials on the phone and how to touch corporate officers for five-figure donations."[66]

Wachtel, drawn into the civil rights movement, may be taken as some evidence of the freedom of the Word to be positively present even among the law's mighty predators. But Wachtel is the exception. And he put his position into service of the poor.

Community

Although lawyers have traditionally been thought of as officers of the court, the bar association's new Rules of Professional Conduct describes them now as "officers of the legal system."[67] The human, communal referent has been dropped in favor of a faceless, abstract, bureaucratic one: "the system." This change in language reflects or may constitute a revision of law practice.

Where law is a medium of community, lawyers' professional responsibility lies in developing, curing, and sustaining the communities of which they are members. And a primary method of legal education is some form of apprenticeship. A person learns to do law by observing its practitioners on location in their settings and by herself becoming a member of communities and engaging, as a lawyer, in the establishment and renewal of the web of responsible relationships.[68]

Where law is conceptual, it is detached from an informing, human community. Instead of a service, it is a business that markets work products. It does not have to be learned within any nexus of community responsibilities, for the only relevant connections are those that hold an abstract system together from within. Law like that can be taught in schools by teachers who need exhibit no binding whatsoever to any community save the theoretical community of scholars. What students may then perceive in law school exemplifying legal practice is institutionally mandated forms of high gossip among strangers. And law, instead of expressing and maintaining community, may then become a tool for shoring up the status quo.

The people I presented in chapter 1 are not depersonalized representatives of an impersonal system. They characteristically belong to communities and aid in the creation and protection of communities. Steve Wizner leads the Yale clinical law program—attorneys, students, and clients—as though it is an extended family and as though law extended the embrace and responsibility of a family. So does Carla Ingersoll, although still a student, make law both protect the homeless and connect them to other students in the law school.

In the midst of high-rise chaos in lower Manhattan, Margaret Taylor creates from her courtroom and the halls outside her courtroom the order of a community of concern and care. And she is continually trying to reform the system and her colleagues so that the people behind the pleadings will be heard. David Harding, both outsider and insider, worked very hard to participate in the tribal community of Warm Springs at the most fundamental level and to allow his judging to express the tribes' best sense of justice. Tim Coulter's vocation is to cause law to protect the communal life and practices of Indian peoples.

John Rosenberg is devoted to the communal, even family, bonds of Appalred. He was instrumental in the creation of the David community. He helped bring Kentuckians for the Commonwealth into being and nurtures its staff of young people; the location of their headquarters in a home suggests the familial quality of John's attorney-client relation with them. He is immersed in the life of Prestonsburg and in the irrepressible insistence that law serve all members of that community.

Individuals count in these instances. This is not a contradiction of community but a realization of it. When Margaret Taylor concentrates attention on the one tenant before her, when Steve Wizner teaches a student the importance of devotion to the single client, and when William Stringfellow gave that devotion to Ramon, they do not thereby undermine or deny communal responsibility. They enact it. Between the judge and the party before her, between the attorney and the client, there is a kind of friendship that is an embodiment of community.

That relationship is, moreover, a kind of appeal to the larger community about its nature, an invitation to affirm its essential character. Henry Schwarzschild's work against the death penalty is instructive in this latter regard. Schwarzschild's identification with Martin Luther King was certainly an act of community. So is his campaign against capital punishment. Except in the instances of people who were innocent in fact and wrongly convicted, prisoners sentenced to die have done terrible things. In opposing the death penalty, Henry is not taking up their cause as criminals. No argument against the death penalty can be made from the acts committed, and rarely, if at all, from the personalities and lives of the convicted. Like King's appeal, Henry's argument is drawn from the nature of the body politic and is addressed to the community's better self.

The Eighth Amendment to the Constitution prohibits the infliction of cruel and unusual punishment. That it does so is a statement of who we are as a people and who we aspire to be. We, the people of the United States, ordain and establish a community that rejects cruelty, even or especially to the least member. If we had not done so, we should have, for the sake of the kind of people we choose to be. Opposition to the death penalty does not require pretending that perpetrators of horrible crimes are anything other than criminals who must be punished in some way. It does require renouncing killing in cold blood, as much wrong for the community as for the individual: We are not that kind of people. It is a form of supplication asking that the community be in fact what it aspires to be. Henry's work has everything to do with community, or it makes no sense at all.

Communities are the ground and goal of Henry's engagements with law, as they are of the law practices of Steve, Carla, Margaret, David, and Tim. For that reason, their work may be described as a kind of Aristotelian politics. Aristotle believed the *polis* to be the form of community that is "the best of all the forms for a people able to pursue the most ideal mode of life."[69] Politics is then the activity of the *polis*, the pursuit of the best form of community.

Such politics is what Paul Lehmann has in mind when he argues that God's action in the world is aptly described as politics, as forming authentic human community. Lehmann points out that the biblical stories are told in political images: the gathering of a people, the bringing in of a kingdom, the coming of a messiah, etc. God is portrayed as doing politics.[70] The discernible outcome of this activity is a redemptive *polis,* a redemptive city or community, characterized by the deliverance of the poor.

Specific communities of faith proceed from the vocation to be anticipatory experiments in the most authentic modes of life. They are indicative of the Word at work in the world. The people of Israel, the disciples of Jesus, Dilsey's community drawn toward Easter, and Baby Suggs's community of the beloved in the Clearing are express types of the politics of redemption. The practices of law I have described, in their enactment of community characterized by deliverance of the poor, are secular types of the same politics.

Professionalism

These practitioners are experts. They are good at what they do. They are lawyerly. This is so in important part because they are constituted and oriented by communities. The reciprocity of their relationship to clients complements and enhances their proficiency.

The professionalism Steve Wizner demonstrates himself and demands of his students begins with close commitment to the person who is a client; clients are not to be objectified, and lawyers are not to gain distance from them. That Carla Ingersoll slept on the train station floor to be with her homeless clients was a function of her professionalism and not the least element in her success.

Because they are his friends, the traditional Indians Tim Coulter represents have led him to become the country's leading expert in the black letter of old treaties. In order to become a good judge, David Harding became a good friend of the Warm Springs tribal members. The friendship Margaret Taylor creates between herself and the parties before her is the expression of her skill as a judge and not its denial; in protection of that friendship and the possibility for it, she deploys statutes and common law precedent professionally and effectively.

Henry Schwarzschild is a skilled advocate for abolition of the death penalty. I do not think Henry has met the people on death row. He is certainly not the pal of any. He is less their advocate than he is the advocate of those who would end capital punishment. In this sense he might be aptly identified as speaking for America's better self. He would likely say, more simply and elegantly, that he is the advocate of principle. Although Henry cannot be made to fit comfortably in the present discussion, he does not necessarily stand as a contradiction to its point. He is very good at what he does, and his professionalism may be read as a function of his community responsibility.

The communal nature of these practices, including the investment of the person of the lawyer, supports their lawyerly quality. This circumstance runs counter to expectation because professionalism is identified with impersonal detachment. (Even as I write this, I have received an invitation to speak at a forum whose sponsors ask "that you distinguish your personal opinions from your professional ones"—as though, like Felix Frankfurter, I could or should.)

Surgeons, it is said, should not operate on those they love because they would lack distance and so might make false moves or bad decisions. The knife is supposed to be surer, steadier in the hands of the dispassionate.[71] For the same reason, it is thought that lawyers should not represent those to whom they are close because, lacking remove, they might provide bad counsel or the wrong kind of advocacy. A detached, hired gun is supposed to shoot more effectively. The purchaser of such services wants success rather than enthusiasm and friendship.

Such professionalism is disembodied and random, and its quality becomes dependent on fees, the interest of the task, competitiveness, or institutionalized duty enforced by threats of malpractice suits and disbarment. These are unreliable guarantors. Perhaps that is why the supreme court of Georgia, concerned about the state of things, directed all attorneys under its jurisdiction to submit to an hour of instruction in professionalism as part of the annually required twelve hours of continuing legal education. Because there is uncertainty about what constitutes professionalism in a vacuum, the course I took—I did enough time in a single sitting to cover three years—was an outrage. It featured a lecturer who taught us the kind of handshakes, telephone manner, upscale clothing, highly polished glass/brass/wood office decoration, classy waiting-room magazines, and expensive personal automobiles we should have in order to convey to clients the aura of success and therefore of competence.

The people I have written about do not require external stimuli or contrived imagery to be proficient. They are tied to their clients or the parties they are to judge by the mutuality of friendship, but the services they render are not the less professional. Indeed, the professionalism is an expression of the friendship and the community involvement of their work. This extension of the communal in the professional is another encouragement to read their work as parabolic of the Word.

Religion places God beyond what can be reached by humans. Correspondingly, it may undermine craft and the care of culture. The religious assumption is that God is to be found in what humans cannot accomplish and do not know; good intention and subjective energy are supposed to give the individual exit velocity and carry him toward God beyond the limits of the actual and the communal. But then sincerity and high feeling may count as compensation for performance lacking in discipline. They may even count as a preferred substitute: the less formal, the more authentic.

The Word, however, does not take up where form, structure, and human ability end, as though it inhabited the interstices of incomplete, inadequate capacities or inhabited realms beyond them. The living, present Word underwrites aesthetic meaning and political justice; it is present in the midst of life and not the periphery, in its structure, not its chaos. To say that the Word became flesh is to say, among other things, that it was made manifest in a particular time and place. It was revealed as having form. The humanity of God is not theoretically, abstractly universal but contextually, specifically human. It takes form and embraces culture.

Robert Frost noted that Jeremiah's sincerity has been questioned "because the anguish of his lamentations was tamable to the form of twenty-two stanzas for the twenty-two letters of the alphabet." But form is of the essence of the Word, as it therefore is of the realization of human freedom and passion. "The Hebrew alphabet has been kept to the twenty-two letters it came out of Egypt with," Frost added, "so the number twenty-two means as much form as ever."[72] Like the Lamentations, prophecy's accomplishment of form—its carefully wrought poetry, its development of lawsuit rhetoric, its professionalism—is the bearer of authenticity and not its contradiction. The artfulness of Mark—the effectively crafted structure—is critical to its substance. Discipline and learning are not despised but nourished.

From what the text of *The Sound and the Fury* presents of Rev. Shegog's Easter sermon, the reader may conclude that the preacher was making deliberate, technically skillful use of his body and of rhetorical devices and that he was giving a trained virtuoso's performance with the instrument of his voice. He began talking like a white man and then took an African-American voice. On this basis to disqualify his sermon as a medium of the Word would be to make a false and religious assumption. It would assume that the Word is inchoate, universal, formless, and therefore only vaguely human. In the event, Shegog's craft is the occasion for the Word's accessibility to Dilsey and her congregation.

In the hands of the skilled practitioners I have talked about, law is made a means for giving expression to the grievances and hopes of people whose voices have not been heard. There is every reason for such practitioners to tend and perfect law and to become accomplished in its use, because law is made a medium of their friendship. They take the language as it is found and make it realize meaning and justice in present communities. In the process the received culture is transfigured and transmitted to the next generation for that generation's own realization of meaning and justice. This is professionalism as a function of the personal and communal and, as such, a political activity of the Word. It is a formation of practice by the humanity of God that makes law animate.

Tension

Proficiency in law comes entailed. Law is not a neutral, benign tool that can be picked up like a hammer and discarded without effect.

John Rosenberg is a supplicant in many ways and much of the time, but when he engages the power of the courts or the power of the legislature on behalf of his clients, he is engaging in a use of force that is certainly not supplication. Mine safety ought to be vigorously pursued. But there is no way to pursue it through law that does not engage the violent power of the state. Requiring small operators to adopt safety measures that drive them out of business is the use of force.

Margaret Taylor is daily engaged in deploying the power of the state. She orders people to appear in court. She orders the transfer of money from one party to another. She orders the eviction of tenants. Granting remedies to landlords or refusing to grant them is an exercise in institutionalized force.

When Tim Coulter wins a judgment that certain lands in New York are the property of one of the Six Nations, he protects the tribe, but he is invoking the force of law against present non-Indian occupants. David Harding brought a greater measure of protective due process to the Warm Springs tribal court, but in doing so he was drawing the alien ways and law of the established powers into the life of the reservation. Steve Wizner is a loving teacher and committed to the creation of a better life for oppressed people, but he is teaching law students how to use the power of the state.

Such instances of the use of force may be easily justifiable and demonstrably praiseworthy. These wielders of power do not act in their own behalf but on behalf of the powerless. Their actions are well intentioned. The uses of force are not mindless or programmatic and tend, admirably, to the episodic. Furthermore, they are particular instances of counterforce—that is, they are fundamentally defensive maneuvers against overwhelming systemic violence.

All these things and more can be said by way of approval or exoneration, if any were needed, but none changes the fact of the events as deployments of the force of law with its background of death. John Rosenberg may ensure that the poor people of Appalachia have a fair fight in court, but it is still a fight. Margaret Taylor may see to it that poor tenants have a hearing in her court, but their landlords do not lend their ears uncoerced. Steve Wizner teaches responsibility, but it is responsibility in the use of power.

American law is a language, an institution, a way of thinking, a mode of organizing life and living together. To become proficient in its use affects the person, often positively. An education in law can certainly be as elevating as an education in any of the humanities. Archibald Macleish proposed that law, like poetry, allows its students to envision "the interminable journey of the human mind."[73] A legal education may also have immediately useful impacts. A student of mine said law had made him a better mechanic. It helpfully changed the way he looked at an engine, analyzed it into constituent parts, and solved the problems of its malfunctions.

But this is also one of the curses of legal education: calculation, the isolation of life into discrete moments and discrete problems to be solved, the resulting sense of omnicompetence. In the famous observation of Thomas Reed Powell, if "you can think about something which is attached to something else without thinking about what it is attached to, then you have what is called a legal mind."[74] Such attachments as we are trained to think about are those internal to the profession. Anything ground into the processes of law is reduced to legally cognizable terms. I still think of an advertisement for a *Medical Atlas for Attorneys* that touted its value for the lawyer:

> More than 2000 drawings expose the entire anatomy—structure by structure from skin to skeleton. . . . Every part of the body is keyed with citations to cases, awards, ALR annotations, and other references which take you directly to the relevant law.[75]

Attorneys are taught to see body parts attached to cases and awards of money damages.

We speak an institutional language fabricated of cliche and label, abstraction and rule. The people who appear in cases are plaintiffs and defendants, p's and d's, lacking human dimension. Partly this is the problem of any profession: A medical atlas for physicians will differ from one for attorneys only by keying body parts to a different argot. Partly this is the limitation of any language: Martha Minow observes that "our minds—and probably our hearts—cannot contain the whole world, and so we reduce the world to short-hand that we can handle."[76]

The effect that the shorthand of law has on the lawyer is therefore a shared and not a singular phenomenon but is especially acute because legal words work so directly and forcefully on the world. They are the power of the state backed by death. The biblical stories repeatedly warn that touching unclean things renders the person unclean. "He who touches pitch shall be defiled." It is impossible that there is not something of Felix Frankfurter in every lawyer. To touch the law is to be touched by its force.

Nor can lawyers avoid legitimating that force. When they are admitted to the bar, lawyers take an oath, in one form or another, that they will uphold the law. Even their presence, like that of the chaplain on the *Bellipotent* in *Billy Budd,* sanctions the system. John, Margaret, Steve, David, Carla, Tim—and Henry, too—cannot avoid being "officers of the system" after all.

To profess the law is not mean. American law is a great, wonderful achievement of Western culture. Much good and much justice have been done with it. Much more will be done. There is every reason for lawyers to render it the endorsement of their person.

But American law has also done much evil and will do more. This is not carping. There is a fundamental, troubling issue here obvious to victims of the legal system but almost invisible to others. William Stringfellow noted how "the American legal system . . . has seemed to me—a white, middle-class, Harvard-educated lawyer—to be civil and fair,"[77] so that any suffering caused by the legal system could be accounted for as aberrational. But Stringfellow then wondered how it must appear to blacks and others for whom "the law, in a quite overwhelming sense, . . . is now, as it always has been, an enemy: a harasser, an invader, an oppressor."[78]

To the extent that victimization is the fruit of shortcomings or failures, it can be cured by shoring up the system. Enforce the law. Where, however, the law itself is the problem, enforcing the law only aggravates the wrong. This is so, for example, in the bearing of the law of equal protection upon Indian tribes. Equal protection jurisprudence has been the great engine of assimilation of minorities into the protection of the constitutional reality. However, assimilation into the jurisdictional monopoly of the American Constitution destroys rather than benefits Native American tribes. The noble achievement and aspiration of equality is, at the same time and without abandoning its goodness and nobility, destructive of tribes. To enforce the beneficial law of equality is wrongly to terminate the tribes.

Under such conditions, critique of law has limited value at best. I am unsure that critique could unravel equal protection beneficial to many minorities from equal protection threatening to the tribes. Even if it could, any critique may only add scope or legitimacy to the thing under scrutiny. I think, for example, of the response to a cigarette advertisement that came to be known as the "Pajama Man" ad. It depicts seven white, well-to-do people: five young women, an older man, and a young man. The setting is airy, white-walled, with CD player, paintings, and a table set with white tablecloth, white china, silver, and four bottles of wine. The young women and older male, all expensively dressed, are seated at table, pausing between courses to smoke. The young man is in the background, clad only in pajama bottoms, his pelvis thrust forward. It is a scene of privilege and fakery. The ad is incoherent except as a—to me deeply offensive—celebration of life, art, sex, women, and wine as and only as objects of consumption. A well-taken assault on it was published in the pages of *Arts Magazine*.[79] The article was accompanied by a reproduction of the ad. Reproducing the ad was the only way the critique could be meaningfully carried out. However, it recirculated the offense and gave it a wider audience. That is the dilemma of criticism.

One version of the dilemma in law is to be found in the law reviews, where critique may not only reproduce the offense but may also lend it legitimacy. Robert Cover observed that the academic lawyer who publishes criticism of court opinions may no more than serve the reality she protests: "Officialdom may maintain its interpretation merely by suffering the protest of the articles."[80]

To write jeremiads against the Supreme Court for the harm it causes may not alleviate and may only exacerbate the injury.[81] The same may be said of an act like that offered by Harry Wachtel, who was prepared to resign his job with the company that was parent to a chain of stores with segregated lunch counters; and of an act like the one Henry Schwarzschild puts before audiences: Refuse to continue representing a person sentenced to the death penalty and walk out of court. Such actions may have no effect on the system and may only justify the decision of others to remain supportively within it. These steps may well be called for and may be the correct choices in given circumstances. They certainly cannot be dismissed. But even they—like any form of critique—will not finally disentangle the lawyer from the thing in law protested. They will not purchase her purity of heart. Nor will they disentangle the good in American law from the evil.

Perhaps disentanglement is as unnecessary as it is impossible. Dietrich Bonhoeffer's life is an example. After the failure of the first attempted coup d'état against Hitler, Bonhoeffer and other members of the resistance concluded that "opposition that took seriously its aim to stop Hitler had to make sure of possessing the instruments of power through which alone he could be restrained."[82]

This conclusion led to a radical change in strategy, for up until then Bonhoeffer had been on the watch for people who would refuse obedience to Hitler publicly and so be dismissed from their posts. "There now came a period when it was of the utmost importance that people of character should remain at the controls in all circumstances and not allow themselves to be displaced. That meant that what had hitherto been a question of character now became a mere bagatelle—a greeting with the Hitler salute, for instance. Instead of refusing this, one had to see that it meant nothing if by it one could get into key positions. That meant that the use of camouflage became a moral duty."[83] To get the necessary power meant getting a foothold in the central Nazi apparatus and maintaining contact with people of questionable character. "Someone had to take on the shady business. And if he, Pastor Bonhoeffer, was not called on to be one of those directly involved, it could at least be his business to set their consciences at rest."[84]

Bonhoeffer could discern the Word at work within the German secret service in the gathering of power to do away with Hitler. If the Word was actively present in Pharaoh's Egypt and Pilate's Jerusalem, it could not be ruled out of Nazi Germany. And cannot be foreclosed from

American law, which is not the law of Egypt or of Rome and certainly not that of Nazi Germany.

There is a duality here, a tension between yes and no, that is an irresolvable paradox in intellectual analysis but is commonly found in experience, where it does not forestall action and may be something more like the usual accompaniment to responsible choice. Stringfellow, from his own perspective, found law to be civil and fair but knew it did not appear so to the people he served in East Harlem. Because of the harm law did, he lived with the question of whether he should resign from the bar.[85] That tension arose from his practice and kept him responsibly, effectively at work.

Mari Matsuda urges that attention be paid to those who have been victimized by law. It is what she calls "looking to the bottom."[86] This is not a hypothetical or abstract exercise but an examination of "the actual experience, history, culture, and intellectual tradition of people of color in America."[87]

What emerges from the "bottom," she reports, is the duality that Stringfellow noted and that I have been addressing. From her own experience and that of others she concludes that one can simultaneously affirm and repudiate American law and that it may be necessary to do so. Those victimized by law believe they "have a right to participate in society with any other person" at the same time they believe "rights are whatever people in power say they are."[88] So were Japanese-Americans embittered when the Constitution did not protect them from incarceration during World War II, but were nonetheless committed to the Constitution. "From behind barbed wire in America's concentration camps, young . . . Nisei volunteered to fight in World War II. They spilled their blood on the beaches of Italy and France because of their faith in American constitutionalism and their demand for recognition as citizens."[89]

The tension gave life to the law: "If trust in the Constitution sustains Japanese-Americans in their uphill battle against racist oppression, then the Constitution for them has become a radical document."[90] In their struggle, those who suffer by law remake and so animate it. This is to follow the precedent of Frederick Douglass in simultaneously striving against and for the Constitutional reality.

The same enlivening of law emerges from the tension between Margaret Taylor's belief that law oppresses the poor and her courtroom action in giving justice to the poor. And from the tension between Tim Coulter's despair about the effect of law on the tribes and his successful practice on their behalf. And from the tension between Henry Schwarzschild's knowledge that capital punishment will not be ended and his continued campaign against it. And from the tension between

David Harding's flunking out of law school and his becoming a judge; and between his being fired as a judge and his continuing commitment to law and to service. And from the tension between John Rosenberg's knowledge that only 3 percent of black lung cases are successful and his continuing to bring them.

So does law come to life. This is not a propensity of law or lawyers, neither of which is naturally tolerant of gaps and disturbances. As Steve Wizner and Carla Ingersoll would hold, into law like this you are pushed, or pulled. Or both.

Annie Dillard writes this: "This Bible, this ubiquitous, persistent black chunk of a best-seller, is a chink—often the only chink—through which winds howl. . . . We crack open its pages at our peril. Many educated, urbane, and flourishing experts in every aspect of business, culture, and science have felt pulled by this anachronistic, semi-barbaric mass of antique laws and fabulous tales from far away; they entered its queer, strait gates and were lost."[91]

ACKNOWLEDGMENTS

THE UNIVERSITY OF GEORGIA Humanities Center and its director, Bernard Dauenhauer, together with the University of Georgia School of Law and its dean, Ronald Ellington, provided grants and time needed to write this book. Both institutions and both people are due hearty thanks.

Obviously I owe much to the people whose stories I have written. The story of Roy Herron, a lawyer and state legislator in West Tennessee, does not appear here. I am nonetheless grateful to him and his family. He, like those whose stories do appear, was long-suffering, open, and uncommonly generous. Watching Roy, Henry, John, Margaret, David, Tim, Steve, and Carla work was a rare privilege.

At the beginning of this book, I took note of the education Native Americans have offered me. In addition to David and Tim, Cecil Corbett, Vine Deloria, Robert Williams, and Les Ramirez have been principal teachers. Symposia on the relationships between theology, law, and the tribes that Cecil and Vine arranged are published in the January/February 1985 and September/October 1988 issues of *Church & Society*.

I also noted the conversation with Robert Cover, too soon cut off. The Cover Study Group, sponsored by the Society of American Law Teachers, and the Cover Conference on Public Interest Law provide occasion for extending in different forms the care he took for people and for justice. The organizers of and participants in those two ventures, some of whom appear in these pages, have importantly shaped my approach to law for the last several years.

As was further registered at the beginning, precedent for studies in law and religion has been set by recent work of others; the text and notes will have provided some indication of my indebtedness to this work. In fact, my education by others and my dependence on them are extensive. And this is so not only in theology and law, and not only in subjects of scholarly inquiry. I want to be explicit about this fact, both to serve full disclosure and to bear witness to the communities who have made the present experiment possible and urgent. To the extent that the dialogic character of my enterprise is not already obvious, I wish to make it so; what follows is not a review of generally relevant work but an attempt to leave a clear trail of particular dependencies.

My happiest, longest-running indebtedness is to June Ball: to the clarity, imagination, and serenity in her art; to her courageous determination to follow—no matter the fashion—her inspiration; and to her keen, intolerant eye for pedantry. For not quite so long a time I have been challenged and nourished by Paul Lehmann, as is apparent from the fact that I have seldom found it possible to write without reference to him and his work. And Coleman Barks has for decades shared freely his rich insights and given my manuscripts close, wonderfully helpful readings.

James Boyd White, in his writing, in conversation, and in acts of friendship, has opened many possibilities for me. It is symptomatic of his generosity of spirit that this book found its way to a publisher through him. Public record of my dependence on him began with my assessment of his book *The Legal Imagination* (1973), published in *University of Chicago Law Review* 44 (1977): 681. Further evidence of it is recorded in "Confessions," *Cardozo Studies in Law & Literature* 1:2 (1989): 185.

In that same piece, I also note (and second and amend) the invitation to robust theological dialogue issued by another practitioner of studies in law and literature, Richard Weisberg. See his "Accepting the Inside Narrator's Challenge," *Cardozo Studies in Law & Literature* 1 (1988): 43–44, 46 n. 15. My choice of a title for this book may have been influenced to some extent by White's *When Words Lose Their Meaning* (1984) and Weisberg's *The Failure of the Word* (1984), the latter of which may be read as a critique of Christendom.

A common interest in the relation of law and the humanities provided my introduction to James O'Fallon. Some material that has found its way into chapters 5 and 6 was first presented as the Colin Ruagh O'Fallon Memorial Lecture at the University of Oregon School of Law and published by that school's law review as "Death and Life in American Law" (*Oregon Law Review* 69 [1990]: 779–95, © 1990 by University of Oregon). The law review is due thanks for its permission to republish the piece, although it has been given substantially different form. That lecture was offered as a tribute to O'Fallon and in memory of his son. O'Fallon's contagious example of courage and of affirmation of life in the face of death emboldened me to undertake reflection on the presence—but also the penultimacy—of death in law.

An early, first take on the results of that reflection were presented to the students and colleagues of Bruce Rockwood at Bloomsburg University. He and they graciously extended hospitality and encouragement to continue the experiment.

The interest in the relation of law and the humanities that I share with O'Fallon also provided my introduction to Aviam Soifer. I first met Aviam at a conference on Faulkner where he delivered a splendid paper, subsequently published as "Listening and the Voiceless," *Mississippi College Law Review* 4 (1984): 319. That paper sent me back to Faulkner and may be what eventually led to the reading of *The Sound and the Fury* presented in this book. More recently, his own work prompted a symposium in which I was a participant. The proceedings are published in *Washington & Lee Law Review* 49 (1991): 381. In between there have been other symposia in which our work is juxtaposed. See *Georgia Law Review* 20 (1986): 811; *Connecticut Law Review* 21 (1989): 849. These publications reveal little of the much good done me by his friendship, by his scholarship, and by fruitful conversations with him and his wife, the filmmaker Marlene Booth. He introduced me to some of the people who appear in these pages and to many of the ideas I wrestle with. When I first imagined this book, I had thought it would begin with the sentence: "Aviam Soifer had called." As I have noted, his telephoned invitation to inaugurate the Cover Study Group was the proximate cause of the research for a central portion of the book. (An article drawn from my work for that session was published as "Law and Prophets, Bridges and Judges," *Journal of Law & Religion* 7 [1989]: 1. Some portions of the article are to be found in a different form in chapter 4; I thank the editors of the journal for permission to use them in this way.) There is an authentic community of scholars, and Soifer is a genuine exemplar of it.

As is Carol Weisbrod, also a fellow traveling symposiast. See, for example, the Connecticut and the Washington and Lee symposia cited above. Conversations with her invariably set me off in new, productive directions, looking for the unexpected where only she knows surprises are to be found. I depend on her work, her habits of thought, and her penetrating, teacher's mind. (Her dean, Hugh Macgill, in addition to his supportive interest in my work, has gently nudged me into lines of inquiry that I would otherwise, wrongly, have failed to pursue.)

Professor Weisbrod is a member of that community of women who have helped make this a fascinating time to be a teacher of law and who have made reading law reviews almost a pleasure. Included in that same company are Martha Minow, Betsy Clark, and Judith Resnik. Professor Minow's work I cite in text and notes, a small indication of a larger dependence. The work of professors Clark and Resnik is not cited, but they, too, are among those responsible for my education and this book. My indebtedness to Minow, Clark, and Resnik is personal as well as professional.

So is my indebtedness to Emily Fowler Hartigan. I have not been able to accommodate all of her criticism of a manuscript of this book, but her comments saved me from error and forced me to reconsider some basics. Her "Parabolic Jokes and the Unknown Law," *Capital University Law Review* 20 (1991): 73, gives a sense of our conversation and of the instruction that, I am thankful to say, she continues to offer. She is one of the modern scholars who have insisted on the relevance of religion to law. See, for example, her affecting performance of that relevance in

"The Power of Language beyond Words: Law as Invitation," *Harvard Civil Rights–Civil Liberties Law Review* 26 (1991): 67.

There is an impressive array of other scholars who share with Hartigan a concern for the connection of law to religion. I am dependent on many of them. Two of the patriarchs (the reference is to stature, not age) are Harold Berman and Thomas Shaffer. A bibliography of Berman's writings in law and religion is to be found in *The Weightier Matters of Law* (1988), a collection of essays (including one by me) offered in tribute to him. Although my interest lies in theology and his chiefly in religion and the history of relationships between religion and law, his example of risk-taking has been an inspiration. His *The Interaction of Law and Religion* (1974) must have earned him the undeserved suspicion of colleagues; it was written at a time when the subject was not included on the list of studies thought legitimate for academic lawyers. His writing helped to change the climate of opinion.

No small responsibility for beneficial change belongs also to Thomas Shaffer, another risk-taker. The brief mention I make of him in the text provides no hint of his great influence in such books as *On Being a Christian and a Lawyer* (1981) and *Faith and the Professions* (1987). Nor does it reveal my considerable indebtedness to him. Portions of this book formed the center of discussions he invited me to hold with his students at Notre Dame in the spring of 1991. (One of his students, Marty Loesch, was good enough to send me his own extensive comments, which helped reshape the text.) Professor Shaffer's kindness in arranging this occasion repeated his similar kindness in arranging a colloquium in 1984 organized around the manuscript for an earlier book of mine. His comments on that work, together with the criticism of the other colloquium participants, are to be found in *Journal of Law & Religion* 3 (1985): 141. His comments on another book of mine are published in *Christian Legal Society Quarterly* 4:1 (1983): 36. All along the way he has provided support, criticism, collegiality, and friendship. Few could understand as well as he how I have followed his lead, if along a different path. I can set this book in relation to work of his by noting that, insofar as I have here made confession of both my belief and my community formation, I have made response to central concerns of his about how believers are to be lawyers. What he commends, I have tried to do.

Others within the Roman Catholic tradition who have made contributions to the relevance of religion for law include Robert Rodes and John Noonan. Their publications have served me well in classes I have taught.

In *The Authoritative and the Authoritarian* (1986), Joseph Vining ventured the proposition—more risk-taking—"that the practice of law today is most like the practice of theology" (p. 187). My response and a hint of my indebtedness to that elegant volume are set out in a review in *UCLA Law Review* 35 (1988): 547. Obviously, I have found his invitation to a rapprochement with theology irresistible. My acceptance of this invitation has been greatly aided by other work of his and by his friendship. Several years ago, when I had not thought to do it and would have shrunk from the task if I had, he urged me to bring the Barthian insight to law. And recently his close reading of a manuscript for this book proved indispensable. (I have not been able to answer all the questions he raised.)

Both Kent Greenawalt and Michael Perry have supported a place for religion in political discourse. Greenawalt's carefully reasoned case is presented in *Religious Convictions and Political Choice* (1988). "Obligation: Not to the Law But to the Neighbor," *Georgia Law Review* 18 (1984): 911, is a response of mine to an earlier entry of his. A conversation with him during a lengthy car ride several years ago helped immeasurably to clarify my thinking about how theology could be said to bear upon law. Long conversations, similarly helpful, with Michael Perry complemented my reading of his books. My introduction to a symposium on one of his books is a sign of my high regard for his work and our conversation. See "Michael Perry and the Sign of Better Times Ahead," *Tulane Law Review* 63 (1989): 1283. I took the opportunity of a later symposium, at which he was the principal lecturer, to begin formally setting out my understanding of Barth. I did so in important part conscious of the need to state my own Protestant heritage over against the moral philosophy and Roman Catholic theology that informs his work. His paper, adapted from his subsequent book *Love and Power* (1991), my paper, and criticism of my work by David Gregory and Oliver Thomas—fellow, valued laborers in the vineyard—is published in *Capital University Law Review* 20 (1991): 1. (Although that paper of mine is not reproduced here, there is some correspondence between portions of my remarks then and some paragraphs of chapter 2. I thank the law review for permission to give sections of those remarks a second, if very different, life.)

The recent work of Alan Freeman and Elizabeth Mensch has taken a thoughtful turn toward theology. Their "The Politics of Virtue: Animals, Theology, and Abortion," *Georgia Law Review* 25 (1991): 923, recognizes some basic, contemporary legal controversies as theological controversies. Along the way to encouraging conversation across the divide of these controversies, they provide a useful summary of recent theology. Their presentation of Barth and Bonhoeffer is remarkably apt and especially welcome.

I have argued that something of the biblical tradition is to be discerned in the work of other critical legal scholars even when theological issues are not to be read on the surface of their work. See my review of *The Politics of Law* (1982) in *George Washington Law Review* 51 (1983): 309. See also my pressing of theology in "Don't Die Quixote," *Texas Law Review* 59 (1981): 787, in which I level criticism at Mark Tushnet. I was indebted to Tushnet's work at the time and have become more indebted to it since. A brief conversation with him after my paper to the Cover Study Group convinced me of the necessity to think through some of the issues addressed in this book. In "The City of Unger," *Northwestern University Law Review* 81 (1987): 625, I undertook an appreciative but critical theological assessment of Roberto Unger's work. Although there is no public record of it, I have been helped in my understanding of the theological potential of critical legal studies—and correspondingly of my own position—by Jay Feinman.

Robert A. Burt published an interpretation of the parables that I have cited and discussed in the notes. This article is all the more stunning because it is a sensitive exegesis of Christian texts accomplished from his own grounding in the Jewish tradition. A thread running through his writing is his concern to give voice to the voiceless. His work was the focal point of a symposium that includes comments of mine and is published in *Washington & Lee Law Review* 42 (1985): 1. His comments on an earlier book of mine are published in *Theology Today*, October 1986, p. 451.

Thomas Grey and Sanford Levinson have importantly raised the issue of constitutional law as civil religion. I have cited here the writings of both and continue to rely on their insights. Professor Levinson's *Constitutional Faith* caused me to think through more carefully the relation of theology to the profession of constitutional law. Some idea of the stimulus of his work can be read in my review of his book in *Michigan Law Review* 87 (1989): 1438. What cannot be read from that review is the influence of continuing conversations with him and with my students about his work. (Grey's work has been part of the same sessions with my students.)

Professor Levinson was on hand when brief portions of a manuscript for this book were presented to a faculty symposium at the University of Texas School of Law. I am grateful for my reception on that occasion, for the responses of participants, and for Michael Churgin's arrangement of it. Professor Churgin read into the manuscript above and beyond the call of duty and offered helpful suggestions. I am grateful also to Zipporah Wiseman, another participant then and in earlier conversations.

The *Michigan Law Review* that put me onto Levinson's *Constitutional Faith* later included me in a unique long-weekend work session on legal story-telling that resulted in the symposium published in *Michigan Law*

Review 87 (1989): 2073. Some of the thoughts embodied in chapter 6 began to take shape then. More important, that event brought me into contact with people—the other participants—who have worked major changes in my approach. Conversation has continued with Derrick Bell, Richard Delgado, Mari Matsuda, and Steven Winter. Professor Winter is not only a productive writer but also a tireless, thoughtful commentator on manuscripts. My reference to Matsuda near the end of the last chapter will serve as a small illustration of the larger education I have received from her. A better illustration is my assessment of her work, along with that of Professors Bell and Delgado, published as "The Legal Academy and Minority Scholars," *Harvard Law Review* 103 (1990): 1855. An editor encouraged me to drop from that piece a citation to Barth on God's preference for the poor. The editor thought the issue of minority scholars in the legal academy had nothing to do with theology. I insisted the citation be left intact, for reasons that should be clear to readers of this book.

Kevin Kennedy, the talented editor-in-chief of the *Michigan Law Review* who conceived and oversaw that session on story-telling, has subsequently died of AIDS. Another, equally promising former law review editor-in-chief, Jay Spears of Stanford, is also dead of AIDS. He, like Kevin, had worked with me on a law review article in a way that made publishing an unexpectedly rewarding delight. There is great and grievous loss in their deaths.

Joseph Singer and Patricia Williams were not present at the Michigan session, but pieces of theirs were included in the resulting publication. They and their work have figured in the reflections that produced this book. The publications of Drucilla Cornell, Allan Macurdy, and Thomas Ross, as well as correspondence or conversations with them, have also been influential.

The *Journal of Law and Religion,* centered at Hamline University, has been uniquely supportive of theological studies in law. I am personally as well as professionally indebted to the editors of that journal for their work: Michael Scherschlight, Marie Failinger, Patrick Keifert, and Howard Vogel, especially Professor Vogel. Howard has been a leading and important voice in the field, and conversations with him on the bearing of theology upon law have provided direction, correction, and inspiration.

Professor Vogel is not alone in doing theology in law. Frank Alexander, who also teaches and publishes legal-theological studies, has lent his imagination and energy to the Council on Religion and Law. Indeed, the council and the gathering interest in law and religion are, in important respects, the fruits of his labor. This book would not likely have come to be without his example and the years of friendship in which we have wrestled with theological subjects. Four other exemplary theologians in law whose scholarship has worked its way into these pages are Ed Gaffney, Fred Gedicks, Andrew McThenia, and John Witte.

Anthony Chase is an accomplished scholar of many subjects within and without law, including theology and popular culture. Comments of his on manuscripts of mine have challenged me to discover more adequate means for addressing Barth. He has ranged widely in his thinking and reading and is able to deploy his learning collegially in the form of apt, provocative criticism. He, like the others whose help I acknowledge, bears no responsibility if, in spite of warnings, I have persisted in error or offense.

Any lawyer had best exercise great care in taking up theology and biblical criticism. For a long time, Horace Allen, Philip Lee, and Alexander J. McKelway have tried to keep me informed and orthodox. Lapses cannot be blamed on them. At McKelway's instance, I was invited to deliver the 1986 Otts Lectures at Davidson College. Those lectures and the research that went into them appeared to me at the time to contain the possibility for a book. That book was displaced by this one in no small part because Professor McKelway pressed me with the need to do an ontology of lawyering. Such a project is quite beyond me, but reflecting on Sandy's urging helped give rise to these pages. He and his wife, Babs, are forever linked for me and my wife with fresh, sustaining memories of the excitement—the music—of theology in Barth's Basel.

Others who have helped me with theology and biblical studies are Ted Lewis, Patrick Miller, and Tim Polk. This brief note of thanks is wholly disproportionate to the time and care of their generous, close attention.

At the University of Georgia, there are communities of scholars, undetermined by departmental boundaries, who have read and commented on manuscripts for me, introduced me to ideas and scholarship, and included me in their ongoing conversations. Those who have played particular roles in the formation of this book are—in addition to those already mentioned—Celeste Condit, Betty Jean Craige, Margaret Dickie, Jim Kilgo, Nancy Rubin, and the monthly Interdisciplinary Study Group; and within the law school, Robert Brussack and Ellen Jordan. I am profoundly grateful to these colleagues for their direct and indirect contributions to this book and for much else besides. Readers of books by my colleague in political science, Lief Carter—for example his *Contemporary Constitutional Lawmaking* (1991) and his *An Introduction to Constitutional Interpretation* (1991)—will understand how dependent I have been upon him, his work, and his friendship. He has been an instructive example for years.

The University of Georgia is the locus of a community of

coconspirators that is something like a family and is certainly the matrix for work like this book. Some of its members I have already named. Four so far unmentioned are Bertis and Katherine Downs and William and Mary McFeely.

Would that others have such friends.

Paul Lehmann once remarked how dogma is that which one generation chooses to pass on to another about what it has found to be essential. This book is a personal entry in partial fulfillment of the responsibility for dogmatics that Paul taught me and that he continues to exemplify.

NOTES

∽∼∿∽

CHAPTER ONE

1. Henry refers to Berea College's "significant abolitionist history." In *Berea College v. Kentucky,* 211 U.S. 45 (1908), the Supreme Court upheld a Kentucky statute that prohibited "white and colored persons" from attending the same school. Berea was fined $1,000 for violating the statute.

2. Robert Stevens, *Two Cheers for 1870: The American Law School,* Perspectives in American History series, vol. 5 (Cambridge: Harvard University Press, 1971), pp. 416–18.

"Rules of admission and preparation were probably nowhere rigorously administered." Lawrence Friedman, *A History of American Law,* 2d ed. (New York: Simon and Schuster, 1985), p. 317. "After the Civil War, the trend toward laxity was reversed" (p. 654).

The Spooner quotation is from the *Worcester Republican,* Wed., Aug. 26, 1835.

Thanks to Carol Weisbrod for the cites.

3. Alexis de Tocqueville, *Democracy in America,* ed. Richard Heffner (New York: NAL-Dutton, 1956), part 1, chap. 12, p. 126.

4. Aviam Soifer has drawn my attention to the Yiddish term *Zitsfleisch*—"the people who sit through to the end."

5. Samson Occom, "Sermon Preached at the Execution of Moses Paul"; attached to Jonathan Edwards, *A Short Account of the Late Spread of the Gospel among the Indians* (1788), p. A3.

6. 319 West 48 St. Realty Corp. v. Slenis, 458 N.Y.S.2d 153, 155–56 (N.Y. City Civ. Ct. 1982).

7. Id. at 155.

8. Id.

9. Id.

10. S.P.S.G. Inc. v. Collado, 448 N.Y.S.2d 385 (N.Y. City Civ. Ct. 1983).

11. Cited in letter by Judge Taylor to the *New York Times,* Thurs., Mar. 19, 1987, sec. A, p. 26, col. 4; discussed below.

12. S.P.S.G. Inc. v. Collado, 448 N.Y.S.2d at 386.

13. Id. at 387.

14. Consolidated Edison Co. of N.Y. v. Branley, Index No. 041263/88 (Civ. Ct. of the City of N.Y., Special Term Pt. II, Jan. 10, 1989).

15. Id. at 3.

16. Id. at 7.

17. See *New York Times,* supra note 11.

18. Hayman v. Pacht, 108 Misc.2d 622, 438 N.Y.S.2d 207, 209 (Sup. Ct. 1981).

19. Tom Goldstein, "Spiegel Takes Lead in Surrogate Race," *New York Times,* Wed., Sept. 18, 1976, p. 29, col. 6. She won the Democratic primary, tantamount to election. She was endorsed by the *New York Times* "because of her litigation experience and scholarship." *New York Times,* Sat., Sept. 11, 1976, p. 18, col. 2.

20. *In re P.,* 92 Misc.2d 62, 400 N.Y.S.2d 455 (Fam. Ct. 1977).

21. *New York Times,* Sun., June 18, 1979, sec. B, p. 8, col. 1.

22. *In re P.* at 460.

23. Id. at 469.

24. In re Dora P., 418 N.Y.S.2d 597 (Sup. Ct. App. Div. 1979). The juvenile was also charged with robbery and assault for taking the complaining witness to a hotel room where, with three companions lying in wait, she stole thirty dollars from him. Judge Taylor first adjourned the hearing on these charges and then dismissed them because P. had been denied a speedy trial in violation of the law. The appellate court reversed this decision as well. By the time the appeal was heard, P. had been placed in a foster home and had then disappeared. On the equal protection issue, the reviewing court held that there had not been a sufficient showing of intentional selective enforcement. And on the due process issue, it held that no right of privacy had been offended.

25. David Harding, "Law, Theology, Culture, and Social Reality," in *Church & Society,* Sept./Oct. 1988, p. 56.

26. Ibid., p. 61.

27. Vine Deloria, Jr., and Clifford Lytle, *The Nations Within: The Past and Future of American Indian Sovereignty* (New York: Pantheon, 1984), p. 213.

28. Robert T. Coulter, "The Moral Crisis in Indian Law," *Church & Society,* Jan./Feb. 1985, p. 24.

29. See Oneida of Thames Band v. State of New York, 771 F.2d 51 (2d Cir. 1985).

30. Vine Deloria, "American Indians and the Moral Community," *Church & Society,* Sept./Oct. 1988, p. 28.

31. Christopher Stone, "Culture and the Law," *Church & Society,* Sept./Oct. 1988, p. 53.

32. Ibid., p. 54.

33. Robert T. Coulter, "A History of Indian Jurisdiction," in National Lawyers Guild, Committee on Native American Struggles, ed. and comp., *Rethinking Indian Law* (New York, 1982), pp. 5, 6.

34. "'. . . the United States Is Violating International Law!'" *Akwesasne Notes,* Summer 1978, p. 28.

35. Robert T. Coulter, "The Failure of Indian Rights Advocacy: Are Lawyers to Blame?" in *Rethinking Indian Law,* p. 51.

36. 1980 Report, pp. 2–3.

37. Indian Law Resource Center, *Indian Rights—Human Rights* 3 (1984).

38. *Akwesasne Notes,* Summer 1978, p. 28.

39. Jerome Frank, "Why Not a Clinical Lawyer-School?" *University of Pennsylvania Law Review* 81 (1933): 907, 913.
Another more recent teacher/judge, Richard Posner, has a somewhat different view. Without conventional legal training, he writes, "a tedious apprenticeship would be required to equip a person to practice law and would not do as well. One should recognize, however, the similarity of conventional legal training to the apprenticeship system that preceded and for a long time coexisted with it. The immersion in judicial opinions and other legal materials that is the hallmark of a legal education provides the student from the outset with a simulacrum of practice; he is like an airline pilot training on a simulator." R. Posner, *The Problems of Jurisprudence* (Cambridge: Harvard University Press, 1990), p. 99.

40. Frank, "Why Not a Clinical Lawyer-School?"

41. Jerome Frank, "A Plea for Lawyer-Schools," *Yale Law Journal* 56 (1947): 1303, 1304.

42. Ibid., p. 1313.

43. Ibid., p. 1344, n. 104.

44. J. Bradway, preface to "A Handbook of the Legal Aid Clinic of the University of Southern California" (1930), p. ii.

45. Frank, "A Plea for Lawyer-Schools," 1303, 1321.

46. Aviam Soifer remembers the "mentors," now his good friends, and their "supervising." According to Soifer, "those were the days when student power was an issue. When Steve and Denny were brought in for interviews as faculty prospects, we who were students in the clinic were suspicious of them. Denny, after all, was a graduate of the U.S. Naval Academy and had held a Southeast Asia ship command. When they joined the faculty and directed the clinic, we would ask for help on a case and they would say: 'Don't ask me, I'm not a Connecticut lawyer.'"

47. Conn. Supreme Court, case no. 13796 (1990).

48. 214 Conn. 256, 571 A.2d 696 (1990). A single dissenting justice would have upheld the trial court.

49. See "Catholic Order Is Helping Homeless in New Haven," *New York Times* (national edition), Jan. 20, 1991, p. 17, col. 1.

50. L. E. Browne, "Esther," in *Peake's Commentary on the Bible* (New York: T. Nelson, 1962), p. 381.

51. That session produced, among other things, a fruitful law review article by Carol Weisbrod that focuses particularly on Vashti. See Carol Weisbrod, "Divorce Stories: Readings, Comments, and Questions on Law and Narrative," *Brigham Young University Law Review* (1991): 143.

CHAPTER TWO

1. In order to draw on Barth's insights for an audience of lawyers, Elizabeth Mensch and Alan Freeman had to fill in the blanks of modern developments in Roman Catholic and Protestant theology. They provide a handy account of Barth. See Elizabeth Mensch and Alan Freeman, "The Politics of Virtue: Animals, Theology, and Abortion," *Georgia Law Review* 24 (1991): 923.

2. George Hunsinger, *How to Read Karl Barth: The Shape of His Theology* (New York: Oxford University Press, 1991), p. 27. The title of this fine volume may prove misleading; it is not a "how to" book for beginners but a sophisticated, complex attempt to organize analysis of the dozen books of Barth's *Church Dogmatics*.

3. For recent work that displays Barth's influence and pays tribute to him, see Alexander J. McKelway, *The Freedom of God and Human Liberation* (Philadelphia: Trinity Press International, 1990); Hans Küng, *Theology for the Third Millennium: An Ecumenical View*, trans. Peter Heinegg (New York: Doubleday, 1988); Philip J. Lee, Jr., *Against the Protestant Gnostics* (New York: Oxford University Press, 1987).

4. The text for the seminar was an early portion of the section in which Barth takes up the subject of ethics under the rubric of the command of God (2 *Church Dogmatics*, part 2, pp. 562–630). Barth addresses the command of God as the starting point for ethics. Here and elsewhere, he is careful to relate the command of God to God's grace and forgiveness: "Openly or secretly (but, as a rule, openly), its imperatives stand on its indicative" (p. 562).

"The Ten Commandments . . . are not independent and cannot be separated from this antecedent [of what God has already done for Israel]. They receive and have from it their specific content. . . . In content each of the commands reflects and confirms the fact that Israel is this people, the people created and maintained by these acts of God. *Thou* shalt! means, *Israel* shall! and everything that Israel *shall* is only an imperative transcription of what Israel *is*, repeating in some sense only what Israel has become by God, and what it must always be with God" (p. 572). (This may explain why, in Christian liturgy, the Decalogue is appropriately read following the celebration of the Eucharist.)

Notwithstanding Barth's dialectic care in elaborating the command of God, it seemed to me then and seems to me now that, with equal dialectic care, the grace and forgiveness of God rather than the command of God ought to be elaborated as the starting point for ethics. My disagreement with Barth proceeded from Barthian premises. If, as Barth demonstrated, Jesus Christ is constitutive of theology—that is, if theology begins and ends in the revealed Word— theological ethics takes its origin from the ultimacy of God's revealed grace, mercy, and forgiveness. Ethics is then indicative or descriptive rather than prescriptive. The foremost example of such an ethics is Paul Lehmann's *Ethics in a Christian Context* (New York: Harper and Row, 1963).

5. William Stringfellow, *A Public and Private Faith* (Grand Rapids: Eerdmans, 1962), p. 18.

6. See the assessment offered by Dietrich Bonhoeffer, "Protestantism with-

out Reformation," *Gesammelte Schriften,* vol. 1 (Munich: Chr. Kaiser Verlag, 1965), pp. 323, 354.

7. Stringfellow, *A Public and Private Faith,* p. 14.

8. Ibid., p. 41.

9. Herman Melville, *Billy Budd Sailor and Other Stories,* ed. H. Beaver (New York: Penguin, 1970), p. 399.

10. Ibid., p. 405.

11. Harriet Jacobs, *Incidents in the Life of a Slave Girl: Written by Herself,* ed. Jean Fagan Yellin (Cambridge: Harvard University Press, 1987), p. 68.

12. Ibid., p. 270, n. 1.

13. Ibid., p. 68.

14. Ibid., p. 69.

15. Ibid., p. 74.

16. Ibid.

17. See, for example, the histories of United States/tribal relations recounted in Francis Paul Prucha, *The Great Father: The United States Government and the American Indians* (Lincoln: University of Nebraska Press, 1984), and William McLoughlin, *Cherokee Renascence in the New Republic* (Princeton: Princeton University Press, 1986).

18. "Letter from the Birmingham Jail," in Martin Luther King, Jr., *Why We Can't Wait* (New York: New American Library, 1964), pp. 77, 96.

19. Page citations are from William Faulkner, *Light in August,* with an introduction by Richard Rovere (New York: Modern Library, 1950).

20. Barth, 1 *Church Dogmatics,* part 2, p. 328.

21. Barth, 4 *Church Dogmatics,* part 2, p. 450.

22. Centuries later the religious-construction impulse still finds expression. It drew the attention of Martin Luther King, Jr., who observed in the white South "the anesthetizing security of stained-glass windows" and "massive religious-education buildings" and wondered what had happened to their builders' "voices of support when bruised and weary Negro men and women decided to rise from the dark dungeons of complacency to the bright hills of creative protest" ("Letter from the Birmingham Jail," pp. 94, 95).

23. On Dietrich Bonhoeffer's understanding of nonreligious interpretation and of religion, see Eberhard Bethge's *Dietrich Bonhoeffer: Theologian, Christian, Contemporary,* ed. Edwin Robertson (London: Collins, 1970), p. 774.

24. Barth once remarked: "Jesus Christ does not fill out and improve all the different attempts of man to think of God and to represent Him according to his own standard" (1 *Church Dogmatics,* part 2, p. 308).

25. Barth, 1 *Church Dogmatics,* part 2, pp. 302–3.

26. Barks's observation immediately rang true, because in fact I had felt that the spines that run up Mount McKinley, as well as the outlying ridges and valleys

we explored, were external reflections of interior places inviting self-discovery. The interplay between things inside and things outside put me in mind of lines from two Robert Bly versions of Kabir ecstatic poems:

> Inside this clay jug there are canyons and pine mountains,
>   and the maker of canyons and pine mountains!
> All seven oceans are inside, and hundreds of millions of stars.
> . . . .
> If you want the truth, I will tell you the truth:
> Friend, listen: the God whom I love is inside.

Robert Bly, ed., *The Kabir Book: Forty-Four of the Ecstatic Poems of Kabir* (Boston: Beacon Press, 1977), poem no. 5, p. 6.

> Thinkers, listen, tell me what you know of that is not inside the soul?
> Take a pitcher full of water and set it down on the water—
> now it has water inside and water outside.

Ibid., poem no. 4, p. 4.

The god inside is the attractive strength, but also the treachery, of religion.

27. In explaining why he climbs mountains, Art Davidson explains that "there are mountains in all of our lives. Whether we climb the earth's highest peaks, hike in gentle hills, or explore the metaphysical ranges of the psyche, most of us are drawn by the archetypal power, beauty, and exquisite wildness of mountains. . . . In my four expeditions to Denali, once making the first winter ascent, I have found myself drawn into its tremendous presence" (foreword to Bill Sherwonit, *To the Top of Denali: Climbing Adventures on North America's Highest Peak* [Anchorage: Alaska Northwest Books, 1990], p. ix). "Denali" is the Native American name for the mountain; "McKinley" the American name. The designation of the national park in which it is located was changed from "McKinley" to "Denali," but the official name of the mountain is still "McKinley."

Mountains—especially, in my experience, Mount McKinley—do have a powerful effect on the spirit that may take different forms. "Generations of Indians had regarded [Denali] as a holy place, treating it with distant reverence and using it as a point of reference. Only after non-Native pioneers—with their passion for discovery, exploration, and conquest—learned of the mountain's existence did people attempt to unravel its secrets. In doing so, it was only natural that they'd find a route to its top" (Sherwonit, *To the Top of Denali,* p. 5). What is "only natural" may be "only natural" to white males who see mountains, like other things, as challenges. It may be "only natural" for Native Americans to regard mountains with respect and awe. One regrettable consequence of taking Denali as a challenge is that trash and human waste have become a real problem on heavily traveled routes to the summit. The need to "conquer" mountains has produced some forms of defacement that are popularly well received—the presidential heads blasted out of Mount Rushmore in South Dakota, for example, and the Confederate war heroes blasted from Stone Mountain, Georgia.

The point in the text is that my experience in the wilderness was a religious experience and that it had mightily to do with the self. In this regard, my experience was not singular. For example, Vern Tejas describes himself as "not religious or superstitious" (p. 236). But the following is reported about his harrowing solo ascent of Denali in winter: "While sleeping alone in a snow cave high on Mount McKinley, Tejas was roused by some sort of disturbance. On awakening, he sensed a presence that made his hair bristle.

"'Good morning,' Tejas said. In Japanese.

"There was no response. Nothing else out of the ordinary happened. But Tejas is certain he received a special visit that day, from the spirit of Naomi Uemura. Just four years earlier, Uemura had become the first climber to climb McKinley alone in winter; he then disappeared while going down the mountain" (p. 235). Also, "Just when things seemed darkest, Tejas began to feel an outpouring of emotional and spiritual support. 'While lying in my snow cave, I could feel the warmth and vibrations of many, many people,' he said. 'I know people were praying for me, wanting me to get back safe and sound'" (p. 251).

28. Victor McTeer, a Mississippi delegate, quoted in Gary Wills, *Under God: Religion and American Politics* (New York: Simon and Schuster, 1990), p. 234. McTeer also noted about Jackson's speech: "White people around me are crying. I mean the men. I'm not talking about no lightweight little white girls. I'm talking about we're-going-to-fight-you-nigger-till-you're-gone white folks. . . . I'm standing there next to this white lady from Mississippi who's there in tears on my shoulder. I realized, 'My God, I'm part of something important'" (p. 233).

29. Barth, 4 *Church Dogmatics*, part 2, p. 284.

The self-projection at the heart of religion is not a question of the experience of individuals only but also—perhaps inherently—of groups. Émile Durkheim, for example, thought religion to be a celebration of the collectivity; the reality behind the immediate objects of worship is an idealized form of society, a projection of feelings of awe toward the social collectivity. E. Durkheim, *The Elementary Forms of the Religious Life*, trans. Joseph Swain (New York: Free Press, 1965), pp. 464–71. Thomas Grey notes that "from Durkheim's conception of religion to a religion of the Constitution is an easy step. The Constitution is an explicit self-representation of society. . . . The Constitution resembles the Bible of the new theologians—a sacred text indirectly representing an ineffable underlying reality." Grey, "The Constitution as Scripture," *Stanford Law Review* 37 (1984): 1, 22, 23.

Judge Richard Posner holds a similar view: "Although most lawyers think of themselves as engaged in rational inquiry rather than religious affirmation, the religious impulse is well-nigh universal; it is particularly strong in the United States; and in many secular Americans trained in law the impulse gets channeled into veneration of the Constitution as a sacred text and a decision to attend one of the churches at which it is worshipped." Posner, *The Problems of Jurisprudence*, p. 150. See generally Sanford Levinson, *Constitutional Faith* (Princeton, N.J.: Princeton University Press, 1988).

30. Barth, 3 *Church Dogmatics*, part 4, p. 479.

31. Paul Davies, *God and the New Physics* (New York: Simon and Schuster, 1983), p. 2.

32. Ibid., p. 223.

33. Barth, 3 *Church Dogmatics,* part 1, p. 6. See further chapter 3 on the Chalcedonian emphasis in Barth and the distinction between Barth and Niebuhr, on the one hand, and Aquinas, on the other.

34. See further chapter 3 on *Aufhebung* as descriptive of the relation between Word and religion.

35. In 1973, *Katallagete,* a sometime periodical, published the transcription of a tape recording of a brief informal talk Merton had given several years earlier to his fellow Trappist monks at the monastery of Gethsemani. In the talk Merton reflected on the experience of time presented in *The Sound and the Fury,* the gathering of the black church members as the calling of the elect, and the Word in the service:

> There are no complications, no funny theology. There is simply the Word of God. . . .
> So all in all, the Easter service in *The Sound and the Fury* seems to me to be an authentic example of the way in which the Word of God is preached: the point is the fulfillment of one's identity *in response to the Word of God preached in a community.*
> *That* is the unburdening and the recollection of the Lamb.

Thomas Merton, "Time and Unburdening and the Recollection of the Lamb: The Easter Service in Faulkner's *The Sound and the Fury,*" *Katallagete,* Summer 1973, p. 15 (emphasis in original). Page citations to *The Sound and the Fury* are to the 1946 Modern Library edition (see chap. 5, note 8).

36. Barth, 1 *Church Dogmatics,* part 2, p. 326.

"The revelation of God is actually the presence of God and therefore the hiddenness of God in the world of human religion. By God's revealing of Himself the divine particular is hidden in a human universal, the divine content in a human form, and therefore that which is divinely unique in something which is humanly only singular" (p. 282).

37. Thomas Merton pointed out that "it is not altogether clear whether Reverend Shegog did what he did on purpose—whether he had some trick up his sleeve. Why did he start out preaching as a white man and then all of a sudden shift to preaching as a black? I don't know. *But it doesn't matter.* That is not the point.

"The point is what Dilsey said, from the start that Easter morning: she is going to church for the unburdening, and while Reverend Shegog is a funny little man, the Lord has used 'cuiser' things than that! The Lord is going to speak to her!" Thomas Merton, "Time and Unburdening," p. 15.

John Pearson in Zora Nea'e Hurston's *Jonah's Gourd Vine* (New York: Quality Paperback Books, 1990) is a philanderer who is prideful about his role and to whom the Word comes nonetheless. "Ah jus' found out whut Ah kin do. De words dat sets de church on fire comes tuh me jus' so. Ah reckon de angels must tell 'em tuh me" (p. 112).

38. Lehmann, *Ethics in a Christian Context*, p. 347.

39. Jacobs, *Incidents in the Life of a Slave Girl*, p. 71.

"We really look away from ourselves, and therefore know ourselves genuinely and freely, only as we really look to Jesus Christ. We do not do so merely as we look formally away from ourselves and beyond ourselves, in a purely formal negation of that figure 'the self,' to an empty beyond." Barth, 4 *Church Dogmatics*, part 2, p. 284.

40. Dietrich Bonhoeffer, *Letters and Papers from Prison*, 3d rev'd ed., ed. Eberhard Bethge, trans. Reginald Fuller (New York: Macmillan, 1967), p. 186.

41. Barth, 4 *Church Dogmatics*, part 2, p. 217.

42. W. H. Auden, "For the Time Being," in *The Collected Poetry of W. H. Auden* (New York: Random House, 1945), p. 465.

43. Barth, *The Epistle to the Romans*, 6th ed., trans. Edwyn Hoskyns (New York: Oxford University Press, 1933), p. 195.

44. Barth, 4 *Church Dogmatics*, part 2, pp. 178–79.

45. Bonhoeffer, *Letters and Papers from Prison*, p. 198. I have changed the word *man* to *human*. I believe the change is consistent with Bonhoeffer's point.

46. Toni Morrison, *Beloved* (New York: Knopf, 1987).

47. I have attempted to state a theology of the natural and its bearing upon law in *Lying Down Together: Law, Metaphor, and Theology* (Madison: University of Wisconsin Press, 1985), pp. 126–38, 181–91 (notes).

48. Barth, *The Epistle to the Romans*, pp. 258–59.

49. Karl Barth, *The Humanity of God*, trans. Thomas Wieser and John Newton Thomas (Richmond: John Knox Press, 1960), p. 49.

50. Ibid., p. 51.

51. Bonhoeffer, *Letters and Papers from Prison*, p. 199.

52. Barth, *The Humanity of God*, pp. 46–47.

Chapter Three

1. Much of Professor Shaffer's work has been concerned with raising the issue of ethics for legal ethics. See, e.g., his *On Being a Christian and a Lawyer: Law for the Innocent* (Provo, Utah: Brigham Young University Press, 1980), *American Legal Ethics: Text, Readings, and Discussion Topics* (New York: Matthew Bender, 1985), and *Faith and the Professions* (Provo, Utah: Brigham Young University Press, 1987).

2. Stringfellow, *A Public and Private Faith*, p. 69.

3. Ibid.

4. Ibid., pp. 70–73.

5. Ibid., p. 70.

6. Ibid., p. 71.

7. Ibid., p. 54.

8. Ibid., p. 72.

9. Ibid.

10. Ibid., p. 73.

11. Ibid.

12. Ibid.

13. Barth, 4 *Church Dogmatics*, part 4, p. 268.

14. Ibid., p. 269.

15. Bonhoeffer, *Letters and Papers from Prison*, p. 155.

16. Ibid., p. 210. "God lets himself be pushed out of the world on to the cross.
. . . Man's religiosity makes him look in his distress to the power of God in the
world: God is the deus ex machina. The Bible directs man to God's powerlessness and suffering" (pp. 196–97). This is not the triumphalist exercise of force
in the name of God.

17. See William Stringfellow, *An Ethic for Christians and Other Aliens in a
Strange Land* (Waco, Texas: Word Books, 1973).

18. Martha Minow, *Making All the Difference: Inclusion, Exclusion, and American
Law* (Ithaca, N.Y.: Cornell University Press, 1990), p. ix.

19. See Paul Lehmann, *Ethics in a Christian Context* and *The Transfiguration of
Politics* (New York: Harper and Row, 1975).

20. Barth, 4 *Church Dogmatics*, part 2, p. 168.
As Gustavo Gutierrez explains, the beatitude "blessed are the poor" is primarily a statement about God: "God loves the poor by preference, not because
the poor are good persons, better than others, or good believers, better than
other believers, but because God is God." Gustavo Gutierrez, "Theology and
Spirituality in a Latin American Context," *Harvard Divinity Bulletin* (June–
August 1984): 4–5. This preference is therefore not a sign of egalitarianism or
of the goodness of the poor but of the "transvaluation of all values" (Barth, 4
Church Dogmatics, part 4, p. 169). The Kingdom of God—the beloved people
which was not beloved—is being brought into existence.
The poor are "all those without status and without power in the world [who
constitute] the society that God has called into life for the humanization of human life" (Lehmann, *The Transfiguration of Politics*, p. 258.

21. Lehmann, *Ethics in a Christian Context*, p. 346.

22. Norman Maclean, "A River Runs Through It," in *A River Runs Through It
and Other Stories* (Chicago: University of Chicago Press, 1976), p. 1.

23. Sanford Levinson, *Constitutional Faith* (Princeton: Princeton University
Press, 1988).

24. Barth, 1 *Church Dogmatics*, part 2, p. 301.

25. Barth, 4 *Church Dogmatics,* part 2, p. 122.

"The reality of Jesus Christ, which includes our own reality, presses in upon us, from its objectivity to our subjectivity, in order that there should be in us a correspondence," not "merely as an imparting of information, but as that which lays claim on us for what is imparted" (5 *Church Dogmatics,* part 2, pp. 303–4). It establishes our freedom for faith: "The freedom to keep to the fact, and orientate ourselves by it, that the alteration of the human situation which has taken place in Him is our own" (4 *Church Dogmatics,* part 2, p. 305). This freedom is not "proffered to us from without . . . but rather . . . is actually made our own. It is the power in whose operation we are motivated and impelled from within, of ourselves, to be in this freedom, and to use it as our own" (ibid.).

26. Barth, *The Epistle to the Romans,* p. 128.

27. Ibid., p. 258.

28. Ibid., p. 136. We should not "try to oppose to the continually threatening anthropomonism a no less abstract theomonism" (Barth, 4 *Church Dogmatics,* part 2, p. 10).

29. Karl Barth, *Christ and Adam: Man and Humanity in Romans 5,* trans. T. A. Smail (*Scottish Journal of Theology* Occasional Paper no. 5, 1956), p. 43.

"Jesus Christ is the secret truth about the essential nature of man" (p. 41).

In Romans, Paul addresses the relationship of Jesus to all men, and "'religious' presuppositions are not once hinted at. The fact of Christ is here presented as something that dominates and includes all men. The nature of Christ objectively conditions human nature and the work of Christ makes an objective difference to the life and destiny of all men" (p. 42). "So it is Christ that reveals the true nature of man" (p. 43).

This is the radical and revolutionary claim, and it is one about humanity. True human nature can be understood only by those "who look to Christ to discover the essential nature of man" (p. 43).

30. Küng, *Theology for the Third Millennium,* p. 233.

31. Barth, 1 *Church Dogmatics,* part 2, p. 298.

32. Barth, 1 *Church Dogmatics,* part 1, p. 327.

33. Ibid. "It has its justification either in the name of Jesus Christ, or not at all. . . . It is not that some men are vindicated as opposed to others, or one part of humanity as opposed to other parts of the same humanity. It is that God Himself is vindicated as opposed to and on behalf of all men and humanity" (pp. 356–57).

34. Ibid., p. 484.

35. Ibid., p. 485.

36. Barth, 2 *Church Dogmatics,* part 2, p. 562.

37. Hunsinger, *How to Read Karl Barth,* p. 86.

38. Ibid., p. 98.

39. See ibid.

40. Ibid., p. 85.

41. Ibid.

42. Ibid., p. 287.

43. See Barth, 4 *Church Dogmatics,* part 3 (2d half), p. 718.

44. See Küng, *Theology for the Third Millennium,* pp. 264–66.

45. See, e.g., Thomas Aquinas, *Summa Theologica,* vol. 30, ed. Cornelius Ernst (New York: McGraw-Hill, 1972), 1a2ae. 113, 10. See also Hunsinger, *How to Read Karl Barth,* pp. 145–46.

46. Hunsinger, p. 40.

47. See Reinhold Niebuhr, *An Interpretation of Christian Ethics* (New York: Meridian, 1958), pp. 109–11, 134–36; *The Nature and Destiny of Man* (New York: Charles Scribner's Sons, 1949), pp. 52–53, 63–64. See also Hunsinger, *How to Read Karl Barth,* pp. 38–39.

48. Reality is "the reality of God, which either includes all possibility or excludes it as an impossible possibility." Barth, 2 *Church Dogmatics,* part 2, p. 536.

49. See Barth, 4 *Church Dogmatics,* part 1, pp. 408–10.

50. Hunsinger, *How to Read Karl Barth,* p. 39.

51. "The transcendent God who yet loves, elects and liberates the world, and lowly man who is yet loved, elected and liberated by Him, are indeed distinct and yet are not separated or two, but one. In Him the covenant between God and man has not merely been kept by God and broken by man, but kept by both, so that it is the fulfilled covenant. In Him there is not the clash of two kingdoms, but the one kingdom of God in reality. . . . In spite of everything, the man who acts and postures. . . , who in wickedness and folly, being blind to what he already is in Jesus Christ, thinks and speaks and acts, and arranges his sorry compromises, and sins, and causes so much suffering to himself and others, is the man who stands in the covenant with God which is already fulfilled. . . . Hence [the people of God] can share neither the enthusiasm of those who regard the old form [of the world] as capable of true and radical improvement nor the scepticism of those who in view of the impossibility of perfecting the old form think that they are compelled to doubt the possibility of a new form. It need judge no man either optimistically or pessimistically because in relation to all, whatever their virtues and accomplishments or their faults and blasphemies and crimes, it is sure of the one fact that Jesus Christ has lived and died and risen again for them too. . . . Because it cannot fear, it cannot hate, and therefore basically, whether it finds it easy or difficult, it can only love. At bottom and in the long run it can only be *pro,* i.e. for men, since God in Jesus Christ is and has decided for them. It cannot be *anti,* i.e. against even individuals." Barth, 4 *Church Dogmatics,* part 3 (2d half), pp. 712, 717–18.

52. "Even as sovereign acts and words of God, as His free acts of rule, judgment, salvation and revelation, these events are also human actions and passions, works and experiences, and *vice versa.*" Barth, 4 *Church Dogmatics,* part 3, p. 63.

53. See Hunsinger, *How to Read Karl Barth,* pp. 189–202, 186–88, 231, 111–12, 212, 290 n. 2.

54. Karl Barth, "Mozart's Freedom," in *Wolfgang Amadeus Mozart,* trans. Clarence Pott (Grand Rapids: Eerdmans, 1986), pp. 53–54. I have followed the translation in Hans Küng's *Theology for the Third Millennium,* p. 284.

CHAPTER FOUR

1. Frank Kermode, *The Genesis of Secrecy: On the Interpretation of Narrative* (Cambridge: Harvard University Press, 1979), p. 27.

2. Luke 8:10 employs *hina.* Krister Stendahl suggests that, on the basis of an underlying Aramaic saying, "both possibilities [*hina* and *hoti*] were open to those who had to render this saying into Greek." Krister Stendahl, "Matthew," in *Peake's Commentary on the Bible* (New York: T. Nelson, 1962), pp. 769, 785. See note 7 infra. He adds that Matthew's "total understanding of Jesus' use of parables comes nevertheless closer to" Mark's sense of *hina*—"the use of parables was a way to reveal and yet to do so in a veiled manner" (p. 786). See also Joachim Jeremias, *The Parables of Jesus,* 3d ed., trans. S. Hooke (London: S. C. M. Press, 1954), pp. 12–15. C. H. Dodd, from whose approach the present text varies greatly, believed that the explanation for speaking in parables attributed to Jesus was in fact "a piece of apostolic teaching." C. H. Dodd, *The Parables of the Kingdom,* rev'd ed. (London: Nisbet, 1936), p. 15.

3. Kermode, *The Genesis of Secrecy,* pp. 33–34.

4. Ibid., pp. 144–45.

5. Ibid., p. 30.

6. The Septuagint was produced in Egypt sometime beginning around 250 B.C. when, as legend has it, Ptolemy II sent for seventy-two scholars from Jerusalem to translate the first five books of the Bible for the royal library. The Septuagint was adopted by the early Christian Church.

7. The full quotation of the passage from Isaiah may be a later expansion informed by the Church's use of the Septuagint. See Krister Stendahl, *The School of St. Matthew and Its Use of the Old Testament* (Philadelphia: Fortress, 1964), pp. 129–33. The phraseology is in accord with the version of Isaiah 6 in the Targum Jonathan. See ibid., pp. 131, 144. The Targums were Aramaic translations of the Hebrew, used by rabbis for popular instruction. Aramaic spread after the fall of Samaria and had become the popular spoken language by the time of Jesus. According to Jeremias, "Mark follows the paraphrase of Isa. v. 10 commonly used in the synagogue and known to us through the Peshitta [a Syrian translation] and the written Targum." Jeremias, *The Parables of Jesus,* p. 13. Stendahl says the Semitic features that distinguish Mark's allusion to Isaiah from the Greek Septuagint seem "to be a survival of that Aramaic form in which the words and deeds of Jesus were originally recounted. The features cannot be interpreted as of direct literary dependence on Semitic Scriptures." Stendahl, *The School of St. Matthew,* p. 146.

8. It seems clear to me that *dabar* as power is pre-Deuteronomic. But see Moshe Weinfeld, *Deuteronomy and the Deuteronomic School* (Oxford: Clarendon Press, 1972), p. 15.

According to Klaus Koch, in *The Prophets: The Assyrian Period*, trans. Margaret Kohl (Philadelphia: Fortress, 1983), "What is heard through Isaiah's lips is Yahweh's *dabar,* and for him this is without doubt the most relevant active force in the metahistorical process. By giving expression to Yahweh's *dabar,* Isaiah moves history. . . . Other talk is mere lip-*dabar,* as it is contemptuously called in 36:5."

9. See, e.g., 29:9–10; Gerhard von Rad, 2 *Old Testament Theology,* D. M. G. Stalker trans. (New York: Harper & Brothers, 1965), 151–55. The prophets' "concern was not the faith, not even the 'kerygma': it was to deliver the message from Jahweh to particular men and women who, without themselves being aware of it, stood in a special situation before God" (p. 129).

10. On the heavenly assembly and the divine lawsuit, see Kirsten Nielsen, *Yahweh as Prosecutor and Judge* (Sheffield: University of Sheffield Press, 1978) and sources cited therein; Frank M. Cross, *Canaanite Myth and Hebrew Epic: Essays in the History of the Religion of Israel* (Cambridge: Harvard University Press, 1973), pp. 186–90; Claus Westermann, *Basic Forms of Prophetic Speech,* trans. Hugh Clayton White (Philadelphia: Westminster Press, 1967); H. Wheeler Robinson, *Inspiration and Revelation in the Old Testament* (Oxford: Clarendon, 1946), pp. 167ff.; George Ernest Wright, "The Lawsuit of God: A Form-Critical Study of Deuteronomy 32," in *Israel's Prophetic Heritage,* ed. Bernhard Anderson and Walter Harrelson (London: S. C. M. Press, 1962), p. 26.

"It is not coincidental that the language of theophany and the imagery of revelation derived from the mythology of the storm god largely fell out of use . . . in prophetic Yahwism. The prophets chose another language, other imagery with which to describe their intercourse with Yahweh, drawn . . . from the concept of the messenger of the Council of 'El. So far as we are able to tell, the prophets did not attempt to suppress in systematic fashion the old hymns and traditions which used the uncouth language of the storm theophany. The attack was on Ba'al and not on the notion that Yahweh controlled the elements of nature. Nevertheless, they used a refined or purged language of revelation, because Yahweh, so to say, no longer used the storm as a mode of self-manifestation." Cross, *Canaanite Myth and Hebrew Epic,* p. 191.

11. On covenant, see George Mendenhall, *Law and Covenant in Israel and the Ancient Near East* (Pittsburgh: Presbyterian Board of Colportage of Western Pennsylvania, ca. 1955); John Bright, *A History of Israel* (Philadelphia: Westminster, 1959), pp. 128–51. On curses, maledictions, and prophecy, see Weinfeld, *Deuteronomy and the Deuteronomic School,* pp. 129–38.

12. A plausible argument can be made that Amos drew upon this lawsuit tradition although, except for 3:7, God is not described as speaking in the heavenly assembly, and, except for one appearance of the word *rib* (7:4), there is no express statement of God undertaking a lawsuit. The book does open with *rib*-like pronouncements against foreign nations (1:3–2:3) and then against Israel: Is-

rael was chosen, redeemed from Egypt, and given the promised land by the mighty acts of God. Nevertheless, her people now "sell the righteous for silver, and the needy for a pair of shoes" (2:6). They make "the Nazirites drink wine" and command silence of the prophets (2:12), all the while making much outward show of religious feasts (5:12ff.). The sentence is destruction (3:13ff.), so certain to be carried out that Amos already sounds a funeral dirge (5:2).

The lawsuit theme emerges more fully in Hosea: "The Lord has a *rib* with the inhabitants of the land" (4:1, 12:2). The indictment charges that "they have broken my covenant, and transgressed my law" (8:1), making Israel a harlot (4:10, 17–18). Although God had brought Israel from Egypt (11:1), "there is no faithfulness . . . in the land" (4:1). Again the sentence is destruction (8:3, 10).

In Micah, lawsuit rhetoric is explicit and concentrated:

> "Hear what the Lord says:
> Arise, plead your *rib* before the mountains,
> and let the hills hear your voice.
> Hear, you mountains, the *rib yahweh,*
> and you enduring foundations of the earth;
> for the Lord has a *rib* with his people, and he will
>   contend with Israel" (6:1–2).

God acted on behalf of his people; their response was to reject justice, kindness, and humble devotion to him (6:3–5, 8). They are sentenced to destruction (1:6–7, 2:3–5, 3:12, 6:14–16).

13. Koch cautions that the celebrated commissioning is not placed at the beginning of Isaiah and therefore should not be overemphasized; if the redactor did not think it primary, neither should we. Koch, *The Prophets*, p. 113.

14. Von Rad, 2 *Theology of the Old Testament*, p. 145.

15. Von Rad said that Isaiah was a failure in the sense that Israel did not repent in response to his prophecy. Ibid., p. 167. So also John Bright, "Isaiah—I," in *Peake's Commentary on the Bible*, pp. 489, 495. I think von Rad and Bright are wrong in this respect. Isaiah—or, rather, the word he proclaimed—was a success. What was said was done. Hearts were hardened. The *dabar* would have failed only if hearts were *not* hardened and Israel had understood and repented. The tale of Jonah is both later and a deliberate counterexample. Jonah prophesied destruction, but Nineveh repented and was spared. Jonah viewed himself as having been duped by God for this reason; i.e., he resented his failure. What he said did not happen. Michael Walzer falsely generalizes that "prophecy aims to arouse remembrance, recognition, indignation, repentance," and implies "a previously accepted and commonly understood morality." Michael Walzer, *Interpretation and Social Criticism* (Cambridge: Harvard University Press, 1987), p. 73. See pp. 73–89. This is a subtle way of attempting to place humans at the controlling center as the occasion and measure of the *dabar* of God.

16. A partial explanation of the ambiguity may lie in the different geographical-political settings of the prophecies. The covenant theology of the northern kingdom required that the people fulfill their treaty obligations or be

punished with destruction (the Ten Commandments). The royal theology of the southern kingdom placed hope in the coming of a messiah whose rule would transform the nation and save it (the Davidic expectation). Micah is substantively illustrative of the northern, more Mosaic influence; Amos of the southern, more Davidic tradition.

Isaiah may be counted within the southern theological tradition; utterances of hope are interleaved among doom-sayings. Sometimes the hope-sayings serve to highlight and reinforce the doom-sayings. (I would argue that this is so of Isaiah 7:7–25, for example.) As a doctoral thesis proposes, "the serious exhortations [to change] in the pre-Deuteronomic classical prophets do not have the function of softening the force of judgment prophecy or of setting up the conditions for a last minute way of staving off the announced judgment. The occasional utterance of a serious exhortation is perfectly consistent with the prophet's task of announcing unconditionally the coming judgment, for the exhortations serve in some way to substantiate and justify Yahweh's decision to bring judgment." A. Hunter, "Seek the Lord: A Study of the Meaning and Function of the Exhortations in Amos, Hosea, Isaiah, Micah, and Zephaniah," Ph.D. diss., University of Basel, p. 277 (St. Mary's Seminary and University, Baltimore, 1982). At other times, however, the hope-bearing texts, cryptic and spare though they may be, cannot be subordinated to the doom-sayings. This is so, I judge, of the texts revolving around the remnant theme—e.g., 10:21–22; 6:13; 7:4. Only a remnant will be left, and that only after Israel is punished, but there will be a remnant, in fulfillment of the Davidic promise.

17. See Nielsen, *Jahweh as Prosecutor and Judge,* pp. 1–26.

18. Robert Cover, "The Supreme Court, 1982 Term—Foreword: Nomos and Narrative," *Harvard Law Review* 97 (1983): 4, 9, 44–45, 47.

19. See Gerhard von Rad, *Deuteronomium-Studien* (Göttingen: Vandenhouk und Ruprecht, 1947); George Ernest Wright, "Deuteronomy," in 2 *Interpreter's Bible* (New York: Abingdon-Cokesbury Press, 1953), pp. 311, 320–23; Weinfeld, *Deuteronomy and the Deuteronomic School,* pp. 158–64.

20. Other biblical books of law, i.e., the other legal corpora, are the Book of the Covenant (Exodus 20:23–23:19), the Holiness Code (Lev. 17–26), and the priestly laws for sacrifice and purity (Lev. 1–7; 11–15). There are other smaller sections. Much ancient law underlay some of the extant sources of Deuteronomy, for example. There was possibly multiple or polycentric law in the "anarchic period of the judges." Weinfeld, *Deuteronomy and the Deuteronomic School,* p. 171. See also p. 338 ("Toroth"). Cover pointed out that Torah "is amenable to a range of meanings that serve both to enrich the terms and to obscure analysis of it." Cover, "Nomos and Narrative," p. 11, n. 31. From the various meanings it attracted in early biblical sources, "law" became associated with the singular, canonized sense of Deuteronomy, and then with life itself in later rabbinics. Israel was "a society founded on law from the beginning." Bright, *A History of Israel,* p. 151. See also pp. 130, 149–51; William Albright, "The Biblical Period," pp. 11–12 (in Finkelstein, ed., *The Jews; Their History, Culture, and Religion* [New York: Harper and Brothers, 1949; reprinted Pittsburgh, Pa., 1955]).

"Deuteronomy rather looks like a last stand against the beginning of legislation." Von Rad, *Theology of the Old Testament*, p. 201.

21. There was before the exile no change in attitude toward or sense of law equivalent to the fundamental change that occurred after the exile. See Bright, *A History of Israel*, pp. 418–28; Cover, "Nomos and Narrative," pp. 11–12. Deuteronomy, especially given the range of materials included within it, is not atypical, even though the Deuteronomistic editing was post-exilic.

22. The law is to be obeyed with all one's heart and, in this sense, in spirit. See the exhortations on justice for the poor, e.g., 15:7.

23. Koch, *The Prophets*, p. 11.

24. "The commandments had been of service to the people of Israel as they made their way through history and through the confusion occasioned by heathen forms of worship." Von Rad, *Theology of the Old Testament*, p. 91.

25. And for this reason it may appear aligned with reward (so Weinfeld and the association of Deuteronomy with wisdom literature).

26. But see 5:8, 11:26. There are, of course, numerous positive relationships between law and prophecy. For example: Deuteronomy 32 is probably an ancient example of the divine lawsuit employed in classic prophecy; there is close association between Deuteronomy and the contemporaneous prophecy of Jeremiah; when the Book of the Law was presented to Josiah, he immediately sought out the word of the prophetess Huldah; the entire book of Deuteronomy is cast as an oration of Moses, who is described as a prophet. Moreover, later in Israel's history, after the exile, beyond the period on which I am focusing, prophecy took a turn toward promise and hope and could even be said, in some ways, to have been replaced by law.

Curse flows from breach of the covenant/treaty. Weinfeld, *Deuteronomy and the Deuteronomic School*, pp. 156–57; Deut. 28:15ff. Weinfeld sees curse and punishment as teaching devices, part of the sapiential approach. Curse and punishment are thereby tamed.

27. See, e.g., Martin Noth, *The Deuteronomistic History*, various trans. (Sheffield: University of Sheffield Press, 1981).

28. G. Wright, "The Book of Deuteronomy," in 2 *Interpreter's Bible*, p. 317: "an older form of the book exists in chs. 5–26; 28 with introduction in 4:44–49. Chs. 27; 29–30 contain old material, but the exact date of their present written form and of their attachment to chs. 5–26; 28 is unknown. It is not improbable that they were already attached to the edition of Deuteronomy which was available to the Deuteronomistic historian when in chs. 1–4 he appended an introduction to his history of Israel in Palestine (Deuteronomy through II Kings)."

29. On the differing northern and southern theological traditions, see note 16 above.

30. Cross, *Canaanite Myth and Hebrew Epic*, pp. 278–85.

31. "Thus says the Lord, Behold I will bring evil upon this place and upon its inhabitants, all the words of the book which the king of Judah has read. Because

they have forsaken me and have burned incense to other gods, that they might provoke me to anger with all the work of their hands, therefore my wrath is kindled against this place, and it will not be quenched. But as to the king of Judah. . . . Regarding the words which you have heard, because your heart was penitent . . . I will gather you to your fathers, and you shall be gathered to your grave in peace, and your eyes shall not see all the evil which I will bring upon this place" (22:16–20).

On the "negative prophetic cycle" in the Deuteronomic history, see Weinfeld, *Deuteronomy and the Deuteronomic School,* pp. 21–26. On the specific text here in issue, see pp. 25–26. Second Kings 22–23 do seem to present a principal challenge to his conclusion about the Deuteronomic literature and national reward that leads him to connect Deuteronomy with the sapiential tradition. Compare the Josiah episode with Weinfeld at pp. 307–19.

32. Deuteronomy is presented as an oration of Moses. It anticipates the later-known outcome of the story about to be told in the Deuteronomist's history.

33. The years of Josiah may have in fact and directly been pivotal for the Deuteronomist historian. See Noth, *The Deuteronomistic History,* p. 73: "Inevitably this reign was of particular significance to *Dtr.* because in it that law which he has placed at the beginning of his history as the authentic exposition of the Sinai decalogue was found in the temple and put into practice by the king."

34. "*Dtr.* elevates the events of Josiah's time to a general norm" (ibid., p. 82). The history ends on a more or less hopeful note. But the purpose of the history is to explain the calamity that befell Israel.

35. Koch maintains: "Since sin builds an inner-worldly sphere of power, it cannot be set aside just because God decides to let 'two and two make five.'" Koch, *The Prophets,* p. 98. I am not so sure. Is God bound by arithmetic? Is sin more powerful than God?

36. See Patrick Miller, *Sin and Judgment in the Prophets: A Stylistic and Theological Analysis* (Chico, Calif.: Scholar's Press, 1982). Miller points out that punishment follows sin, but not as the necessary working-out of an impartial fate. The matter is one of correspondence, and correspondence is a function of appropriate justice. Punishment is the consequence of God's power.

37. I should add that there is here no institutional separation of the judge from the violence of law, no mechanism separating the judge's responsibility from the violent act of his judgment. See Cover, "Violence and the Word," *Yale Law Journal* 95 (1986): 1601, 1613–16. See also Martha Minow on the terrorism of King Solomon. Minow, "The Judgment of Solomon and the Experience of Justice," in Cover and Fiss, *The Structure of Procedure* (Mineola, N.Y.: Foundation Press, 1979), p. 447.

38. "The events . . . under King Josiah . . . are an especially important part of the historical presuppositions to *Dtr.'s* work. . . . These events determined his own view of the history of Israel and of what should have been the case but was not." Noth, *The Deuteronomistic History,* p. 80. Josiah's reign showed "how things should have been done all along" (ibid., pp. 73–74).

39. Law is a gift and is good. Paul, e.g., is not antinomian.

Much has been written about the relation of law and prophets. Protestant Christians from the time of Luther to the middle of the last century thought of the prophets as exponents of Mosaic law. Julius Wellhausen showed that prophecy was not preceded by law. Wellhausen, *Prolegomena to the History of Israel,* trans. Black and Menzies (New York: Meridian Books, 1957). Subsequent scholarship demonstrated that ancient types of law were early taken up by the Israelites, well before the prophets. See, e.g., Albrecht Alt, "The Origins of Israelite Law," in *Essays on Old Testament History and Religion* (Sheffield, England: Journal for the Study of the Old Testament, 1989), p. 79. B. Gemser maintains that the prophetic context was a frame of mind or general Israelite fascination with law. B. Gemser, "The Rib or Controversy-Pattern in Hebrew Mentality," in *Wisdom in Israel and the Ancient Near East,* supplements to *Vetus Testamentum,* vol. 3, ed. Noth and Thomas (Leiden: E. J. Brill, 1960). Even so, Koch suggests that the appropriate historical sequence is "first the prophets, then the law." Koch, *The Prophets,* p. 3. On the general conversation about the relation of law and prophets as well as the theological and historical misunderstanding that has attended that conversation in the Christian tradition, see, e.g., von Rad, *Theology of the Old Testament,* pp. 3–4, 390–409. My own immediate point about law in the prophets is limited and formal.

40. "According to . . . Martin Buber, the perpetual enemy of faith in the true God is not atheism (the claim that there is no God), but rather gnosticism (the claim that God is known)." P. Lee, *Against the Protestant Gnostics* (New York: Oxford, 1987) (quoting Buber, *The Eclipse of God,* trans. Goodman [New York: Harper, 1952], p. 175). A claim to knowledge of God is a false claim because God reveals himself as hidden. All knowledge of God begins and ends in his hiddenness. See Barth, 2 *Church Dogmatics,* part 1, p. 183.

41. The word does what it says. That was one of the tests of its authenticity. If what a prophet said did not come to pass, it had not been spoken by a true prophet (Deut. 18:22). But history was not finally dispositive.

There was a second test. If what a prophet said did come to pass but the prophet urged idolatry, his word would still be false and not a word of God (Deut. 13:1–5). The prophet must be one who had "stood" in the *sodh,* the heavenly assembly (Jer. 23:18). The true prophetic word is realized in, but not fully accounted for, by history. This is another way of saying that faithful reflection of the *sodh*—the other world—is preeminent. True prophets are attendant upon that world, and, if they are, they will be grounded in this one.

Neither test for the authenticity of prophecy was contemporaneously determinative. The test of history required waiting to see how things turned out. The test of standing in the assembly was not empirically available. In both instances, a decision about the authenticity of a prophetic utterance had to be made in the event unaided by rules of thumb. This was a matter of faith. And faith is the work of the word.

42. Both prophecy and law take history as occasion and subject. Calum Carmichael even goes so far as to maintain that the law of Deuteronomy is drawn from historical texts in the sense that it is judgment about events in literary his-

tory. Calum Carmichael, *Law and Narrative in the Bible: The Evidence of the Deuteronomic Laws and the Decalogue* (Ithaca, N.Y.: Cornell University Press, 1985), p. 17. More plausibly, Barth observed: "Everything God wills is an exact expression of the fact that those of whom He wills it are His own—an exact counterpart of the 'great and terrible things' which God had already done. . . . The Ten Commandments and the various ceremonial, legal and moral enactments, are not independent and cannot be separated from this antecedent. . . . And in content each of the commands reflects and confirms the fact that Israel is this people. . . . *Thou* shalt! means, *Israel* shall! and everything that Israel *shall* is only an imperative transcription of what Israel *is*, repeating in some sense only what Israel has become by God, and what it must always be with God." Barth, 2 *Church Dogmatics*, part 2, p. 572.

43. According to Gen. 18:17–19, "the Lord said: 'Shall I hide from Abraham what I am about to do, seeing that Abraham shall become a great and mighty nation, and all the nations of the earth shall bless themselves by him? No, for I have chosen him, that he may charge his children and his household after him to keep the way of the Lord by doing righteousness and justice; so that the Lord may bring to Abraham what he has promised him.'"

If hearts are hardened, perhaps the reason for speaking becomes problematic. And why put the prophecy in writing? Von Rad thinks the prophet wrote for future audiences whose hearts would not be hardened. Von Rad, *Theology of the Old Testament*, p. 43. I have my doubts about this explanation. Von Rad cannot conceive that prophecy was not uttered for the benefit of some human audience. Is this not a way of trying to salvage human causation?

44. See also above and 7:5, 11:9; Exodus 4:21, 9:12, 10:1. "There is no tolerably uniform, consistent pre-history of the concept of hardening the heart. Nevertheless it is certain that from the very first Israel believed the act of deluding or hardening the heart to be prompted by Jahweh, and this is in one way or another the background to Isaiah's saying." Von Rad, *Theology of the Old Testament*, p. 153.

45. Is God merely complying with due process, i.e., looking his victims in the eye and addressing them, like a Hollywood Western sheriff, before he pulls the trigger?

Surely God is not "one of those people . . . who explain what they are doing as they are doing it, like Dale Carnegie or Norman Vincent Peale; part of their ideology is technique. To them the method is just as intoxicating as the message." Saul Bellow, *More Die of Heartbreak* (New York: Morrow, 1987), p. 175.

46. The saying's conclusion that there would eventually be an abundant harvest undoubtedly gave hope to the early Church, which may have witnessed more falling away and choking than harvest.

47. Joel Marcus, "Mark 4:10–12 and Marcan Epistemology," *Journal of Biblical Literature* 103:4 (1984): 566.

"Both in Mark and the Dead Sea Scrolls, the autonomy that can be ascribed to human beings in matters of perception is severely limited. In Mark 4:9, 23 not *all* are exhorted to hear, but only 'he who has ears to hear'—let *him* hear. Only the one who, in the terms of the parable of the sower, is good soil will be addressable, will be able to hear; only the one to whom God has given ears can hear. . . . With regard to Mark 4:24, 'take heed what you hear,' it should be noticed that this warning is framed by 4:23 and 4:25, both of which imply that 'hearing' is not something that one can simply *decide* to do" (p. 562; citations and footnotes omitted). (Aviam Soifer makes the fertile suggestion that rich soil implies accretion and therefore the role of the past.)

Marcus also notes that "there is a 'mysterious interpenetration' between faith and the grace shown in revelation. . . . This is clear from the healing of blind Bartimaeus, in which Jesus says to him, '*Your faith* has saved you' (10:52). . . . Still, . . . the process that culminates in the healing is set in motion by the appearance of Jesus on the scene and the hearing of 'the things concerning Jesus' (5:27; cf. 10:47). Thus the initiative for revelation remains with God, but proclamation and faith have roles to play within the initiative" (p. 562, n. 20). On the question of human faith and God's self-revelation see further above, chapter 3.

Isaiah, too, may be interpreted more than one way. Isaiah does decide to be a messenger from the heavenly court—"Here I am! Send me" (Is. 6:8). But at this point, he has already been admitted to the proceedings of the heavenly court.

48. The parable could be read as human thwarting of the Word, which loses power in some instances. Thus there is ground on which the Word cannot bear fruit. See also 6:5–6 ("And he could do no mighty work there, except that he laid his hands upon a few sick people and healed them. And he marvelled because of their unbelief"). On the word in relation to the demonic powers, see below.

49. Karl Barth, *Community, State, and Church* (Garden City, N.Y.: Doubleday, 1960), pp. 110–11.

50. Ibid., p. 115. Professor Anthony Chase has correctly noted to me that it would be wrong to remove the drama and existential meaning from the life of Jesus among other humans. And he helpfully cites the observation: "The cross was not devised by God, but by sinful men. Their purpose simply failed to thwart God's purpose." Edward Schillebeeckx, *Paul the Apostle* (New York: Crossroad, 1983), p. 29. My comments in the text are not meant to remove either the reality and particularity of Jesus' life or responsible human participation in his death. I would no more strike the drama and existential meaning from Jesus' life than from the lives of the lawyers I have written about or from Dilsey's life. There is human reality and responsibility here. As I say, however, the "I" is also an "I but not I." It is the mystery—which remains a mystery—of our responsible action together with God's active, loving priority. See note 68 infra.

51. Ibid., pp. 116–17. See also Marcus, "Mark 4:10–12 and Marcan Epistemology," p. 558.

52. See Robert Wilson, "Mark," in *Peake's Commentary on the Bible* (New York: T. Nelson, 1962), pp. 799, 804.

53. What, then, is to be said of my interpreting this text on the incapacitation of interpretation?

54. "The 'mystery of the kingdom of God' thus has to do with God's strange design of bringing the kingdom in Jesus Christ, yet unleashing the forces of

darkness to blind human beings so that they oppose that kingdom." Marcus, "Mark 4:10–12," p. 567.

55. Jeremias, *The Parables of Jesus,* p. 158.

Marcus puts it this way: "Rather than being a normative Torah exegete, he is the Son of God, whose coming is the powerful irruption of the kingdom of God. He not only interprets the scriptures; he also fulfills them." Marcus, "Mark 4:10–12," p. 563, n. 22.

56. Such a reading may be supported by the Dead Sea Scrolls (see Marcus, "Mark 4:10–12," p. 564) as well as by other New Testament usage—Romans 11:25, for example. I join Marcus in taking exception to Wrede's proposal that what is given is Jesus' identity, his messianic secret. William Wrede, *The Messianic Secret,* trans. J. C. G. Greig (Greenwood, S.C.: Attic Press, 1971), p. 60. But I depart from Marcus's reading that the mystery is "something that has already put in an appearance in the Gospel" (p. 565), so that what is given to them is the parables. He would have the text read: "To you disciples the mystery of the kingdom of God has been given in parables, but for those outside the reason that everything is in parables is so that they may indeed see but not perceive" (p. 565, n. 33).

57. Christians are to remember "that Jesus as attested by Scripture is Jesus the Jew," and that the Church "exists in special community with the Jews. In Paul's words, it is grafted onto the branch which is Israel." Robert Osborne, "Is the Church Political?" *Katallagete* (Fall 1987): 63.

Also the Church—and I—must listen to George Steiner and his comments on two other troublesome biblical texts. One is Exodus 4:24. God sought to kill Moses. Steiner glosses: "to mean that God suffers gusts of murderous exasperation at the Jews, toward a people who have made Him a responsible party to history and to the grit of man's condition. He may not have wished to be involved; the people may have chosen Him, in the oasis at Kadesh, and thrust upon Him the labors of justice and right anger. It may have been the Jew who caught him by the skirt, insisting on contact and dialogue. Perhaps before either God or living man was ready for proximity." George Steiner, *Language and Silence: Essays on Language, Literature, and the Inhuman* (New York: Atheneum, 1970), p. 142.

The other text is Exodus 33:22–23. God reveals his backside to Moses: "This may be the decisive clue: God can turn His back. There may be minutes or millennia—is our time His?—in which He does not see man, in which He is looking the *other way.* . . . When God's back parts are toward man, history is Belsen" (ibid.).

The Treblinka death camp was destroyed by a Jewish uprising. "What the documents tell us is that in the dark of God's absence, certain men, buried alive, buried by that silence of Christianity and Western civilization which makes all who were indifferent accomplices to the Nazis, rose and destroyed their parcel of hell" (ibid., p. 167).

58. For example, the intrusion of the story of the sick woman into the story about the child invites interpretive connections. A menstrual disorder of twelve years' standing is cured, and the older woman is returned to society ritually

clean; a prepubescent twelve-year-old girl is restored and, no longer unclean, is welcomed back into society. The girl, identified as "the child," is addressed by Jesus as "little girl." The change, says Kermode, "distinguishes her as approaching, from the other side, the condition of the cured woman, a healthy sexual maturity." Kermode, *The Genesis of Secrecy*, p. 132. "My point is absolutely not that Mark is here 'saying something' about sexuality; only that by looking at the twinned narratives in this way we might see how a text can as it were cultivate structural oppositions. . . . This text seems to be continually interested in providing instances of a generalized opposition between clean and unclean. . . . Between the opposites clean and unclean there are inserted—intercalated—figures of sexual or magical force. We can safely say that these stories do not have the same meanings we should have found in them had they been told *seriatim*" (ibid., p. 133).

59. Ibid., p. 134.

60. Ibid., p. 115.

61. Ibid., p. 143.

62. Ibid., p. 66.

63. Ibid., pp. 67–68. Once again so sharp a text apparently invited dulling, and some early manuscripts have variant endings that include the appearance of the risen Jesus.

64. In a well-drawn, well-taken reflection upon Mark 4:11–12 (and related texts, especially the parable of the Prodigal Son) in which he likens the role of the Supreme Court to that of Jesus telling parables, Robert Burt notes that the parables are not intended to be accessible to listener or reader. "They are designed to raise questions more than answer them, to confound rather than to confirm prior understanding, and particularly to accomplish this in order to raise doubts among their listeners about whether they are among the elect or remain outside among those who 'hear and hear, but understand nothing.'" Robert Burt, "Constitutional Law and the Teaching of the Parables," *Yale Law Journal* 93 (1984): 455, 469. "The strategy . . . is not simply to confound or to raise self-doubts for their own sake; the strategy is to heighten the listeners' sense of their own vulnerability." All are outsiders. Through acknowledgment of vulnerability, they may find a way inside. "The premise of the methodology is that when the listeners acknowledge their vulnerability, they will see the answer that Christ represents" (p. 471).

65. See also 14:51–52. Jesus is arrested. The disciples flee. "And a young man followed him, with nothing but a linen cloth about his body; and they seized him, but he left the linen cloth and ran away naked."

66. All Mark does, all that can be done with words in the circumstance, is to tell the story. And not even that is done on the wholly original motion of the teller. Mark 1:2–3: "As it is written in Isaiah the prophet, 'Behold I send my messenger before thy face / who shall prepare thy way; the voice of one crying in the wilderness. . . .'" John the Baptist is a textual function of the "as it is written." But that is also the function of Mark. The silence with which the text leaves

us is textually correspondent to the empty tomb. It also corresponds to Jesus' own silence when Pilate examined him.

67. Coleman Barks responded to a manuscript version of this chapter with the comment, "I'd say the empty space is the Presence of Christ. That's what the Twelve have, and what the parables don't. Maybe that's what you're saying, too." It is, but for the fact I'd say Christ is present to the Twelve and present in the parables. The parables are a compatible textual medium of this mysterious presence. The Twelve understand the Word with them as little as they understand the Word in the parables. In both instances, willy nilly, they are confronted by the Word. I think the story of the Twelve and the parables, like the story at the end of the Gospel, is a way Mark has found to create the possibility of confrontation by the Word in reading. The text gives readers a place for recognizing that they, too, like the Twelve and like the audience for the parables, are confronted by the Word. The text does what words can do to invoke this possibility. Mark is parabolic in this sense. And the parables are prototypical.

By suggesting breaks, disturbances, empty places, silences as a revelatory location of the Word, I run the risk of a particular misunderstanding which I am particularly anxious to avoid. The religious view is that God exists beyond our knowledge at the edges and fringes of the real world, beyond the daily and the secular at the periphery of life. I mean not to take this view.

The breaks to which I refer are openings that radiate from the mystery in the midst of life. In them the Word is disclosed as always, already powerfully present. We are shown and recalled to the transcendent Word at the center. The action is that of discerning the body of Christ in the sacramental elements, discerning the Word present in the communal breaking and eating of bread.

68. Barth, 4 *Church Dogmatics,* part 3 (1st half), p. 113. See also Barth, 1 *Church Dogmatics,* part 2, pp. 499–500.

This chapter has emphasized the otherness of the Word. At the end of the previous chapter I said that to read the priority of the Word as excluding place for humans and human agency would be to commit error. The attention I give individuals and their particular practices performs a repudiation of this mistake.

Now I must point out the possibility for making the opposite mistake: It would be an error to read the otherness of the Word as determined by human perspective. To say "the Word is wholly other" raises the question: "wholly other than what?" Is the Word wholly other than all things human? If so, if the Word is everything we are not, we are conceptually determinative of the Word. The Word is what we are not, whereby what we are not is the operative factor. And God, once again a function of religion, is a projection of a negative image of ourselves.

Barth criticized Schleiermacher's religious notion of contemplation and the sense of being grasped. "Barth did not criticize that sense of being grasped as being without an object but that it knew the object only as something that was presupposed in the process right from the start. It is that kind of understanding which Barth opposes with the concept of God being non-contemplative, beyond contemplation, a concept which signifies that in regard to 'every stance which humans take towards God, God is something other, unique, special, new'" (Eberhard Busch, "God Is God: The Meaning of a Controversial Formula and the Fundamental Problem of Speaking about God," *Princeton Seminary Bulletin,* 1986, pp. 106–7).

How can speech about God be free of an express or implied first personal pronoun?

Eberhard Busch says it cannot, absent intervention: "We humans cannot overcome the dilemma that we are in fact dealing with ourselves every time we talk of God. This dilemma is overcome only when it is none other than *God* who makes God known to us. And no matter how we humans say 'God,' it is only when God is revealed to us *through God* that we are not dealing with ourselves. Who God is becomes known only in God's own self-definition" (p. 110).

There are possibilities for speaking about God.

One is touched upon by Alexander J. McKelway in his helpful book, *The Freedom of God and Human Liberation* (pp. 54–68). I have said that there is no identity between the human reality of the biblical words and the reality of God. McKelway notes how the biblical words may speak of God by means of their contingency. The Bible maintains its power and integrity by refusing to identify itself with the free Word of God. McKelway points out that "because scripture bears witness to the fact that no human word can itself be the word of God, we find in the Bible something like a self-deconstruction" (p. 65). One example of "the Bible's metacritical self-correction" is "its notorious application of gender to God." McKelway writes: "That such references arise out of patriarchal co-optation of the name and image of God cannot be denied in light of the pervasive and oppressive androgyny of the canon. Nor can it be denied that in the church male pride and presumption has all too willingly adopted this usage, and in doing so, made itself liable to the warning of Luther that God holds in judgment 'those pot-bellies' and 'high and mighty' who violate God's name. Yet in scripture itself, this chauvinism becomes subject to clear and consistent criticism, as for instance in the first and second commandments and in such prophetic declarations as 'I am God and not man, the Holy One in your midst.' . . . The Old Testament's refusal to apply male sexual activity to God likewise indicates the Bible's absolute rejection of what its metaphoric language about God might otherwise indicate" (p. 65).

Similarly, Robert Cover cited the example of the manner in which the biblical stories of the patriarchs both lay out mandatory rules of succession and subvert them: "divine destiny is likely to manifest itself precisely in overturning" the rule (Cover, "Nomos and Narrative," p. 22. Compare the charging of Native American morality with stories of the Trickster, often but not exclusively Coyote.)

The use of counterimages for God in the Bible ("a woman in travail") or in proclamation (Rev. Shegog's "de widowed God") is a form of self-correction and even self-subversion that may indicate how nonbiblical words, too, may be speech of the Word. But caution is once again called for. Self-correction embedded in our texts may not be speech about the Word. It may be a put-on, at one extreme, or an exercise in religion, at the other.

I dwell on the subject a little longer because of its importance for law as well as other languages in which we might try to speak about God.

George Steiner called attention to "alternity": "the 'other than the case,' the counter-factual propositions, images, shapes of will and evasion with which we charge our mental being and by means of which we build the changing, largely fictive milieu for our somatic and our social existence" *(After Babel: Aspects of Language and Translation* [New York: Oxford University Press, 1975], p. 222).

Steiner's notion of alternity proved suggestive to Robert Cover and the elaboration of his concept of *nomos* ("Nomos and Narrative," p. 9). By *nomos* Cover intended a normative universe, composed in large measure of stories of origin and destiny. Within a *nomos,* law functions as a bridge between reality and alternity, between existing worlds and worlds that might be, a bridge of "committed social behavior which constitutes the way a group of people will attempt to get from here to there" (Robert Cover, "Folktales of Justice," *Capital University Law Review* 14 [1985]: 179, 181. The selection of *nomos* as a conceptual medium for jurisprudence undercuts governmental claims to a monopoly of jurisdiction. Commitment and stories of origin are more decisive for law than is the state.)

In Cover's universe, if law is a bridge from what is to what might be, importance attaches to both termini, the real as well as the alternative worlds between which law stretches. If thought and action are not well grounded in reality at one end, they become merely utopian and insular. If they are not well hitched to alternity, the vision that constitutes the other end, they lose the potential for transformation; they surrender "law to the overpowering force of what is and what is dominant" ("Folktales of Justice," p. 203). If only in their and our tales, judges have the responsibility to maintain the tension between reality and alternity. Judges must be politically circumspect and refrain from acts that test definitively their capacity to transform a given world. But they must also "be other than the King not because of the need for specialization in dispute resolution, but because of the need to institutionalize the role of the Prophet" (p. 189). The king, the state, the established powers must be reminded of a different order, the other world at the further end of law.

All of us live—should live—between reality and alternity: "Myth is the part of reality we create and choose to remember in order to *reenact.* . . . History is the countermove bringing us back to reality, requiring that we test the aspiration objectively and prudentially. History corrects for the scale of heroics that we would otherwise project upon the past. Only myth tells us who we would become; only history can tell us how hard it will really be to become that" ("Folktales of Justice," p. 190).

The idea of alternity, as it is realized in Steiner's and Cover's writing, is elevating and moving. I am elevated and moved by it. But alternity is not the otherness of the Word. Alternity is an imagined world; a world imagined by us. Its content is ours. Alternity is paired with reality, but the Word is not paired with words. The Word is wholly other because unpaired. (The Word and words—God and man in Jesus—is not a conceptual opposition that "can be reinterpreted as some form of nested opposition" [J. M. Balkin, "Nested Oppositions," *Yale Law Journal* 99 (1990): 1669, 1676]. However, human speech about the Word may well proceed in the language of nested opposition.)

Paul Ricoeur refurbishes the notion of ideology by establishing its pairing—or nested opposition—with utopia (*Lectures on Ideology and Utopia,* ed. G. Taylor [New York: Columbia University Press, 1986]. Utopias are one of the forms of alternity, and I have spilled much ink celebrating and attempting to realize them.) There is no escaping ideology, Ricoeur notes; no one, including its critics, can be free of it. There is no merely descriptive thinker. Curse though it may be, ideology makes a positive contribution, for persons and groups need a concept of self-identity, a certain order, and ideology meets this need by preserving an integrating identity. The preservation becomes pathological when it freezes what exists into schematization and rationalization.

Ricoeur identifies utopia as our breakout from engulfing ideology. Someone within the process takes responsibility for judgment by assuming a utopia, the glance from nowhere that allows us to judge what exists. Utopia gives us distance. But there is a pathology of utopias as of ideologies. Utopias can border on madness and become disjoined from present reality, thus severing the obligation to resolve society's given problems.

Ricoeur concludes that we are caught in the oscillation between ideology and utopia: "We must try to cure the illnesses of utopia by what is wholesome in ideology . . . and try to cure the rigidity, the petrification, of ideologies by the utopian element. It is too simple a response, though, to say that we must keep the dialectic running. My more ultimate answer is that we must let ourselves be drawn into the circle and then must try to make the circle a spiral" (p. 312).

Utopia and ideology form a complementary, polar pair. They are dual aspects of imagination. Utopia is fantasy exteriorized nowhere, but it comes from within.

It is true and invaluable that "a particular human culture can represent a source of 'otherness'—the imagination itself—that persists even in a world that other modes of thought and desire have made almost uninhabitable" (Thomas R. Edwards, "The Stars in a Suitcase," *New York Times Book Review,* Sept. 11, 1988, p. 7, col. 1, reviewing Paul West, *The Place in Flowers Where Pollen Rests*). It is equally true that such otherness remains *our* other and cannot but be colored, even or especially by our bodies: "Rather than describing our human capacity to imagine as transcendent, imagination could be described as a bridge, connecting the known and the unknown, what is to what has been and could be. Our leaps of imagination are a product of our astonishing capacity to form mental images of things which are not present to our senses, or of things never before wholly perceived or encountered in reality. Our sensibility, receptivity, readiness of feeling and awareness are what lead us to the foot of this bridge, and our ability to traverse the bridge of imagination, to guess at and form images to describe what the universe might have been or would be like *if*. . . does not exclude our bodily knowledge, and is, rather, an extension of our livingness, our sentience" (Rachel Koenig, introduction, *Interviews with Contemporary Women Playwrights* [New York: Beech Tree Books, 1986], p. 10).

Unlike alternity and Utopia, the Word is unpaired.

Is prophecy to be paired with kingship? "It is fair to say that the institution of prophecy appeared simultaneously with kingship in Israel and fell with the kingship" (Cross, *Canaanite Myth and Hebrew Epic,* p. 223. See also p. 343). There were no prophets without kings and no kings without prophets. If prophecy and kingship are complements, the word spoken by Isaiah was institutionally singular in the sense that it was not dependent on the king. That is, it did not state an alternity or utopia in Ricoeur's sense. It did not extend the reality of the thing prophesied against. It was an expression of the Word.

Busch observes that God is the subject who "never becomes the object of human understanding and its disposition. But does Ludwig Wittgenstein's assertion then not become the last thing we can say in theology, namely, 'you should remain silent about the things you cannot speak about' ["Whereof one cannot speak, thereof one must remain silent"]?" ("God Is God," p. 107). If Wittgenstein's proposition applies to God, says Busch, "in knowing that we *cannot* speak of God we already *speak* of God" (p. 108). That knowing, however, must be communicated; otherwise one either remains merely silent or speaks about God but with fingers secretly crossed.

Genuine communication—with sound or silence—has a context. Wittgenstein observed that a "theology which insists on the use of *certain particular* words and phrases, and outlaws others, does not make anything clearer (Karl Barth). It gesticulates with words, as one might say, because it wants to say something and does not know how to express it. *Practice* gives the words their sense" (Ludwig Wittgenstein, *Culture and Value*, ed. G. H. von Wright [Chicago: University of Chicago Press, 1980], p. 85). In the Isenheim altarpiece, John the Baptist is depicted pointing to the crucified Jesus. Barth kept a reproduction of the painting just above his desk and referred often to John, who was for Barth an image of the role of theology: the word/practice that bears witness—gesticulates—to the Word.

Like expressive words, expressive silence is not simple. The Native American tradition is predominantly oral and makes extensive use of silence, as did Martin Luther King, Jr., in his sermons. Some forms of jazz also employ silence and make explicit the sense in which music is a shaping of silence. The equivalent in painting and sculpture is the negative space (Henry Moore's sculpture is an example). These silences and negative spaces belong to performance but are also possible on the page. Martha Minow remarks about W. S. Merwin's abrupt, one-line "Elegy"—"Who would I show it to"—that, in stating the impossibility of statement, it communicates: "And the silence, between strangers, between author and reader has indeed been broken. Conversation where there had been silence may best begin this way, in expressions of what has been and perhaps remains inexpressible" (Martha Minow, "Many Silent Worlds," *Western New England Law Review* 9 [1987]: 197, 204).

But silence as a form of speech is no guaranteed formula for speaking about God. The silence is still our silence, shaped by us. Also there are kinds of silence—like Franz Hals's twenty-seven tones of black paint—and distinctions must be drawn. Silence can be an exercise of power—a choice not to listen—as when a court is silent and denies jurisdiction. Or it can be imposed and be an enforced response to oppression. It can be the wordless force of pain. Or it can be an evil, irresponsible failure to oppose inhumanity.

The end, and therefore the beginning, of Mark is exemplary of silence/self-critical speech, also of ethical action. It speaks about God but so as to refuse to identify words or silence with the Word. The next two chapters explore the Markan example.

CHAPTER FIVE

1. Barth, *The Epistle to the Romans,* p. 425.

2. Barth remarks upon "secular parables," those "in the secular sphere, i.e. in the strange interruption of the secularism of life in the world." Barth, 4 *Church Dogmatics,* part 3 (1st half), p. 117.

3. Ibid.

4. See chapter 4, n. 68.

5. William Shakespeare, *King Lear,* in *The Yale Shakespeare,* ed. Tucker Brooke and William Lyon Phelps (New Haven: Yale University Press, 1947), act 1, scene 1, lines 86–93.

6. The lines of Steiner that prompted my reading of *King Lear* are: "Must, as a rigorous nihilism will have it, 'nothing come of nothing'? Or can we attach some substantive consequence, some weight other than that of metaphoric pathos, to the concept that the excess of wholly present but unsayable meanings in Cordelia's silence is that of art, of poetics, when these 'go about their Father's business'?" Steiner, *Real Presences,* p. 213.

7. Ibid.

8. William Faulkner, *The Sound and the Fury* and *As I Lay Dying* (New York: Modern Library, 1946), p. 310.

9. Toni Morrison, *Beloved* (New York: Knopf, 1987), pp. 89, 259, 261.

10. See, e.g., Steiner, *Real Presences,* pp. 212–13.

11. Ibid., p. 181.

12. Ibid., p. 214.

13. Ibid., p. 225.

14. Ibid., p. 4.

15. W. H. Auden, "For the Time Being," in *The Collected Poetry of W. H. Auden,* pp. 405, 450–54.

16. James Boyd White, "What Can a Lawyer Learn from Literature?" (book review), *Harvard Law Review* 102 (19XX): 2014, 2018.

17. 1 John 4:19.

18. Dean Rusk, as told to Richard Rusk, *As I Saw It* (New York: W. W. Norton, 1990), pp. 419–20.

19. The two were reconciled. Their work on the book was the medium for this reconciliation. Richard approached the project out of deep pyschological need and with dread, and he wondered whether "some ghosts [are] better left undisturbed" (Rusk, *As I Saw It,* p. 626). It became a "father-son journey." His father had been a stranger whom he had now come to understand. He concluded: "There is mystery to my father's life, given his inscrutability and the awesome

complexity of human beings. But wherever he is buried, for me at least, there will be no mystery in that coffin, no corroding doubt" (p. 627).

The reconciliation between that father and son may be symptomatic of a larger reconciliation within the nation and between the United States and Vietnam. The great slab, like a huge gravestone, tucked away in the D.C. Mall to serve as a memorial to Americans killed in Vietnam draws many people and many tears. Perhaps only now are we looking into that tomb.

20. Paul Vallière, quoted in Lehmann, *The Transfiguration of Politics,* p. 286 (emphasis in original).

21. Taylor Branch, *Parting the Waters: America in the King Years, 1954–63* (New York: Simon and Schuster, 1988), p. 723.

22. Ibid.

CHAPTER SIX

1. Steiner, *Real Presences,* p. 10.

2. James O'Fallon and Cheney Ryan, "Finding a Voice, Giving an Ear: Reflections on Masters/Slaves, Men/Women," *Georgia Law Review* 24 (1990): 883, 888.

3. Ibid., p. 889.

4. 17 U.S. (4 Wheat.) 316, 431 (1819).

5. Stringfellow, *An Ethic for Christians and Other Aliens in a Strange Land,* p. 111. "Every sanction or weapon or policy or procedure—including law where law survives distinct from authority—which the State commands against both human beings and against the other principalities carries the connotation of death, implicitly threatens death, derives from and symbolizes death" (p. 110). On the violent, jurispathic nature of courts, see Robert Cover, "Nomos and Narrative," *Harvard Law Review* 97 (1983): 4.

6. 329 U.S. 459 (1947).

7. Id. at 467.

8. Id. at 468.

9. Id. at 470.

10. See Robert M. Cover, *Justice Accused: Antislavery and the Judicial Process* (New Haven: Yale University Press, 1975).

11. 329 U.S. 459 at 470–71.

12. See Ronald Dworkin, *Taking Rights Seriously* (Cambridge: Harvard University Press, 1977); "Seven Critics," *Georgia Law Review* 11 (1977): 1201.

13. 329 U.S. at 470. An episode outside the text of the opinion should be noted. "Operating through a Harvard classmate and influential member of the Louisiana bar, Monte E. Lemann, Frankfurter secretly tried to secure executive clemency for Willie Francis." Arthur Miller and Jeffrey Bowman, *Death by Installments: The Ordeal of Willie Francis* (New York: Greenwood Press, 1988), p. 124. Frankfurter wrote to Lemann, and Lemann wrote to the trial judge in

the case. Frankfurter circulated a copy of Lemann's letter to his colleagues on the Court. An accompanying note from Frankfurter did not disclose his role in generating it. Lemann's attempts failed.

In his concurring decision, Frankfurter said he was bound by the "consensus of society's opinion," which permitted a second execution attempt (329 U.S. at 471). In the letter written at Frankfurter's undisclosed instance, Lemann argued that public standards of decency warranted clemency: "The further punishment of Francis is not as important as adherence to the highest standards of decency and humaneness which a large and informed body of public opinion feels would be betrayed by Francis's execution." Miller and Bowman, *Death by Installments,* p. 127. Frankfurter's sentiment and Lemann's argument cannot be reconciled.

14. See James Boyd White, *Justice as Translation: An Essay in Cultural and Legal Criticism* (Chicago: University of Chicago Press, 1990).

15. In a rich textual analysis of another Frankfurter opinion, James Boyd White finds that the justice's rhetoric first claims that the due process clause creates "a vacuum that the judge must fill; his next claim is that he is the kind of judge who can fill that vacuum." White, *Justice as Translation,* p. 108 (discussing Frankfurter's opinion in Rochin v. California, 342 U.S. 165 [1952]). Ultimately, "he simply establishes his conscience as the ultimate standard" (p. 108). White wonders how a lawyer might engage such a judge in conversation, i.e., in the kinds of arguments that lawyers make to and with each other. "One might think of this opinion as establishing a writing assignment: How should you write to this judge? How could you stir this sensibility to act?" (p. 110).

How would a lawyer stir the sensibility of a justice who establishes as the standard his stomach's capacity to retain its contents? What would you write?

Barrett Prettyman describes Frankfurter's decision as "torn from the soul," and says, apparently with admiration, that it "stands as a monument to judgment over feeling." Barrett Prettyman, *Death and the Supreme Court* (New York: Harcourt, Brace & World, 1961), p. 120.

16. Bowman and Miller, *Death by Installments,* p. 91.

17. City of Richmond v. J. A. Croson Co., 109 S. Ct. 706 (1989).

18. DeShaney v. Winnebago County Dept. of Social Services, 109 S. Ct. 998 (1989).

19. Employment Division, Dept. of Human Resources v. Smith, 110 S. Ct. 1595 (1990).

20. In this regard, it is to be noted that on May 4, 1990, Florida's electric chair malfunctioned: "Flames and smoke leaped from the electrodes attached to the head of the condemned prisoner, Jesse Tafero, on the first pull of the switch, and three surges were required to kill him." "Electric Chair Tested on Vat of Water," *New York Times,* Wed., July 25, 1990, p. A8, col. 1. An associate professor of electrical engineering from Auburn University was called in to test the chair. He attached the head electrodes to a colander and the leg electrodes to a pipe, applied the current, and declared that the chair "works as it is supposed to." An

attorney for death row inmates commented: "It proves it works real good on a colander."

21. The attempt at quantification that is a central feature of the practice of law and economics would be a type of the abandonment of responsibility if it replaced judgment with algorithmic cost-benefit analysis that reads human relationships in the social-science terms of market transactions.

22. Joseph Vining provides an inventive, disturbing analysis of the loss of mind, the loss of person, behind court opinions as well as legislation. Joseph Vining, *The Authoritative and the Authoritarian* (Chicago: University of Chicago Press, 1986).

23. Patricia Williams, "On Being the Object of Property," *Signs* 14 (1988): 13.

24. Steiner, *Real Presences*, p. 215.

25. Vining, *The Authoritative and the Authoritarian*, p. 192.

26. Stanley Fish, *Doing What Comes Naturally: Change, Rhetoric, and the Practice of Theory in Literary and Legal Studies* (Durham, N.C.: Duke University Press, 1989), p. 302.

27. Ibid., p. 203.

28. See, e.g., Symposium, "Legal Storytelling," *Michigan Law Review* 87 (1989): 2073.

29. Williams, "On Being the Object of Property."

30. Mari Matsuda, "Public Response to Racist Speech: Considering the Victim's Story," *Michigan Law Review* 87 (1989): 2320.

31. Derrick Bell, *And We Are Not Saved: The Elusive Quest for Racial Justice* (New York: Basic Books, 1987).

32. See Deloria and Lytle, *The Nations Within*, p. 213.

33. See Ball, "The Legal Academy and Minority Scholars," *Harvard Law Review* 103 (1990): 1855.

34. See White, "What Can a Lawyer Learn from Literature?"

35. James Boyd White, *The Legal Imagination*, abridged ed. (Chicago: University of Chicago Press, 1985), p. 247.

36. O'Fallon and Ryan, "Finding a Voice," p. 899. Opponents of abortion ask whether the fetus has a voice, and whether it, too, should be heard.

37. Ibid. In a comment on a manuscript version of this chapter, Emily Fowler Hartigan counterposed that "the crucial question is will we stop telling the story *until* it is heard?"

38. I employ here the version presented in Miller and Bowman, *Death by Installments*. A somewhat different version is to be found in Prettyman, *Death and the Supreme Court*, pp. 90–128.

39. It was Wright's only argument before the Supreme Court. Prettyman says "DeBlanc flew to Washington to sit at the counsel table, but Wright made the oral presentation" (*Death and the Supreme Court*, p. 114). Henry Schwarzschild

talked to Judge Wright about the *Francis* case some years later. Schwarzschild was told, and reported to me, that DeBlanc was not on hand for the argument at the Supreme Court owing to the fact that he had sent his suit out to be cleaned and had not received it back.

40. 329 U.S. at 470.

41. Digested from Miller and Bowman, *Death by Installments.*

42. Narrative in and of itself—narrative as such—is not a type of alternity. Narrative is not an unaffecting medium, and various claims have been advanced for its significance: that there is a necessary connection between story and experience essential to humanity, history, life itself; that to say what *is* always requires telling a story; that narrative reflects or supplies the necessary order of things.

Frank Kermode's proposal about the opacity of narrativity and its stimulation of the hermeneutic impulse is one of the provocative, illuminating claims about the independent significance of narrative. Another is Mikhail Bakhtin's insight into the capacity of narrative to realize polyphony, by which he meant narrative's realization of a plurality of independent consciousnesses or characters whose voices sound together with the equally valid voices of the author and other characters. Polyphony is an ethical and political as well as aesthetic reality. It extends beyond the work of art, for just as there is no nonparticipating viewer of events within the narrative, so can there be no nonparticipating reader of it. The polyphony possible in narrative is then a representation "of human 'languages' or 'voices' that are not reduced into, or suppressed by, a single authoritative voice: a representation of the inescapably dialogical quality of human life at its best" (Wayne C. Booth, Introduction, in M. Bakhtin, *Problems of Dostoevsky's Poetics,* ed. and trans. Caryl Emerson [Minneapolis: University of Minnesota Press, 1984], p. xxii).

For all its potency, however, narrative is a medium—affective and independently significant, but a medium nonetheless. It has limits. Among them:

Narrative does not create the conditions for realization of its subject, does not create the polyphonic will to grant other voices their autonomy.

Nor does a story equip its readers to grant the validity of other stories. Part 4 of John Steinbeck's *East of Eden* begins this way:

> I believe that there is one story in the world and only one, that has frightened and inspired us. . . . Humans are caught in their lives, in their thoughts, in their hungers and ambitions, in their avarice and cruelty, and in their kindness and generosity too—in a net of good and evil. I think this is the only story we have and that it occurs on all levels of feeling and intelligence. . . . There is no other story. A man, after he has brushed off the dust and chips of his life, will have left only the hard, clean questions: Was it good or was it evil? Have I done well—or ill?
>
> We have only one story. All novels, all poetry, are built on the never-ending contest in ourselves of good and evil.

John Steinbeck, *East of Eden* (New York: Viking, 1986), pp. 541, 543.

The one story as Steinbeck and others see it is impressive and moving. But narrative has no protection against—and may stimulate—monopoly, the belief that there is only one story and that the one story is my or our story.

Then, too, story bears no relationship to the storyless, those whose world is consumed by pain or political oppression: "The severely handicapped do not [have a story]; nor do the addicted, the poverty-stricken, the hungry, the imprisoned, and many other[s] . . . whose lives are structured not by the syntaxis of story but by immediate needs of bewilderment at the unrelatedness of things" (Tracy Lischer, "The Limits of Story," *Interpretation* 38:1 [1984]: 31).

Narrative is a richly accommodating medium but is an expression of the Word only when it has been made the medium of the Word. The Markan text is narrative that denies the inherent, ultimate efficacy of narrative and, in this sense, is not opaque (as Kermode thinks), but transparent.

43. See Ronald Dworkin, *Law's Empire* (Cambridge, Mass.: Belknap Press, 1986).

44. William McFeely, *Frederick Douglass* (New York: Norton, 1991), p. 168.

45. Frederick Douglass, "We Ask Only for Our Rights: An Address Delivered in Troy, New York, on 4 September 1855," in *The Frederick Douglass Papers,* vol. 3, ed. J. Blassingame (New Haven: Yale University Press, 1985), pp. 91–92.

46. Douglass, "What to the Slave is the Fourth of July? An Address Delivered in Rochester, New York, on 5 July 1852," in *The Frederick Douglass Papers,* vol. 2, ed. J. Blassingame (New Haven: Yale University Press, 1982), p. 359.

47. Ibid., p. 383.

48. Ibid., p. 368.

49. 60 U.S. (19 How.) 393 (1857).

50. See Adler and Gorman, "Reflections: The Gettysburg Address," *New Yorker,* Sept. 8, 1975.

51. Ulysses S. Grant, *Memoirs and Selected Letters,* ed. Mary McFeely and William McFeely (New York: Library of America, 1990), p. 749.

52. 109 U.S. 3 (1883).

53. 163 U.S. 537 (1896).

54. Geoffrey Stone et al., *Constitutional Law,* 2d ed. (Boston: Little, Brown, 1991), p. 493.

55. 305 U.S. 337 (1938).

56. R. Kluger, *Simple Justice: The History of Brown v. Board of Education and Black America's Struggle for Equality* (New York: Knopf, 1976), p. 132.

57. Buck v. Bell, 274 U.S. 200, 208 (1927).

58. Mark Tushnet, *The NAACP's Legal Strategy against Segregated Education, 1925–1950* (Chapel Hill: University of North Carolina Press, 1987), p. 146.

59. Aviam Soifer may have preserved the possibility for development of equal protection jurisprudence in the future by exploring its juridical history of affording protection to groups. See, e.g., his articles "On Being Overly Discrete and Insular: Involuntary Groups and the Anglo-American Judicial Tradition,"

Washington & Lee Law Review 48 (1991): 381; Sobeloff Lecture: "Freedom of Association: Indian Tribes, Workers, and Communal Ghosts," *Maryland Law Review* 48 (1989): 350; "Toward a Generalized Notion of the Right to Form or Join an Association: Indian Tribes, Workers, and Communal Ghosts," *Case Western Reserve Law Review* 38 (1987–88): 641.

60. Steiner, *Real Presences,* p. 17.

61. Ibid., p. 9.

62. Ibid., p. 8.

63. Barth, 4 *Church Dogmatics,* part 2, p. 168.

64. Gutierrez, "Theology and Spirituality in a Latin American Context," p. 4.

65. Branch, *Parting the Waters,* p. 581.

66. Ibid., p. 582.

67. "Preamble: A Lawyer's Responsibilities," *ABA Model Rules of Professional Conduct* (1983, as amended through 1991).

68. But see Posner, *The Problems of Jurisprudence* (several times noting that classroom legal education does teach how to be a lawyer).

69. Aristotle, *Politics,* 1200.b.27–29 (bk. 2, i, 1) (Loeb Classical Library 1967).

70. Lehmann, *Ethics in a Christian Context,* pp. 74–87, 347.

71. But see Aviam Soifer's reflections on the surgeon in *Billy Budd* in "Status, Contract, and Promises Unkept," *Yale Law Journal* 96 (1987): 1916, 1930, 1955–57.

72. Robert Frost, "The Constant Symbol," quoted in White, *The Legal Imagination,* p. 218.

73. Archibald Macleish, "Apologia," *Harvard Law Review* 85 (1972): 1505, 1510.

74. Quoted in Thurman Arnold, "Criminal Attempts—The Rise and Fall of an Abstraction," *Yale Law Journal* 40 (1930): 53, 58.

75. *American Bar Association Journal* 52 (1966), opposite p. 788.

76. Martha Minow, "Foreword: Justice Engendered," *Harvard Law Review* 101 (1987): 10, 72.

77. Stringfellow, *An Ethic for Christians and Other Aliens in a Strange Land,* p. 84.

78. Ibid., p. 85.

79. Jerry Saltz, "Imitations of the Lifestyles of the Rich and Famous," *Arts Magazine,* Dec. 1988, p. 17.

80. Cover, "Nomos and Narrative," p. 89.

81. Sacvan Bercovitch argued that the railing of Puritan preachers against their congregations for their backsliding and failure to fulfill their destiny played as a form of self-justification, an extension and adaptation of the culture rather than its transformation. Sacvan Bercovitch, *The American Jeremiad* (Madison: University of Wisconsin Press, 1978), pp. 92–98.

An especially complex and controversial example is put by Richard Weisberg. A lawyer in Nazi-occupied Paris, Joseph Haennig, who had defended a Jew, published a treatise on the definition of a Jew. He was using his skills as a lawyer in an attempt to save people from being rounded up for deportation. To this end his treatise argued that the burden of proving Jewishness should be borne by the state in cases of individuals with no more than two Jewish grandparents. Haennig's action was liberally intended but, says Weisberg, "taken as a paradigm, [it] raises dreadful questions." Richard Weisberg, *The Failure of the Word: The Protagonist as Lawyer in Modern Fiction* (New Haven: Yale University Press, 1984), p. 1. Weisberg contends that, instead of fundamentally challenging the existence of racial laws as he should have, Haennig helped "to create a language in the service of" the legal superstructure driving thousands of French citizens to death. His legal word "now gently advanced the monstrous cause by making it debatable" (p. 2).

82. Bethge, *Dietrich Bonhoeffer,* p. 532.

83. Ibid.

84. Ibid., p. 533.

85. See William Stringfellow, "A Lawyer's Work," *Christian Legal Society Quarterly* 3 (1982): 17.

86. Mari Matsuda, "Looking to the Bottom: Critical Legal Studies and Reparations," *Harvard Civil Rights–Civil Liberties Law Review* 22 (1987): 323, 324.

87. Ibid., p. 325.

88. Ibid., p. 338.

89. Ibid., p. 339.

90. Ibid., p. 340.

91. Annie Dillard, "Luke," *Antaeus* 63 (Autumn 1989): 41.

INDEX

Affirmative action, 138
AIDS, 23, 171
Allen, Horace, 172
Amos, 79; and *rib*, 188 n. 12; 3:8, 117; 5:4, 112; 9:11, 111
Appalachian Research and Defense Fund of Kentucky, 16–17, 19–24
Aquinas, Thomas, 103
Arts Magazine, 161
Auden, W. H., 132

Baby Suggs, 4, 73, 90–95, 99, 106, 140; parable, 133; politics of redemption, 155; and religion adopted by the Word, 103; self-giving, 152; and unsayable meaning, 130–31, 135. See also *Beloved*; Morrison, Toni
Bakhtin, Mikhail, 207 n. 42
Ball, June, 165
Barks, Coleman, 73–75, 80, 166; and empty place, 198 n. 67
Barth, Karl, 128, 151; and Aquinas, 103; on Calvin, 91; command and ethics, 178 n. 4; critique of religion, 4, 78–79, 81; distinction between religion and Word, 76; humanity of God, 91–92, 104; and Mozart, 104–6; and Niebuhr, 103; on Pilate, 121–22; the poor, 171; Ten Commandments, 194 n. 42; theological method, 102; Word and religion, 76, 84; and resurrection, 88; sec-
ular reading, 129; specificity of Word, 98
Bell, Derrick, 171
Bellow, Saul, 194 n. 45
Beloved, 93–94
Beloved, 1, 4, 90–95, 97, 129–30, 140. See also Baby Suggs; Sethe
Bercovitch, Sacvan, 209 n. 81
Berea College, 8; *Berea College v. Kentucky*, 175 n. 1
Berman, Harold, 168
Bethge, Eberhard, *Dietrich Bonhoeffer: Theologian, Christian, Contemporary*, 179 n. 23
Biblical law codes, 190 n. 20
Billy Budd, 76–77, 160
Black lung, 22–23
Bly, Robert, 180 n. 26
Bonhoeffer, Dietrich, 106, 151; call to life, 94; life and death of, 99; life for others, 98; on power, 162; on redemption, 87, religion and secular life, 90
Booth, Marlene, 167
Boyd, Graham, 65–66
Branch, Taylor, *Parting the Waters*, 135, 152–53
Bright, John, 189 n. 15
Bradway, John, 63
Broad form deeds, 19–20
Brown v. Board of Education, 57, 146, 149
Brussack, Robert, 172
Buber, Martin, 193 n. 40